Character Disturbance

The Phenomenon of Our Age

Character Disturbance

The Phenomenon of Our Age

DR. GEORGE SIMON

Parkhurst Brothers, Inc., Publishers
LITTLE ROCK

www.parkhurstbrothers.com

Parkhurst Brothers books are distributed to the trade through the Chicago Distribution Center, a unit of the University of Chicago Press, and may be ordered through Ingram Book Company, Baker & Taylor, Follett Library Resources and other book industry wholesalers. To order from the University of Chicago's Chicago Distribution Center, phone 1-800-621-2736 or send a fax to 1-800-621-8476. Copies of this and other Parkhurst Brothers, Inc., Publishers titles are available to organizations and corporations for purchase in quantity by contacting Special Sales Department at our home office location, listed on our website.

Printed in the United States of America

12 11 10 9 8 7 6 5 4

Library of Congress Control Number: Consult publisher's website.

ISBN: Hardcover: 978-1-935166-32-0 [10 digit: 1-935166-32-8]
ISBN: Trade Paperback: 978-1-935166-33-7 [10-digit: 1-935166-33-6]

This book is printed on archival-quality paper that meets requirements of the American National Standard for Information Sciences, Permanence of Paper, Printed Library Materials, ANSI Z39.48-1984.

Design Director and Dustjacket/cover design:
Wendell E. Hall

Page design:
Shelly Culbertson

Acquired for Parkhurst Brothers, Inc., Publishers by:
Ted Parkhurst

Editor:
Roger Armbrust

Proofreaders:
Bill and Barbara Paddack

For Sherry,

whose heart is truer than any I know,

and who inspires me daily to be

a better person. And for all those silent

but committed souls of noble character,

upon whom the very survival

of freedom depends.

Acknowledgements

I'm deeply grateful to my wife, Dr. Sherry Simon, and my entire family not only for their unwavering support, patience and understanding, but also for the invaluable lessons they have taught me about conducting a life of meaning and character.

I owe a supreme debt to the hundreds of weblog readers, workshop attendees, online reviewers, and other supporters who have taken the time to write and share their experiences. Their insights and comments have helped me to clarify perspectives and to modify my work to better address their needs.

This book draws from the works of many theorists and researchers. I am particularly indebted to Theodore Millon, Stanton Samenow, and Robert Hare for their remarkable contributions to the understanding of personality and character.

Finally, I'd like to thank Ted Parkhurst of Parkhurst Brothers, Publishers for his understanding, support, and encouragement, as well as Roger Armbrust for his expert editing and kind suggestions for clarifying my message.

Table of Contents

Preface

Imagine you recently read a newspaper article about a young girl who suddenly and inexplicably lost her eyesight. Her frantic parents took her from doctor to doctor, specialist to specialist, and clinic to clinic, yet no one could find the reason for her blindness. In desperation, one day they decided to take her to a psychologist. After months of traditional psychoanalysis, the therapist revealed that the child's blindness resulted from severe emotional trauma. It seems that several months before, while riding on the school bus, this young lady just happened to glance at a boy seated with some friends across the aisle. She thought to herself: "This guy is really cute." Before long, she also began thinking things like: "I wonder what it would be like to kiss him." But almost immediately after having these thoughts, she started to feel badly. She began fretting about what kind of horrible person she must be to entertain such "impure" thoughts. She worried that they could only lead to other impure urges and temptations, and even perhaps some impure action on her part. Eventually, she became consumed with guilt and shame. She remembered times in the past when she had looked at boys, and how hard it was to resist impure thoughts and urges. Surely worse would follow, she feared, if she didn't keep herself in check. Shortly after this incident, she lost her vision.

When she first saw the psychologist, this troubled little girl didn't even remember the bus incident. She certainly didn't remember what she was thinking or feeling at the time. She'd even forgotten how deeply the incident unnerved her, and how she dealt with her anxiety over the situation. The psychologist helped her see that she had "repressed" her memories as a way of easing the intensity of her emotional pain. Her lengthy analysis eventually helped her not only recover her memory of that fateful day's events, but also enabled her to re-connect with her conflicted emotions. She came to realize this: She was so deeply distressed by what she thought were her unforgivable, impure desires that she actually believed it was better not to see at all than risk having such thoughts about boys again.

Once she had confessed her sins to the doctor and he did not condemn her, the young girl slowly began to feel better. She took heart in the notion that he appeared to accept her just as she was. She slowly began to feel that she wasn't such a horrible person after all merely for the kinds of thoughts she sometimes had about boys. In time, she came to believe that the level of her fear, guilt, and shame was excessive and unwarranted, given the nature of the situation. No longer believing that simply having thoughts about kissing boys was as evil as she once did, she allowed herself to see again.

Now, I would pose to you, the reader, the same question I ask of professionals and non-professionals alike at every one of the hundreds of workshops I've given over the past 25 years. How many scenarios similar to the one I described have you read or heard about in the last year? How about the past five years? How about the past, 10 – 20 – 30 years? It should come as no surprise that the answer I get is always the same: ***zero***. What should shock you, however (and always gets the attention of my audiences), is this: *Almost all of the principles of classical-psychology paradigms stemmed from various theorists' attempts to explain this and similar phenomena* (sometimes referred to by adherents to these theories as "hysterical" blindness).

You see, in Sigmund Freud's day, *some* individuals actually suffered from such strange maladies. It's important to note, however, that these extreme psychological illnesses were *never* widespread phenomena. But in the intensely socially repressive Victorian era, cases appeared of persons experiencing extraordinary levels of guilt or shame merely for being tempted to act on a primal human instinct, and displaying pathological symptoms as a result. If there were a motto or saying that might best describe the "zeitgeist" (i.e.

social or cultural milieu) of that time it would be: "Don't even *think* about it!" So, some individuals were quite unnecessarily consumed with excessive guilt and shame about their most basic human urges. Freud treated some of these individuals, most of whom were women, typically subjected to more oppression than men. He eventually coined the term "neurosis" to describe the internal struggle he believed went on between a person's instinctual urges (i.e. *id*) and their conscience (i.e. *superego*), the excessive *anxiety* or nervous tension that often accompanies this internal war, and the unusual psychological *symptoms* a person can develop when attempting to mitigate (i.e. through the use of marginally effective *defense mechanisms*) the intense emotional pain associated with these inner conflicts. He then developed a set of theories and constructs that appeared to adequately explain how his patients developed their bizarre maladies. In the process, however, *he also came to believe that he had discovered universal, fundamental principles that explained personality formation and the entire spectrum of human psychological functioning.*

Many of the constructs and terms first articulated by Freud, and several other "psychodynamic" theorists who followed him, found their way into common parlance over the years. For a significant period of time, these tenets also gained widespread acceptance by mental health professionals. And many of the principles of what I refer to in this book as "traditional psychology" still enjoy a fair degree of acceptance, not only among professionals but also among lay persons. This is true despite the fact that, in recent years, several of the most important assumptions and doctrines have been proven completely false or significantly flawed.

Not only are some of traditional psychology's central tenets of questionable validity, but also times have changed dramatically since the days of Sigmund Freud. If a motto or saying best befits our modern era's zeitgeist, it would be much like the once popular commercial that urged: "Just *do* it!" As a result, highly pathological levels of neurosis (as exemplified by the girl who went blind simply because she "lusted" after a boy she found attractive) have all but completely disappeared, especially in industrialized free societies. Instead of being dominated by individuals overly riddled with unfounded guilt and shame (i.e. "hung-up" as children of the '60s used to say), modern western culture has produced increasing numbers of individuals who aren't "hung-up" enough about the things they let themselves do.

So, today we are facing a near epidemic of what some theorists refer to as *character disturbance.* Neurosis is still with us, but for the most part at *functional* as opposed to pathological levels. That is, most people today experience just enough apprehension and internal turmoil when it comes to simply acting on their primal urges, that they don't in fact "just do it." Instead, they experience sufficient anticipatory guilt or shame to restrain their impulses and conform their conduct to more socially acceptable standards. So, one can easily say that their neurosis is *functional.* It's largely what makes society work.

Freud used to say that civilization is the cause of neurosis, and given the climate of his time, it's easy to see how he came to that conclusion. In a sense, he had a point; but his observation was more than a bit narrow-sighted. True, the prohibitions any society imposes on the unrestrained expression of primal urges can give rise to a fair degree of anxiety in some of us. And, a brutally oppressive culture can breed excessive degrees of neurosis. But in large measure, *it's most people's* ***capacity*** *to become unnerved when contemplating acting like an animal (i.e. their capacity to be "neurotic" to some degree) that makes civilization itself possible.* So, it's precisely because significant numbers of people still get a little "hung up" when they contemplate punching someone's lights out, or have some apprehension and qualms of conscience when they think about taking something that doesn't belong to them, that there's any degree of civilization left at all.

Today many types of professionals span a wide variety of disciplines that deal with mental health issues and personal problems of one variety or another. Most of these professionals have *never* encountered — let alone treated — a case of "hysterical blindness," pseudo-paralysis, or any similar phenomenon. In fact, it's becoming increasingly rare for professionals to encounter a case of neurosis at a highly pathological level of intensity. Therapists rarely deal with problems that stem from a conscience so overactive or oppressive that it causes a person to develop bizarre or severely debilitating psychosomatic or other pathological symptoms. Instead, mental health clinicians in all disciplines increasingly find themselves intervening with individuals whose problems are related to their dysfunctional *attitudes* and *thinking patterns*, their shallow, self-centered relationships, their moral immaturity and social irresponsibility, and their habitual, *dysfunctional behavior patterns*. All of these stem from an *underdeveloped conscience* and reflect significant ***deficiencies or disturbances of character***.

This wouldn't be so much of a problem if it weren't for the fact that many mental health professionals not only are trained primarily in classical theories of human behavior, but also cling to beliefs about human nature and the underpinnings of psycho-social dysfunction that originally emanated from these theories. For this reason, they often attempt to use the tenets and the principles that flow from more traditional paradigms to guide them in their efforts to solve today's very different kinds of psychological problems. In short, they attempt to understand and treat character disturbance with approaches and methods originally designed to treat extreme levels of neurosis.

Retaining outdated notions about why people do the things they do can put anyone — lay persons and mental health professionals alike — at a great disadvantage when it comes to understanding and dealing with the disturbed character. Even some of our more modern frameworks for understanding human behavior are inadequate to address the phenomenon. The problem is compounded by this fact: It's not "politically correct" to consider people's emotional and behavioral problems as stemming from or reflecting deficiencies in their character. So, sometimes problems actually rooted in character pathology might be framed as almost anything else (e.g., an "addiction," ADHD, Bipolar Disorder, a "chemical imbalance," etc.). Their symptoms can be somewhat managed with medication or other forms of treatment. Then, if at least some degree of change is observed, that mere fact validates the perspective that disease of some sort — as opposed to character — caused the problem. Sometimes, professionals actually do recognize personality or character disturbances, but regard them as unchangeable or untreatable. So, they target issues other than character concerns in therapy. At other times a professional's over-immersion in traditional paradigms will prompt them to view everyone — even the most severely character-disturbed individual — as neurotic, at least to some degree, and then attempt to treat their purported neurosis. But the reality is this: ***character disturbance is one of the most pressing psychological realities of our age; it's becoming increasingly prevalent; and it's an entirely different phenomenon from neurosis, requiring a different perspective to adequately understand and treat.***

Understanding character disturbance requires viewing human beings, and the reasons they do some of the things they do, in a very different light. Further, character disturbance simply can't be dealt with effectively using traditional approaches. The tools and techniques that have proven effective in treating character disturbance are radically different from those originally developed to treat neurosis.

Over 14 years ago, I wrote *In Sheep's Clothing: Understanding and Dealing with Manipulative People* to help both therapists and average folks understand what certain people are really like, and how they manage to manipulate and control others. The book has grown increasingly popular every year since its first printing, has been translated into several foreign languages, and consistently draws highly laudatory reviews from professionals as well as lay persons. The comments are generally of a similar nature. Readers report that once they cast off old notions about the nature and behavior of the manipulative persons in their lives, "got it" with respect to what really makes such individuals "tick," and adopted not only a new perspective for understanding such persons but also a new set of rules and principles to guide their relationships with them, their circumstances dramatically improved. This kind of feedback has been more than edifying for me, and inspired me to write this book. *In Sheep's Clothing* was about one type of disturbed character. This book is about all of the various disturbed character types you are likely to encounter in your life. *In Sheep's Clothing* briefly delved into the general topic of character disturbance. This book takes a much deeper look at this significant and disturbing phenomenon, its growing prevalence, and some of the socio-cultural features of the current era responsible for promoting it.

My primary purpose in writing this book is to help you (1) cast off faulty assumptions that can place you at a distinct disadvantage, and (2) understand the real reasons disturbed characters behave the way they do. It's important to recognize that disturbed characters differ dramatically from neurotics on almost every imaginable dimension of interpersonal functioning. They don't hold the same values, believe the same things, harbor the same attitudes, think the same way, or behave in the same manner as neurotics. This book will help you understand why you might have had such a difficult time dealing with the disturbed characters in your life, what makes these individuals so different, and why aid you might have sought, hoping to deal with problems involving them, proved inadequate.

As with *In Sheep's Clothing,* I've written this book in a concise manner, easy to read and understand. It should be equally helpful to the layperson as well as the professional who is primarily versed in or aligned with traditional perspectives. I have deliberately not included mounds of difficult-to-understand scientific research data and have attempted to translate sophisticated and highly technical material into simpler, yet reasonably accurate language. My intention was not to craft an authoritative and comprehensive textbook-style treatise on human nature, personality, or psychopathology. Rather, I present principles and perspectives derived from years of experience working with disturbed characters and their victims, illustrate those principles with real-life examples, and support the most important contentions and perspectives with relevant research findings when appropriate or necessary.

My secondary purpose in writing this book is to expose character disturbance for the significant social problem that it is, and address some of the socio-cultural influences responsible for it. I am not the first to sound the alarm on the issue, and I hope I will not be the last. In their book on character strengths and virtues, the eminent psychology pioneers and researchers Christopher Peterson and Martin E.P. Seligman address the issue directly:

> "After a detour through the hedonism of the 1960's, the narcissism of the 1970's, the materialism of the 1980's and the apathy of the 1990's, most everyone today seems to believe that character is important after all and that the United States is facing a character crisis on many fronts, from the playground to the classroom to the sports arena to the Hollywood screen to business corporations to politics."[1]

But no problem can be resolved until it's fully acknowledged and adequately defined. That's the first step. The second step is to take a serious look at the characteristics of our social milieu that contribute to the problem. This book will do both.

I have been working with disturbed characters for over 25 years now. Yet I know that much of what I assert in this book is likely to be controversial. When I first started doing workshops on manipulators and other problem characters, especially with professionals, several attendees were uncomfortable with my perspective. Some even walked out! That's because a lot of what I had to say challenged some longstanding notions and deeply-held beliefs about why people experience psychological problems in the first place, and how professionals must assist them in achieving mental and emotional health. But time and recent research has validated much about the perspective I introduced those many years ago. These days, it's very common for me to see many heads in the audience frequently nod in approval as I articulate the principles I've adopted to understand and deal with disturbed characters. It's also common for individuals who have already been to one of my workshops to come back again several times for "refreshers" on the tenets I will outline in this book. One of the more frequent comments I get from professionals involves how much more satisfying working with disturbed characters has become after they adopted some of these principles.

But old notions and biases aren't easily shed, so I still expect some controversy and debate. The same was initially true for *In Sheep's Clothing.* But I am confident that — if you approach the concepts I will introduce with an open mind, allow my disturbed-character descriptions to *validate your experience,* accept the reality that our very different times have spawned problems the major helping professions have only recently begun to face by developing sound paradigms, and at least try out some of the principles and tools I will outline — you'll be better prepared to understand and deal with the individuals in your life who display significant character pathology.

There are two principal reasons I felt it imperative to write this book at this time. First, I have come to a deep realization about how serious the problem of character disturbance has become, and the degree to which it undermines the very foundations of our free society. For the past 15 years, I have been working with some of the most severely disturbed characters, most of whom have been incarcerated at some point in their lives, and several of whom have been incarcerated multiple times. You should know that the United States has a higher percentage of its population incarcerated than any industrialized country, and that percentage is increasing. You should also know that contrary to popular belief, it generally takes some very serious and/or chronic misbehavior to end up incarcerated. Yet, prisons and jails are overcrowded, and the judicial system is overburdened. Although very few may be incarcerated who don't necessarily need to be, many others lead lives of wanton major social norm violations for which they rightfully could have been sanctioned many times, but weren't because of the scarcity of space and resources. I've also worked with many individuals who, although they engaged in no major societal transgressions and do not have criminal records, nonetheless harbor significant deficiencies of character. I've increasingly counseled individuals who didn't begin functioning in a truly responsible manner until they were in their late 40s, 50s, or even 60s. (I recently attended a discussion group in which a group member discussed his problematic relationship with a brother who, even at age 67, continues to exercise little control over his impulses and engages in deeply irresponsible behavior!)

The greatness of American society has deteriorated dramatically in recent years because of our culturally-spawned character crisis. There is a saying often attributed to Alexis De Tocqueville: "America is great because she is good; and if America ever ceases to be good, she will cease to be great." De Tocqueville never actually said this, yet the saying contains a powerful truth. The overall character of a country can be no better than the collective character of its constituents. I grew up in an era of unprecedented American greatness, in significant measure spawned by the distinctive character of what Tom Brokaw rightly called "the greatest generation." I have now lived long enough to witness what I regard as the tarnishing of the best American ideals; and although I am no longer shocked by it, I am nonetheless outraged. I'm mostly outraged because I still see our unique brands of free expression and free enterprise as the last, best hope for improving the human condition. But even our founders knew that ***freedom and character are inextricably interdependent***. John Adams adamantly asserted that "no government" deliberately designed to be limited in power and scope would be "capable of contending with human passions unbridled by morality and religion." He further noted that the American "constitution was made *only* for a religious and moral people," and that "it is *wholly inadequate* for the government" of people "of any other" character.[2]

In the absence of sound individual conscience, society is naturally tempted to legislate its way out of the problems that ensue, imposing rules and restrictions that inevitably increase the role, size and scope of government, and limit individual freedoms. While it may seem like a necessary evil, such attempts to legislate social responsibility *never* really fix the problem; they only set the stage for both economic and cultural deterioration. So, it bothers me greatly that the populace's complacency and denial, with a fair amount of aiding and abetting by some mental health professionals, in recent times have all allowed this character crisis to surreptitiously and steadily spin out of control, to fray our culture's once distinctly noble fabric, to erode the integrity of our national character, and to hasten our country's fall from greatness.

Sometimes I wonder just how many fast-talking politicians, greedy executives, and crafty religious "leaders" — finally caught in their lies and indiscretions, failed relationships, or major corporate scandals — it will take for us to realize how much character and integrity really matter. For a long time, it seems like we had resigned ourselves to the notion that people simply can't be any better or do any better than we've come to expect. But the second major reason I felt compelled to write this book now is this: I know from years of experience that the problem of character disturbance is not at all hopeless. There are some straightforward things we can do to address the cultural contributors to the character crisis. There are interventions we can initiate at the individual level to encourage a person to develop the character they need to function responsibly in society, and to form healthy, happy, intimate relationships. From a therapist's perspective, the interventions necessary are not of the same sort that one would use to deal with neurosis. Nor are they easy, given the challenging nature of the problem. But *there is hope* for dealing effectively with the disturbed character, especially once you know and accept the approach that's necessary to deal with the problem.

When I was developing *In Sheep's Clothing*, the cognitive-behavioral therapy (CBT) revolution was in its infancy. Today, it has become more widely accepted. Nonetheless, many individuals who outwardly assert that they understand and accept the tenets of cognitive-behavioral theory still have a hard time divorcing themselves from outdated and ineffective paradigms. Furthermore, although they might readily focus on a person's distorted cognitions, some clinicians have an aversion to aligning themselves with the most important aspect of the cognitive-behavioral model: focusing on and modifying *behavior.* As a result, they often don't fully and faithfully implement the principles of CBT (doing largely CT instead of C**B**T). This is a genuine shame because CBT has demonstrated its superiority to other forms of intervention when it comes to treating persons of disturbed character. The principles advanced in this book are very much in harmony with the principles of CBT.

We are all in this vast human experiment together. Like it or not, ours is an extremely interconnected and interdependent world. My personal mission for the last several years has been to call attention to a significant social problem, and to inspire people to address and overcome it. This book is the culmination of my most recent efforts toward that end.

At a fundamental level, we are all savages seeking the survival of the fittest. But we also have within us the power and capacity to elevate ourselves and inspire others to a much higher plane of functioning. Doing so, however, requires the development of *character.*

Introduction

Personality and Character

This is a book about character, and the disturbances of character it seeks to examine differ in significant ways from the various personality disturbances we'll discuss. Therefore, it's important that we clearly distinguish and define these two terms. It's common to hear *personality* and *character* used in a manner suggesting that they are virtually synonymous. Even professionals frequently employ the terms interchangeably. Although the two words are related, I think it not only important but also helpful to draw a firm distinction between these two concepts. A close look at the terms' origins and the evolutions of their meanings will help clarify the working definitions we'll employ throughout this book.

Traditional Conceptualizations of Personality

The word "personality" derives from the Latin word *persona,* which means "mask." In the ancient theater, males played all the roles, including those of female characters. Also, the art of dramatizing situations and conveying emotion was not as evolved as it is today. So actors used masks of various types not only to denote gender, but also to depict and emphasize various emotional states. Classical psychology theories borrowed the term "persona" because they generally conceptualized *personality* as the social "mask" a person wears to conceal the more authentic or "true" self.

Classical theories of personality also conceptualize all individuals as fundamentally struggling with *fears* of various kinds, especially fears of social rejection, condemnation, or abandonment. These theories regard basic human needs, desires and emotions as universal, and potential environmental "threats" to them as ever-present. So, the theories postulate that (1) to a greater or lesser extent, everyone struggles with fears that those basic wants and needs will be thwarted in some way; and (2) people fear that they might encounter disappointment and disapproval if they ever reveal their true wishes and desires. Classical theories also propose that people engage in certain stylized but unconscious ways of "defending" themselves against a potentially hostile and rejecting world, and in the process end up estranged from their more authentic selves. The classical model, then, sees personality as an *unconsciously constructed façade* — a mask that hides the genuine person behind a veritable wall of defenses. This conceptualization still has some value when it comes to understanding personalities who are best thought of as *neurotic* (more about this later).

Traditional theories of personality also postulate that a person wouldn't need to hide his or her authentic self behind the façade of personality if our environments weren't so hostile, cold, or rejecting. In other words, everyone would be "authentic," healthy, and without defensive armor if the world didn't force so much emotional trauma into our lives. From traditional perspectives, it's the slings and arrows of life that have the greatest influence in shaping personality. Traditional theories view everyone as *essentially the same* underneath their structure of defenses. Furthermore, the types of defenses a person most likely will employ are seen as logical growth — responses to the kind and severity of traumatic experience to which they've been subjected, especially during their formative years. Within traditional frameworks, the various personality types are defined primarily by the cluster of defenses they have learned to employ.

A More Contemporary Conceptualization of Personality

More recent conceptualizations, most eloquently described by the eminent theorist and researcher Theodore Millon, generally define personality as an individual's distinctive and relatively engrained "style" of interrelating.[3] Such conceptualizations of personality often incorporate a multi-dimensional perspective: They recognize a person's constitutional predispositions (i.e. hereditary, hormonal, temperamental, and other biological factors), environmental factors (e.g., early learning, significant life events, peer and role-model influences, degree of nurturance available, etc.), and a *dynamic interaction* between what the world teaches a person and how they are predisposed to respond to events. Multi-dimensional personality theorists believe all the aforementioned factors contribute to a person's distinctive manner of perceiving, relating to, and interacting with others and the world at large.

The multi-dimensional perspective of personality better explains how some individuals can develop very dysfunctional personalities, despite being reared in relatively benign, supportive environments; whereas others can develop remarkable and admirable character despite experiencing the most egregious circumstances. If you recall, traditional theories assume this: Underneath, we're all the same, and we'd be perfectly healthy and authentic individuals if it weren't for the fact that we grew up in a world full of pain, rejection, and emotional trauma. Within the multidimensional framework, both the environment and an individual's innate predispositions play roles. The weight various factors might carry in shaping personality varies considerably from person to person. The choices a person makes about how to best cope with life's challenges also play a role. In short, the multi-dimensional model allows for the increasing scientific evidence that we are not all the same. Each of us has a unique collection of traits. Some developed as a result of learning, some we were simply endowed with by nature, and some developed as a result of the dynamic interaction between our innate predispositions, the environment in which we were raised, and the choices we've made. And the model also allows for the fact that, once our "preferred" ways of thinking and behaving congeal and become ingrained, they fairly much define who we are as individuals. Personality, therefore, is seen — not so much as a false-face or a pretense — but rather as a stable set of traits, preferred thinking and behavior patterns that define our unique *style* of interaction over a wide variety of situations, and for most of our lifetime.

So, the multi-dimensional conceptualizations of personality are more comprehensive than the classical definitions. They also appear more accurate and useful when we try to understand the thinking and behavior patterns of individuals best described as *character-disturbed* rather than *neurotic*. This will become increasingly evident to you when we take a more in-depth look at the nature of character disturbance and its vast differences from neurosis.

Character

The word "character" derives from both Old French and Greek words meaning to engrave or furrow a *distinctive mark*. The word has been used to denote the most distinguishing traits of overall personality that uniquely define or "mark" an individual as a social being. Most especially, the term commonly reflects an individual's positive personality aspects — those *socially desirable qualities* and virtues such as self-control, ethics, loyalty, and fortitude.

As mentioned before, it's not uncommon for professionals as well as lay persons to use the terms "character" and "personality" interchangeably. It's also not uncommon for folks to speak of character as if it were synonymous with *strength* of character. Many also erroneously equate the terms *personality disorder* and *character disorder* (I'll have more to say about this later). But, again, this is a book about character and the social and psychological consequences of significant disturbances or deficiencies of character. So it's of paramount importance that we highlight the key differences between someone who possesses all of the various traits and quirks of a certain *personality* and someone whose dominant personality features reflect significant deficiencies or defects in their *character*. Therefore, in this book, the term "character" will refer to those *distinct aspects of personality* that reflect the presence and strength of a person's virtues, personal ethics, social conscientiousness, and depth of commitment to respect-worthy and meritorious social conduct.

CHAPTER 1

Neurosis and Character Disturbance

Before we can even begin a meaningful discussion about the differences between neurosis and character disturbance, it's important to understand the strengths and limitations of any scientific or philosophical metaphor. We simply can't have a discourse about the important matters of life without theories, definitions, and constructs. But in the end, absolute truth is illusive. Some might say it's unknowable. We have to settle for "metaphors" that, indicated by evidence, approximate the incomprehensible truth as closely as possible.

Some metaphors appear more ideally suited to understanding and dealing with various aspects of reality. For example, Sir Isaac Newton tried to explain the phenomenon we know as gravity, as well as planets' motion and orbits, with the "law" that every material object attracts every other in proportion to their mass, and in inverse proportion to their distance from one another. In a competing "metaphor" for explaining the same phenomenon, Einstein proposed that what appears as one body attracting another is really the distortion or warping of "space-time" (a concept so complex it's far beyond the scope of this book); and that all clusters of matter (including particles of light) simply follow the resulting "curvature" of distorted space-time. A landmark test of Einstein's theory during a solar eclipse demonstrated convincingly that his metaphor provides a more accurate description of gravitation. Newton's metaphor, however, still works very well when you're trying to plot a course for a rocket to the moon, or determine an orbital path around the earth. So, there are still situations in which the Newtonian metaphor is useful, despite its limitations. And neither Einstein's metaphor nor Newton's gives us the whole truth about gravity. We still don't really know exactly what it is or how it works.

Social science metaphors are no less subject to limitation or appropriate application than any other scientific metaphor. And any metaphor can become problematic when we over-generalize it, or stretch it to fit or explain phenomena it was never really meant to explain. Most branches of science have come to grips with this. All encompassing explanations of reality such as string theory, the theory of everything, or the unified field theory are still illusive. So, for the most part, scientists apply various theories in the areas they appear to suitably explain. But in the social sciences, we've been slow to recognize and deal with limits to some of our traditional explanatory models.

Traditional psychodynamic metaphors still apply and have value when you're trying to understand or deal with the phenomenon we call "neurosis." But the evidence is mounting that such metaphors are inadequate at best, and potentially counterproductive or even harmful at worst, when we're trying to understand or deal with character disturbance. The constructs of neurosis and character disturbance are themselves only metaphors. Each attempts to describe a psychological reality we cannot adequately or completely define; but we have to attempt to give it some structure if we're to understand it at all. The terms themselves are not reality; they're metaphorical ways we attempt to describe some aspects of reality. And each way has its strengths and limitations, as well as areas of applicability and areas of poor fit.

I find it useful to conceptualize neurosis and character disturbance as constructs lying at different ends of a continuum. A representation of this concept is provided in the following diagram:

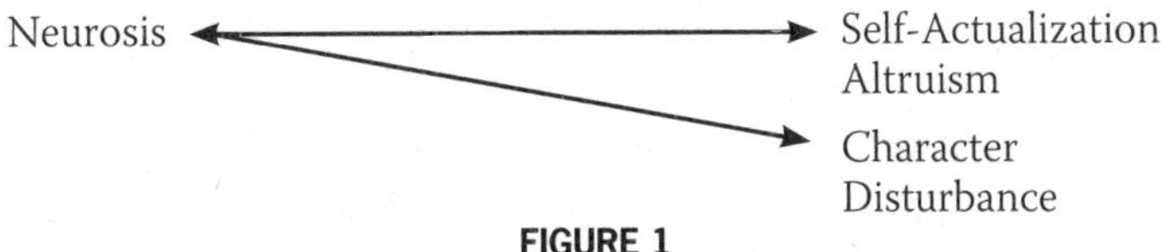

FIGURE 1

At first glance, the representation depicted above might appear a bit confusing. It's important to realize, however, that very few individuals have ever walked our planet who could rightfully be considered so socially and morally evolved (e.g., Jesus, the Buddha) that they're considered truly altruistic. By altruistic, I mean that their commitment to selfless, humanistic behavior is not rooted in pangs of guilt for doing otherwise, or in an unacknowledged selfish desire for admiration or immortal reputation. Altruists, by definition, are individuals who *freely* and completely commit themselves to advancing the greater good. They are not neurotic because they have no driving desire to avoid guilt or shame for doing otherwise. Also, they're not out for personal glory or to be revered by society. By definition, altruists simply, freely, and nobly choose to subordinate their own selfish desires for the good of all.

Fully *self-actualized* (altruistic) individuals are extremely rare indeed; some assert they don't really exist. That's because most people restrain their baser instincts out of a sense of guilt and/or shame for doing otherwise. It's theoretically possible to be without neurosis and not be character disordered, but the absence of neurosis usually results in some degree of character disturbance. That's because without potential pangs of guilt or shame influencing our decisions, most of us would act in socially irresponsible ways. So, character disturbance and neurosis are at opposite poles of a continuum, with *each individual personality falling somewhere along the continuum.* And, as you might expect, personalities rightfully classified as more neurotic will differ significantly from those rightfully classified as more character-disturbed on several dimensions.

The framework advanced here ultimately views character disturbance as a crucial *dimension* of personality. It varies in degree and results from a number of shaping influences that affect an individual's personality development. For example, there are people who started out in life with some degree of neurosis; but extraordinary pain and trauma "hardened" their hearts, *solidifying* their preferred styles of coping to such a degree that their neurosis eventually became relegated to their souls' deepest recesses. In such individuals, any neurosis they harbor can usually only re-emerge when they are truly "broken down" by sufficiently humiliating or spirit-fracturing life events, abject failures of their coping style, or sufficiently intensive and confrontational therapeutic techniques. But some individuals were never very neurotic to start with. Either they didn't experience the usual neurosis-fostering and civilizing experiences like most of us, or their innate predispositions prevented those typical civilizing influences from impacting them as such influences impact most of us.

Disturbance vs. Disorder

Throughout this book you will see the following terms: "personality disturbance," "personality disorder," "character disturbance," and "character disorder." It's important to recognize that not all problematic aspects of personality or character rise to the level of a true disorder. For a disturbance of personality and/or character to be considered a disorder, it must be of such intensity, inflexibility, and intractability that it impairs adaptive functioning in a wide variety of situations. I've included a more in-depth discussion on this in the next chapter.

Key Neurotic vs. Disturbed Character Differences

Character-disturbed personalities differ from neurotic personalities on almost any dimension of interpersonal functioning imaginable. The differences greatly affect how they function in interpersonal relationships, as well as how they respond to therapeutic interventions. It's virtually impossible to list all of the ways disturbed characters and neurotics differ, but I think it's helpful to examine some of the more significant ones (summarized in the chart on page 60):

- **Anxiety**. Disturbed characters are significantly different from neurotics with respect to their levels and quality of anxiety. Anxiety is the primal emotion (i.e. fear response) we experience when we feel threatened in some way. It has always been thought to play the most important role in both creating and maintaining neurosis. When our fear is rooted in a specific, identifiable circumstance — such as being in a room filled with a lot of people, having to take a test, or coming face to face with a snake — we call it a *phobia*. When our apprehension does not appear connected to a specific thing or circumstance, is unidentifiable, unknown, or unconscious, we call it *anxiety*.

  Psychodynamic theorists of all persuasions give pre-eminence to anxiety's role in all forms of neurosis. Individuals who are overly anxious, excessively apprehensive, inordinately fretful, or too easily unnerved can suffer a host of maladies either directly caused or exacerbated by their anxiety. Further, therapists have traditionally thought neurotic "symptoms" — whether stress-related ulcers, tension headaches, avoidance of crowds or open places (i.e. agoraphobia), obsessive worry, desperate actions to prevent abandonment, etc. — to be rooted in anxiety.

  It's also noteworthy that, whether a fear is conscious and specific (i.e. a phobia) or unconscious or unidentified, research indicates that there is a common essential factor in getting rid of it: exposure. When phobic clients undergo treatment with behavioral or cognitive-behavioral methods, they are encouraged to systematically come into increasing contact with the very situations they fear, thus gaining an increased sense of personal empowerment, and reducing their apprehension levels. In traditional psychotherapy, clients gradually come into conscious contact with, and therefore "face," their previously unconscious fears in the safe, supportive, accepting atmosphere promoted by the therapist; and their fears are eventually reduced.

Anxiety is minimally present or plays a negligible role in the disturbed character's problems. In some cases, it's absent altogether. Character-disordered individuals are notoriously nonchalant about the things that upset most other people. Some, especially the aggressive personalities (more about them later) appear to *lack adaptive levels* of fearfulness.[4] They don't get apprehensive enough about their circumstances or their conduct. They're not unnerved enough at the prospect of conflict, and they readily leap into risky situations when others would hesitate. For the most part, disordered characters don't do dysfunctional things because some past trauma has them too "hung-up" to do otherwise. Instead, they do them because, unlike neurotics, they lack the capacity to get hung-up enough to think twice about their behavior, inhibit their impulses, or restrain their conduct. A little of the neurotic's typical apprehension would go a long way toward helping the disturbed character be more cautious or hesitant when it comes to frequently doing the things that cause problems.

For several reasons that I have never fully understood, traditionally-minded therapists, as well as relatively neurotic individuals, appear determined to ascribe fears and insecurities to disordered characters that simply don't exist. They will frequently misinterpret the behavior and motivations of character-disordered individuals and frame their behaviors inaccurately. For example, some disordered characters have a *passion* for novelty and a *craving* for excitement. So they constantly seek shallow, intense, short-lived, and high-risk sexual involvements and other interpersonal entanglements. But this characteristic thrill-seeking behavior is often framed as a "fear" of intimacy or commitment. This mistake is made because it's difficult for neurotic individuals (or traditionally-minded therapists for that matter) to imagine why a person wouldn't necessarily prefer a stable, intimate relationship over multiple risky encounters, unless they were in some way apprehensive about the prospects of engaging in something more substantive. This kind of thinking also reflects a long-held, but never proven, tenet of classical psychology: Everyone will naturally gravitate toward the healthiest life choices unless they are hung-up by unconscious fears that stem from past emotional trauma. It's also possible that some therapists are so married to their traditional metaphors about the nature of human behavior that, even when they encounter a "square peg," they still try to fit it into the proverbial round hole.

- **Conscience**. The neurotic individual is basically a person with a very well-developed conscience or superego. Sometimes that conscience can be overly active to the point of being oppressive. Neurotics have a huge sense of right and wrong, and always want to do what they think is the most correct. They can sometimes set impossibly high standards, engendering a significant amount of stress. Neurotics are also prone to judge themselves overly harshly when they fail to meet their own expectations. They take on inordinate burdens, carrying the world's weight on their shoulders. When something goes wrong, they quickly ask themselves what more *they* can do to make the situation better.

  The disordered character's conscience is remarkably under-developed and impaired. Disturbed characters don't hear that little voice that urges most of us to do right, or admonishes us when we're contemplating doing wrong. Or if they do hear it, they can easily ignore it, silence it, or put it in a "lock box" (i.e. *compartmentalize* it). As opposed to persons with a sound conscience, they don't push themselves to take on unattractive burdens and responsibilities; and they don't hold themselves back when they want something they really shouldn't have.

In the most severe disturbances of character, conscience is not simply weak, underdeveloped, or flawed, but *absent altogether*. The little voice most of us have simply isn't there, and the capacity to even form a conscience is grossly deficient. Robert Hare aptly named his book about the most severely disordered character, the psychopath, *Without Conscience*.[5]

It's hard to imagine individuals with no conscience at all. And as mentioned earlier, our traditional psychology metaphors have conditioned us to believe that underneath it all, we're all the same. Most folks find it unimaginable that some people are simply not "normal." That's why psychopaths are able to prey on the unsuspecting so effectively. Their victims dupe themselves with their inability to accept that the predators they've been dealing with are heartless and devoid of normal human empathy. It's very important to realize and accept that not everyone is the same. Not everyone has an active, mature conscience. All the disordered characters have deficiencies of conscience. They vary from those whose conscience is markedly immature to those with no conscience at all. Such individuals can do others great harm with absolutely no compunction. Those who fail to recognize this are extremely vulnerable.

Lacking a mature conscience, possessing a diminished capacity to experience distress in the face of injury to others, and deficient in empathy, many disturbed characters don't experience genuine remorse for their hurtful acts, whether acts of commission or omission. They might have some after-the-fact and practical regret for a behavior, especially if it results in some clear and appreciable cost to them. But because they don't have a healthy conscience, there's nothing to keep them from acting on their destructive impulses in the first place. So any practical regret for their own behavior is usually too little and comes far too late.

- **Shame and Guilt**. Because they are persons of conscience, neurotics can experience high (and sometimes toxic) levels of both shame and guilt. Shame is the emotional state we experience when we feel badly about *who we are.* Guilt is the emotional state we experience when we feel badly about *what we've done.* Neurotics tend to judge themselves harshly, so they're quick to feel ashamed when they fail to measure up to their own high standards and the self-image they try to maintain. They're also quick to feel guilty when they think they've fallen short, done something poorly, or caused injury to someone else.

  Most neurotics' levels of shame and guilt are adaptive to some degree. I have encountered a few neurotics who experienced such toxic levels of shame and guilt growing up that it led them to develop truly pathological symptoms. But even these individuals rarely experienced the extreme levels of guilt or shame necessary to produce the kinds of bizarre psychological phenomena Freud used to treat. Most neurotics are not sick from unreasonable or extreme levels of guilt or shame. But they are hypersensitive to these feelings. They are quick to feel badly about themselves when they've done something that reflects negatively on their character; and they're too quick to beat themselves up emotionally when they think they've committed unpardonable sins.

  Disturbed characters lack sufficient pangs of guilt or shame when they do things that are harmful or hurtful. Such feelings can only emanate from a well-developed conscience, which, as we discussed earlier, they lack. So, shamelessness and guiltlessness are two of the disturbed character's most distinguishing features. They don't feel badly enough about the kind of person they are when they repeatedly do things that negatively affect or injure others. They also don't feel badly enough about the harmful things they do, at least not badly enough to keep from doing them over and over again. If they were able to experience enough guilt or shame, they might refrain from doing socially harmful things in the first place, or from doing the same wrongful acts repeatedly.

The plethora of books dealing with shame and guilt that dominated the self-help and "recovery" market of the '60s, '70s, and even '80s, was largely written ***by, for, and about*** neurotics. Shame and blame were the names of their game, and most of those books blamed toxic levels of guilt and/or shame for a wide variety of psychological problems that damaged a person's self-esteem. These books largely made us believe there was no such thing as good shame or healthy guilt. Some authors and theorists later relented regarding guilt, acknowledging that at least some measure of guilt is necessary to keep us civilized. But even today, the dominant opinion about shame (and supported by empirical research), casts it as a bad thing, period. The general consensus seems to be this: While it's a relatively good thing to feel badly about something harmful you've *done*, feeling badly about oneself — about whom one literally is — is *never* a good thing.

But after working for many years with disturbed characters, I quickly came to question the validity of this premise.

Most of us experience some genuine self-disgust with the *kind of person* we might find ourselves becoming when we engage in behaviors disordered characters display. This is precisely what prompts us to change our ways, and restore a self-image we can live with. I've known many individuals who made significant changes in their characters. But when they did so, it was not only because they regretted their irresponsible behaviors, but also because they became unsettled enough with the person they had allowed themselves to become (i.e. became too ashamed of themselves) that they decided to change course. So, it appears that one must have the capacity to experience both shame and guilt in order to forge a sound character. As is usually the case, however, it's a matter of degree. When individuals experience toxic and unwarranted levels of either guilt or shame, there can indeed be a negative impact on psychological health.

Some professionals (and non-professionals) take issue with positions I outlined above. They insist that even disordered characters actually do feel guilt and shame, but that they effectively utilize — or perhaps over-utilize — certain "defense mechanisms" such as "denial" and "projection" to assuage any emotional pain. This is largely because they still adhere to the tenets of classical psychology (i.e. that *everyone* is to a greater or lesser degree neurotic, if they are not in fact psychotic, and that all individuals are fundamentally the same at a deeper psychological level). So, it's impossible for them to imagine how anyone could behave so shamelessly unless they were, in fact, defending themselves against real pain *underneath* it all. I'll address the pitfalls of the all-too-common tendency to over-extend and over-generalize classical psychology's metaphors in more depth later in the book. But it's important to remember that — although a disordered character's failure to acknowledge or "come clean" about wrongdoing can be viewed as a "state of denial" prompted by feelings of shame and guilt — such a perspective is often inaccurate. And it's potentially dangerous when trying to deduce the true nature of their problems and degree of character pathology.

Being embarrassed at being uncovered or found out is not the same as feeling genuine shame. Shame is one of those mechanisms that *make a person think twice* about doing something wrong in the first place. Moreover, a person who truly feels ashamed is certainly not likely to do the same things over and over again with no compunction. Character-disturbed people will sometimes claim they didn't come clean with themselves or others, or didn't seek help for their problematic conduct, because they were too ashamed to do so. This is often simply a lie they tell. They know a neurotic person is likely to find such an explanation more acceptable than the truth about their lack of motivation to change.

Individuals overly invested in human behavior's classical explanations also tend to misinterpret the careless, reckless, impulsive propensities of criminal behavior. They might assume criminal individuals had a subconscious desire (arising out of pangs of conscience) to be stopped when their seemingly thoughtless actions lead them to be easily apprehended. There has never been any empirical support for this notion, but that has not kept some from adhering to it. As I have stated several times already: Using metaphors that once appropriately described some neurotic behaviors to explain a disordered character's behavior almost always puts a person at a disadvantage when trying to understand or intervene in troublesome situations. A key thing to remember: Whereas neurotics have a propensity to experience guilt and shame too readily and with too great an intensity, the exact opposite is true for the disturbed character.

- **Level of awareness**. The distress neurotic individuals experience generally stems from emotional conflicts that are mostly *unconscious.* A woman experiences an unexplained "funk." She doesn't know it's related to her suppressed feelings of grief and loss re-surfacing near the anniversary of her mother's death. If she *did* know it, she might not even need to see a therapist to help her sort out why she was suddenly feeling so blue. A man with an ulcer is unaware that his obsessive worry over losing his job, in turn fueled by his deep-seated mistrust of authority figures, arises out of his experience with his abusive father. If he *were* aware of it, he might never have needed to knock on the counselor's door. Neurotics are often in considerable emotional turmoil; but the deeper roots of their distress, and sometimes even the very nature of their emotions, are often unknown to them.

  The problems the disordered character experiences might be so ingrained that they fairly "automatically" occur. However, it's important to remember that the disordered character is *fully conscious* of his problem behaviors. He not only knows exactly what he's doing, but also is fully aware of his *motivations* for doing it.

Lying is one of the more common and problematic behaviors of the disordered character. Sometimes this lying is done so "automatically" that the disturbed character finds himself lying without thinking much about it, and even when the truth would have done just fine. That doesn't mean he doesn't know he's lying. He knows. He just does it so often and so readily that he doesn't give it a second thought.

In my classical training I was taught never to ask clients "why" they did something because it would likely "throw them on the *defensive*" and they would be "afraid" to disclose. So, in my early work with disturbed characters, even though I was very interested in the motivations for their behaviors, I did not ask them directly why they did what they did. A fair amount of the time, when I did broach motivation issues, they would reply with something like: "To tell you the truth, doctor, I really don't know," or "That's what I'm in therapy to find out." This, of course, would reinforce the old notion that one of the major tasks for therapy would be to "uncover" the unconscious underpinnings of the conduct, so they could eventually "see" and understand the reasons for their behavior and "work through" their "issues."

What a surprise it was for me to learn that disordered characters are most often keenly aware, not only of their actions, but also of their motivations for them. This has proven to be true despite the fact that they might use the manipulation and impression-management tactics of "playing dumb," "feigning ignorance," or "feigning innocence" to skirt responsibility. I eventually learned (as have other colleagues and researchers in the area of character disturbance) that most of the time "I don't know" doesn't really mean the disturbed character is oblivious about his actions. It almost always means something else. It can mean:

- "I never really think about it that much."
- "I don't like to think about it."
- "I don't want to talk to you about it."
- "I know very well why I did it, but I certainly don't want you to know. That would put you in a position of equal advantage with me, or possibly even give you an advantage over me — having my number, so to speak — and I won't be able to manipulate you as easily or manage your impression of me."
- "I hope you'll buy the notion that I'm basically a good person whose intentions were benign. That I simply made an unwitting mistake, oblivious about the harm I caused; and that I am willing to increase my awareness with your guidance." (This kind of implied message is the epitome of effective *manipulation and impression management,* and it's amazing how many times it is successfully "sold.")

So, "I don't know" can mean any of the above and a whole host of other things. But in the case of the disturbed character, it ***rarely***, truly means "I don't know." So I no longer accept it for an answer. And once I politely but firmly stopped taking it for an acceptable response, I immediately started getting explanations that made much more sense. Most importantly, the games of manipulation and impression management my character-disordered clients tried to engage me in diminished dramatically.

Realizing how hoodwinked I had been by accepting their initial non-explanations for behavior helped me become dramatically aware of how expert disordered characters generally are on the subject of neurosis, as well as the mindsets of many mental health professionals, especially those steeped in traditional paradigms. They know very well how neurotics tend to think. They know the attitudes neurotics hold, and the naiveties that make them vulnerable to tactics of manipulation and impression management. They often know the neurotics in their lives better than those neurotics know themselves. They're also frequently quite "couch broken" (i.e. have made the rounds to many professionals and become very familiar with psychological concepts, terms, and paradigms); and they know what to say that might be easily believed, especially if it's not scrutinized carefully. So, they can manipulate even a seasoned professional.

These days, I focus very little attention on the underpinnings of behavior, even though it's sometimes very helpful to know what all the nefarious motivations might be. I primarily assume that the disordered character is very aware — not only of his behavior but also the reasons for it. So I direct attention mostly to the behavior itself with an emphasis on changing it.

- **The role of feelings**. When a neurotic person seeks counseling for one reason or another, you can safely assume some emotional issues need to be attended to or resolved. Perhaps those feelings have been long repressed. Perhaps those feelings are very mixed and conflicted. In any case, helping persons establish deeper contact with their feelings and sort through their troubled emotions represents the hallmark of traditional psychotherapy. Regardless of the neurotic individual's problems, traditional psychotherapy almost always devotes considerable focus to the person's *feelings*.

The disturbed character's problems with functioning well in a social context are not so much a consequence of the way he feels, but the way he *thinks*. It's his ill-gotten *attitudes*, erroneous and distorted thinking patterns, and dysfunctional core beliefs that lie at the root of problems. Awareness of this fact has in recent years spurred a revolution in therapeutic approaches.

The term *cognitive-behavioral therapy* refers to an orientation founded on the principle of an inextricable relationship between a person's core beliefs, attitudes, and thinking patterns and that person's behavior. For example, say a man's core beliefs include the view that any woman is naturally inferior to him, is designed by nature to be submissive, is a rightful personal possession if involved in a serious relationship with him, and has value only as a sexual object or toy. One would not be particularly surprised to learn that this man had a history of abusive conduct with his wife or girlfriend. *How we think in large measure determines how we will act.* When dealing with disordered characters, their kinds of problematic thinking become the bigger issue to address, as opposed to how they are feeling.

One of the ways that folks become embroiled in abusive or exploitive relationships is by falling prey to concerns about the way their character-disordered partner is feeling. For example, they might focus all too much on why their partner seems angry all the time, wondering what they might have done to engender such ire. They almost never consider that the brandishing of anger is sometimes a tactic that character-disturbed individuals use to manipulate and control others, as opposed to a genuine feeling. What's more, they don't consider that it's their abuser's attitudes toward them, their value system, and their distorted manner of thinking about things that constitutes the main problem, and might be the precipitant of any unwarranted anger in the first place. If they manage to lure their partner into counseling, and the counselor is of the traditional mindset and primarily focuses on "feelings," things are not likely to get much better. They *may possibly get worse* as the non-character-disordered party bares his or her soul in the counseling process and exposes even more of his or her vulnerability to the abusive party.

When I first began using more appropriate methods to counsel character-disordered persons, a frequent comment I heard from clients was, "I don't think you really care." This kind of comment really put me on the defensive (as it would any good neurotic) initially. After all, I was a therapist, and I was supposed to be a warm, empathic person dedicated to helping alleviate human misery. It took me awhile to realize that a comment like that was often a counter-therapeutic and manipulative tactic on the disturbed characters' part. They wanted to get me to align with their point of view on things, to justify their conduct, and most especially to see if they could convince me that they deserved just as much sympathy as those they had brought great pain. Of course I *cared.* But I also came to know that if I were to *care properly* and *therapeutically* for the disordered characters I was working with, I would have to confront the real impediments to their inner psychological health and healthy interpersonal functioning. That meant calling them on their tactics and letting them know that the genuineness of my "caring" would become all too evident in time. That would be through my unwavering dedication to challenging and helping them correct the distorted thinking patterns that had made a mess of their lives and the lives of others for too many years already. The door was always open to more traditional feelings-based counseling after character issues were resolved. Many did indeed walk through that door when the time came. That made me a believer in the notion that, when it comes to dealing with significant disturbances of character, focusing on feelings is not an exercise in "caring," but rather a perfect example of *enabling.*

In a later chapter, I will outline several of the major thinking errors disordered characters have in common, and the dysfunctional social attitudes those erroneous ways of thinking breed. Knowing disturbed characters' frequent dysfunctional thinking patterns is crucial to understanding their problematic behavior, and learning how to confront and deal with them effectively.

- **The role of defense mechanisms**. Neurotics are thought to use a variety of intra-psychic *mechanisms* to *defend* themselves against the experience of emotional pain, and especially to alleviate anxiety associated with conflicts between their primal urges and their consciences. Almost everyone has heard of these classic "defense mechanisms." Such mechanisms, by definition, operate *unconsciously.* That is, the person doesn't deliberately engage in an action, but rather the unconscious mind employs the mechanism so the conscious mind never has to experience the pain in the first place. Here's the reason neurotic individuals develop problematic symptoms: These unconscious tools of anxiety mitigation, though powerful, are neither adequate, nor are they always fully adaptive ways to mitigate emotional pain. Many times, the symptoms the neurotic individual brings to the therapist's attention result from residual anxiety — or the emotional pain left over after ineffective use of one or more of the typical defenses. At other times, people might seek help because their defenses have become increasingly inadequate or have begun to break down, letting their emotional pain underneath rise to the surface. In those cases, it's the emotional pain that brings someone into treatment. All successful therapies for neurosis depend upon building a trusting rapport with the therapist, so that an atmosphere of safety and encouragement allows clients to relax their defenses and reveal their inner pain or emotional conflicts.

Disordered characters engage in certain behaviors so "automatic" that it's tempting to think they do them unconsciously. On the surface, these behaviors often so resemble *defense mechanisms* that they can be easily misinterpreted as such, especially by individuals overly immersed in traditional paradigms. However, on closer inspection, many of these behaviors are more accurately regarded as *tactics* of *manipulation, impression-management,* and *responsibility-resistance* (much more about this later).

In workshops, I always illustrate the contrast between a true "defense" mechanism and a tactic of manipulation and responsibility-avoidance using the concept of "denial." One of the 10 most commonly misused terms in mental health (more about this later), denial can indeed be an unconscious defense mechanism. Let's take the example of a woman who has been married to the same man for 40 years. She has just rushed him to the hospital because, while they were out in the yard working, he began having trouble speaking and looked in some distress. The doctors then tell her that he has suffered a stroke, is now virtually brain-dead, and will not recover. Yet, every day she is by his bedside, holding his hand and talking to him. The nurses tell her that he cannot hear, but she talks to him anyway. The doctors tell her he will not recover, but she only replies, "I know he'll pull through, he's such a strong man." This woman is in a unique *psychological state* — the state of *denial.* She can hardly believe what has happened. Not long ago she was in the yard with her darling, enjoying one of their favorite activities. The day before, they were at a friend's home for a get-together. He seemed the picture of happiness and health. He didn't even seem that sick when she brought him to the hospital. Now — in a blink of an eye — they're telling her he's gone. This is far more emotional pain than she can bear just yet. She's not ready to accept that her partner of 40 years won't be coming home with her. She's not quite ready to face a life without him. So, her unconscious mind has provided her with an effective (albeit most likely temporary) *defense* against the pain. Eventually, as she becomes better able to accept the distressing reality, her denial will break down. When it does, the pain it served to contain will gush forth and she will grieve.

Now, let's take another example of so-called "denial." Joe, the class bully, strolls up to one of his unsuspecting classmates and engages in one of his favorite mischievous pastimes — pushing the books out of her arms and spilling them on the floor. It just so happens that the hall monitor catches the event and sternly hollers: "Joe!" to which Joe, spreading his arms wide open and with a look of great shock, surprise, and innocence on his face retorts: "Whaaaat?" Does Joe really not understand the reality of what has happened? Does he actually think he didn't do what the hall monitor saw him do? Is he in some kind of altered psychological state? Is his possible altered state brought about by more emotional pain than he could possibly stand to bear? Is he so consumed with shame and/or guilt for what he's done that he simply can't allow himself to believe he actually did such a horrible thing? More than likely, none of the aforementioned possibilities is correct. Joe is probably more concerned that he has another detention hall coming, which means another note to his parents, and possibly even a suspension. So, he's got one long-shot *tactic* to try. He'll do his best to make the hall monitor believe she didn't really see what she thought she saw. The hallway was crowded. Maybe it was someone else. Maybe it was just an "accident." If he *acts* surprised, innocent, and righteously indignant enough, maybe, just maybe, she'll begin to doubt herself. He hopes that, unlike him, she might be just *neurotic* enough (i.e. has an overactive conscience and excessive sense of guilt or shame) to think she might have misjudged the situation. Maybe she'll even berate herself for jumping to conclusions or for causing a possibly innocent person unwarranted emotional pain. This tactic might have worked before. Maybe it will work again.

This preceding example is based on a real case. It is noteworthy that when "Joe" realized that he simply couldn't manipulate the hall monitor, he reluctantly stopped "denying," saying: "Well, maybe I did do it, but she had it coming because she's always bad-mouthing me to her friends." Now, we could engage in some discussion about the other tactics Joe is using to continue the game of manipulation and impression management, but the most important thing to recognize is this: Unlike what happens in the case of real psychological denial as the defense mechanism, in Joe's case we don't see an outpouring of anguish and grief when the denial ends. The reason is simple. Joe was never "in denial" (the psychological state) per se in the first place. He was simply *lying.* He eventually stopped lying because it wasn't getting him anywhere. He moved on from the tactic of lying to excuse-making and playing the victim, also effective tactics of manipulation and impression-management.

I can't stress this enough: The "denial" of the unfortunate elderly woman mentioned above is nothing like the "denial" of Joe the school bully. One is truly an ego *defense mechanism*; the other a *manipulation and responsibility-resistance tactic.* One is an unconscious mechanism of protection from deep emotional pain; the other is a deliberate, calculated lie. Yet many professionals (as well as lay persons) use the same term to describe these very different behaviors. And because they presume there is only one type of denial, whenever their clients display behavior like Joe's, they regard it as a sign of shame-based, unconscious denial. I can't count the number of times clinicians have spoken to me of clients who are still "in denial" about one problem behavior or another, when what they were really describing was a client still "lying and manipulating" as part of the game of impression management and responsibility-resistance. As a result, they end up wasting precious time and missing the mark in multiple sessions designed to help their clients "come out of their denial."

It's important for both lay persons and clinicians not only to know the difference between a true defense mechanism and a tactic of responsibility-avoidance and interpersonal manipulation, but also to know how to appropriately respond to these very different types of behaviors. I presented the principal tactics manipulators use and how to respond to them in *In Sheep's Clothing*.[6] In a later chapter, we'll take a more in-depth look at those tactics, as well as other responsibility-avoidance and impression-management maneuvers used by the various disordered characters.

- **The genuineness of *style*.** Some of the more prominent traditionally-oriented theorists have conceptualized the neurotic personality as essentially a fraud. The neurotic's true self was thought to be hidden behind a social façade. So, a particularly gregarious person might be perceived in reality as quite shy and interpersonally anxious "underneath" the social face he or she presents, and to "compensate" for this social insecurity with feigned sociability. Similarly, bullies have been perceived as cowards underneath their brash exterior, and haughty individuals viewed as compensating for low-self esteem. In short, their outward presentation is an unconsciously constructed "front" to mask their inner insecurities. Classical theorists also believed they could essentially define the principal personality types by the defense mechanisms they typically used to protect their true selves. Even relatively recently, this kind of conceptualization was articulated in David Shapiro's landmark work *Neurotic Styles*.[7] He eloquently describes the various personality "styles," but still views them as essentially an expression of a person's neurosis.

  Have you ever noticed the consistency in these traditional notions about a very different kind of reality lying underneath the façade? They always involve an outward appearance that's not very appealing, and a more pitiable reality underneath.

In other words, traditional notions about personality tend to view egomaniacs as really having low self-esteem underneath, bullies being scared little kids underneath, and abusers being traumatized victims underneath it all, etc. But you've probably never heard a devotee of classical perspectives claim that a shy person is really a ravenous animal underneath it all, wanting to jump the bones of everyone they meet. Or that a particularly sensitive person is really a vicious monster with a heart of stone underneath. I think we're too quick to align with psychology metaphors that have outlived their usefulness for this reason: Most of us still don't like to face the unpleasant things in life, and want to explain them away with a perspective that makes the unnerving more palatable. After all, genuine *denial* is one of the things neurotics do best!

While it might be true to some extent that a neurotic is quite different under the exterior, with the disturbed character, ***what you see is what you get***, unless a deliberate con game is being played. With respect to primary personality traits, there is no pretense. Disordered characters are who they are, as unfortunate as that may be, and often to the core.

I once worked in a residential treatment program that specialized in young persons already displaying significant disturbances of character and conduct. One day, a young man was admitted who, within minutes of arrival, began listing on a notepad program improvements he thought the staff needed to make. He wanted to present this list to the facility administrator and demanded an audience to discuss matters. Steeped in traditional psychological theories, the head nurse — when this young man's treatment plan was fashioned — recalled his haughtiness, and proposed a first treatment goal of increasing his sense of self-esteem. She assumed, as is common to neurotics and devotees of traditional perspectives, that his pompous attitude simply *must* have been a *compensation* for underlying feelings of inferiority. But in time, it became quite apparent that this young man in fact had no feelings of inferiority. Rather, he possessed only a deeply-rooted sense of superiority and *entitlement* common to individuals over-indulged and over-valued all their lives — people who end up as deeply disturbed characters.

- **Self-esteem**. The discussion above alludes to another very key difference between neurotics and disordered characters. Neurotics have significantly damaged self-images, typically arising out of a deflated sense of self-worth or self-esteem. The neurotic often feels defective in some way, and therefore not truly lovable. Sometimes this impaired self-esteem can lead to a profound sense of inadequacy and serious weaknesses of character. Sometimes it prompts the neurotic to try hard to please others, and to do their very best to "earn" approval. If not excessive, this tendency can provide a critical incentive to behave in socially acceptable or responsible ways. In other words, when people think their self-worth largely depends on how clearly they demonstrate their value to society, they can be motivated to conduct themselves in a manner that increases the likelihood of benefitting the greater good.

  Disordered characters have an inflated sense of self-worth. They see themselves as superior to others. As a result, they often feel *entitled* to use and exploit others as they see fit. As noted earlier, their ego-inflation is not rooted in underlying feelings of insecurity or inferiority. It's not a pretense. They really do think they're something special and above the common throng. And, their sense of superiority fuels their attitudes of entitlement. Later in this book, we'll take a deeper look at one type of character disorder, the psychopath, in which this disturbing trait is present to its most pathological extreme.

  In a later chapter, I'll also be introducing a critical distinction between the concepts of self-esteem and self-respect. This distinction will hopefully not only give some additional clarity to self-esteem's definition, but also will help explain why there's often such confusion and misunderstanding about how and why some people's self-image gets bent out of shape.

- **Response to adverse consequence**. Neurotics try very hard to effect positive outcomes, and they easily become anxious and upset when things go badly. They are *hypersensitive to adverse consequence.* A co-occurring trait accompanying this hypersensitivity is the tendency to make *internal attributions* about the reasons for problems. When a neurotic worker doesn't get the "good job" comment she craves from her boss, she might well beat herself up with self-criticism. When the neurotic therapist doesn't see positive change in her therapy group, she might well berate herself as a sub-standard counselor. Neurotics always want things to be right with the world, and they get internally unnerved when things go wrong. They want the world to be at peace, for everyone to love them, and for everyone's dreams to come true. When things go badly, they take it hard. They're unnerved by the cruelty and unfairness of life, and feeling inordinately responsible, they take it upon themselves to make things better. When things go poorly, they chide themselves, question themselves, conduct an internal debate about how they might do things differently, and try all the harder to make things right. Even when it's fairly impossible to blame themselves for a painful happenstance (e.g., a natural disaster or catastrophe), they still question and prod themselves about what they can or should do to make the situation better. And they're deeply affected by any unintended adverse consequences of their own actions, and strive to make amends.

  Disordered characters are largely unaffected and *undeterred by adverse consequence.* They have a characteristic imperturbability when it comes to dealing with the negative fallout of their behavior. They are typically not unnerved by situations that would make the neurotic upset. More importantly, they remain undeterred about their basic way of handling things. They might even be strengthened in their resolve to keep doing just as they have been doing, despite the objective fact that their way is clearly not working.

A co-occurring character trait is the disordered character's tendency to make *external attributions* whenever anything bad does happen. They see others and circumstances outside themselves as the source of problems. So, even if they've lost another job, had another marriage fall apart, run into legal difficulties, or even lost their freedom (if they have become incarcerated), they take it in stride. They never blame themselves, and keep on behaving the same way they've always behaved, despite where it's gotten them. They even pride themselves in the notion that they will remain who they are, doing things as they've always done, despite the hardships in their lives, including those often resulting from their own behavior.

- **Level of internal discomfort**. Neurotics are also different from character disorders on another very key dimension. In large measure, they experience the signs and symptoms of their neuroses as unpleasant and unwanted. Perhaps an individual has been worrying to the point that he's developed an ulcer, and is now in frequent gastric distress. Perhaps this circumstance has slowed him down at work, making him less productive. He still drives hard like always, but his frequent bouts of pain have stymied his usual effectiveness. It's very likely that he does not like the person he has become as a result. Clinicians say that it is *ego-dystonic* (unpalatable to his image of himself) for him not to be performing at his best. What's more, he doesn't like his symptoms either (i.e. the pain of his ulcer). As a result, he will likely take the initiative to get some help. He wants the problem gone, to be out of pain, to be at his best again; and he'll probably do what he has to do to make things better again. If he seeks help from a therapist, he'll even be open to changing some things about himself so he'll be a better person and have fewer disturbing symptoms. He'll likely be motivated to at least try what the therapist suggests, to regard the therapist's guidance as valuable as he begins to gain relief, and to remain in treatment until he has overcome his problem and doesn't need therapy services anymore.

Disturbed characters also display telltale signs and symptoms of their disorder. Lying, conning, manipulating, defaulting on social obligations, etc., are several of the disordered character's defining features. The negative attitudes they hold, the distorted way they tend to think, and the irresponsible ways they tend to behave are likely to be greatly upsetting to others. But these things are what clinicians call *ego-syntonic* to the disordered character. That is, the disordered character doesn't see anything wrong or disturbing about them. Moreover, he is not upset by the kind of person he has become as a result of these characteristics. He likes who he is and how he operates. Others may complain that he tends to use and exploit people. His answer might be that gullible or weaker people deserve to be taken advantage of. As he sees it, if others have a problem with him, it's because *they* are all screwed up. When someone points out one of his most disturbing characteristics, he might retort: "You got a problem with that?" Disturbed characters also don't seek help in the manner neurotics do. Rather, they're more often dragged into counseling by distraught neurotics who are in some kind of relationship with them. Disturbed characters are rarely in the kind of inner distress that prompts most people to seek and appreciate guidance or counseling on their own.

- **Needs in treatment**. Another important difference between neurotics and disordered characters is what they need most from any kind of therapeutic experience. This is, perhaps, one of the most important points I need to make for the benefit of therapists. Because neurotics are struggling with inadequacies, insecurities, and emotional conflicts, they both crave and need positive regard as well as supportive guidance. In short, they need *help*. Also, because many of their unresolved issues are mostly rooted in the unconscious, neurotics both need and benefit from *insight*. They literally don't know what they're doing to perpetuate their difficulties. So they benefit greatly from listening to their counselors *interpret* the "dynamics" of their circumstances, thus shedding "new light" on their situation. Because they were largely unable to come to such insights on their own, they not only seek help but also appreciate it when they get it in the forms of new insights, emotional support, and guidance.

  In contrast to insight-deficient neurotics, disordered characters are already keenly aware of the ways their thinking and behavior cause problems. There isn't one thing anyone can say or bring to their attention that they haven't heard a thousand times before from a variety of sources, or experienced in a variety of circumstances. In many of my workshops, I introduce the trite little saying: "They already *see*; they simply *disagree*." They're just not disturbed enough by their way of doing things; or they may have been successful enough getting their way by doing those things, so they're resolved not to change that modus operandi. Because they do the things they do so automatically and habitually, it can seem like they're unaware. But doing things that are second nature to a person is not the same as doing things in which the motivations are truly unknown or unconscious. When it comes to the behaviors that cause problems in the lives of others, disordered characters *know what they're doing* as well as their motivations for doing it. But they're so comfortable with their way of doing things, and do them so habitually, that they don't give their behavior a second thought. So, what they really need within the context of any relationship (whether it be a therapeutic relationship with a counselor or any other relationship) is not so much *help* and *insight* as benign yet firm *confrontation, limit-setting,* and most especially, *correction.* I frame the things they need the most in any interpersonal encounter as "corrective emotional and behavioral experience." By this I mean they need an encounter which directly confronts and challenges their dysfunctional beliefs, destructive attitudes, and distorted ways of thinking; and which stymies their typical attempts at manipulation and impression management. This is done by setting firm limits on their maladaptive behavior, and *structuring the terms of engagement* in a manner that prompts them to try out alternative, more pro-social ways of interrelating, which can then be reinforced. Doing this resolutely but without hostility or other negative emotion is a genuine art.

Some therapists say it's impossible to effectively treat disturbances of character. This is a truly sad misconception. Disturbed characters can be treated, but it's virtually impossible to treat them effectively with the methods most therapists learned to treat neurosis. It's like a physician trying to do delicate brain surgery with a dentist's appliances. It doesn't matter how well-trained the physician is, or how carefully she conducts the surgery. If the tools and implements she uses are those made for orthodontics, the outcome will likely be bleak. The outlook would be even bleaker if the physician held the belief that all human maladies arise from different forms of tooth disease (analogous to the absurd but still all-too-commonly-held notion that *all* maladaptive human behavior or personality dysfunction are forms of neurosis). Character disturbance can in fact be treated, but because it's such a very different phenomenon from neurosis, the endeavor requires an approach radically different from those developed to treat neurosis. Even when using the proper tools, treating disturbed characters is a particularly challenging and difficult endeavor. But it's truly an impossible task when therapists insist upon viewing and intervening with the disturbed character as they would a neurotic.

Here's another reason clinicians have long believed that personality and character disturbances couldn't be treated: They rarely tried addressing core character issues directly in therapy. Rather than focus on the dysfunctional coping "style" that begot an individual's problems and symptoms in the first place, therapists often gave attention to the problems and symptoms themselves. To address character issues directly — instead of focusing on problems communicating, what a person's memories of childhood are, or how they were parented, etc. — a therapist would need to confront, for example, how a person's inflated self-image, fueled by their egocentric thinking and attitudes of entitlement, leads them to chronically exploit and demean people in relationships, and how it causes other problems. It's impossible to ameliorate a condition you ignore. Giving a person's dysfunctional personality style center stage in therapy is essential to helping change it.

The last big reason some clinicians think it's impossible to effectively treat disturbed characters is because of their own over-immersion in insight-oriented techniques. They spend inordinate time trying to get their clients to "see" the folly of their ways. They might even have the vanity to think that, if they only find the right way to frame things, or make their case in a more eloquent, convincing, or empathic way than any therapist before them, they can make their client finally "get it." They waste a lot of time and energy on this. And when the effort fails, rather than question the appropriateness of adopting the insight-oriented approach, they ascribe the failure to the seriousness and intractability of their client's disturbance.

When I first began treating disturbed characters, cognitive-behavioral therapy (the paradigm of choice) was still in its infancy. But clinicians are increasingly coming to appreciate its value, especially in dealing with such problems. And using the tools arising out of cognitive-behavioral paradigms is just the beginning. Treating character disturbance is relatively new territory, and the tools and techniques needed to address it are still very much in the developmental stage.

- **Impact of symptoms and behavioral "style."** Neurotics generally develop "symptoms" (e.g., stress-exacerbated ulcers, phobias, etc.) that are *self-distressing* and *self-defeating.* Neurotics make themselves miserable and stymie their own well-being as a result of their insecurities and hang-ups. Their way of coping with stress (i.e. their coping *style*) is inadequate and negatively impacts their own personal development. By contrast, disordered characters' symptoms (e.g., problematic attitudes, thinking patterns, antisocial behaviors, etc.), for the most part negatively impact others. The way the disordered character behaves makes everyone else's life difficult. Their methods and tactics might be self-defeating in the long-run, but they're certainly intended to be — and for a time often are — ruthlessly self-advancing, usually to everyone else's detriment. So profound truth lies in this old adage among mental health professionals: If clients are miserable, they're probably at least to some degree neurotic; and if they're making someone else miserable, they're probably at least to some degree character disordered.

The chart on the next page outlines the significant differences between neurotics and disturbed characters:

NEUROTIC	CHARACTER DISORDER
Anxiety is a major factor in symptoms/self-presentation.	Anxiety plays minor role or is problematically lacking.
Conscience is very well-developed, overactive.	Conscience is under-developed or lacking.
Excessive guilt/shame.	Insufficient guilt/shame.
Problems arise from *unconscious* conflicts.	Problem behaviors are habitual but deliberate.
Conflicted emotions at root problems.	Problematic thinking patterns, attitudes, and behaviors create difficulties.
Use defense mechanisms to mediate anxiety/ emotional pain.	Use behaviors and tactics to shirk responsibility.
Authentic self hidden behind defenses.	Self-presentation is authentic but problematic.
Damaged self-esteem.	Inflated sense of self-worth.
Hypersensitive to adverse consequence.	Undeterred by adverse consequence.
Needs/benefits from insight.	Has awareness. Needs correction.
Ego-dystonic symptoms and coping patterns.	Ego-syntonic symptoms and coping patterns.
Self-defeating coping patterns.	Coping patterns meant to be self-advancing and victimize others.

FIGURE 2

CHAPTER 2

Major Disturbances of Personality and Character

Personality traits of one variety or another help define every one of us as a unique individual. But at times, such traits are of a quality, intensity, intractability, or cluster in such a manner that they cause significant problems in everyday functioning. Then that personality is said to be disturbed, or in the more extreme cases, disordered. The official psychiatric diagnostic manual employs some very stringent guidelines to determine whether a person qualifies for a personality disorder diagnosis. Further, the manual attempts to be as objective as possible, using only observable behavioral criteria to delineate the various personality disorders.

This book's purpose is *not* to provide definitive diagnostic criteria about distinct disorders of personality per se. It's a book about character, and specifically about disturbances of character. It is meant to be as accurately descriptive as possible, but not technically diagnostic in nature as we illustrate the major personality types and disturbances of character. The various types depicted differ in the degree they represent a problematic level of interpersonal and social functioning.

Several personality types have been generally recognized by researchers and professionals for many years. More traditionally-oriented theorists still regard the various personality styles as different manifestations of neurosis.[8] Theorists who share this perspective view the various outward behavioral manifestations of personality as a set of compensations for, or false representations of, a much different and unconscious underlying reality. More contemporary thinkers view at least some personality patterns as genuine manifestations of an individual's conscious, but habitual and preferred way, of relating to the world.[9]

Now, a major question arises about how to decide to what degree a person's preferred way of coping represents a "neurotic" style or a disturbance of character, especially when, on the surface, it's often difficult to tell the difference. Biological science recognizes the difference between phenotype (the outward appearance of an organism) and genotype (it's genetic makeup). It just so happens that some creatures are genetically very different from one another, but look identical and even behave in a similar manner. If you're a biologist or genetic scientist, you can resolve the issue by typing the DNA. But judging personality is a bit more complex.

We must take into account two important factors when trying to decide whether we're dealing with a relatively neurotic personality or a person of genuinely disturbed character. First, some personality types are more often associated with varying degrees of neurosis, and others with varying degrees of character disturbance. So, once you know the major personality types (as we'll be exploring shortly), you can make some preliminary judgments about the kind of person you're *probably* dealing with. But to move beyond probability to a greater sense of certainty, you have to look at the cluster of characteristics, presented in Chapter 1, that distinguish character disturbance from neurosis. For example, if you encounter an egoistic, pretentious person, you could entertain either the notion that they are a character-disturbed individual, or a neurotic whose pretentiousness is a façade masking underlying insecurity. But if this person chronically displays egocentric thinking and other thinking errors, reveals attitudes of entitlement, uses various tactics of responsibility-avoidance, routinely exploits others, persists in the behavior pattern despite adverse consequence, already shows a high level of insight, and — despite bringing repeated pain into the lives of others is completely comfortable with the kind of person he or she is, etc. — you can be a lot surer you're dealing with a character-disturbed narcissist. Keep the aforementioned guidelines in mind as we take a look at the major personality disturbances, with special emphasis on those types most often associated with significant deficiencies of character.

The figures below outline some essential dimensions of the more common interpersonal relating "styles" or personality types. They are a greatly simplified representation of the principal styles and dimensions of functioning that Millon outlines in several of his works.[10] Two of the represented domains of interpersonal functioning involve (1) whether a person primarily finds satisfaction of emotional needs in external sources (i.e. is emotionally dependent) vs. internal sources (i.e. is emotionally independent), and (2) whether the interpersonal style of relating has been primarily shaped and maintained by what the person actively does (i.e. the "active" dimension) as opposed to what he or she fails to do (i.e. the "passive" dimension). The axes depict varying degrees along a continuum with respect to these two dimensions. Most individuals achieve a healthy balance on all these dimensions. Some get "stuck" in a state of ambivalence, never really resolving the developmental task of solidifying a balanced style of relating. And, of course, the personality traits of most individuals are neither so extreme nor inflexible that they cause interpersonal dysfunction. Those personalities whose relating styles significantly impair their ability to function adaptively are considered *disordered*.

BASIC PERSONALITY "STYLES"

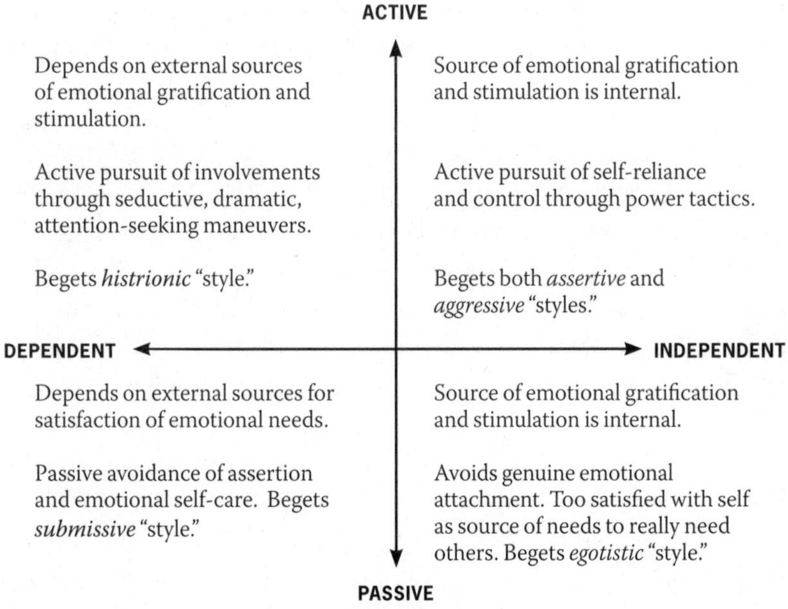

ACTIVE

Depends on external sources of emotional gratification and stimulation.

Active pursuit of involvements through seductive, dramatic, attention-seeking maneuvers.

Begets *histrionic* "style."

Source of emotional gratification and stimulation is internal.

Active pursuit of self-reliance and control through power tactics.

Begets both *assertive* and *aggressive* "styles."

DEPENDENT ←→ **INDEPENDENT**

Depends on external sources for satisfaction of emotional needs.

Passive avoidance of assertion and emotional self-care. Begets *submissive* "style."

Source of emotional gratification and stimulation is internal.

Avoids genuine emotional attachment. Too satisfied with self as source of needs to really need others. Begets *egotistic* "style."

PASSIVE

FIGURE 3

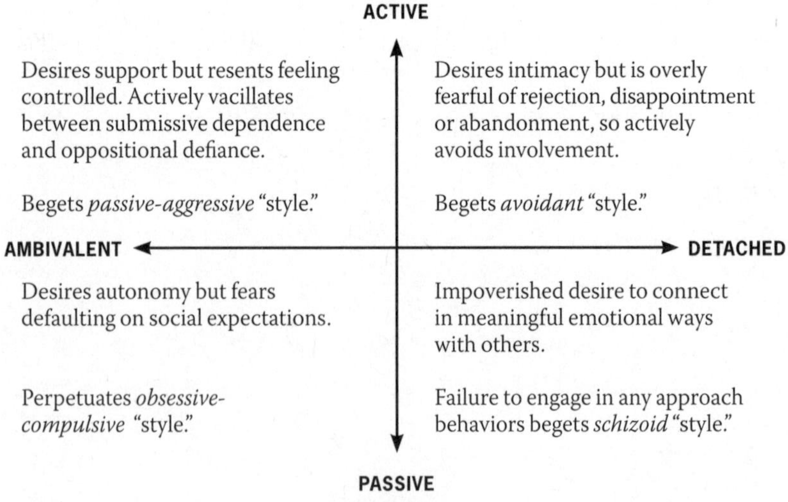

ACTIVE

Desires support but resents feeling controlled. Actively vacillates between submissive dependence and oppositional defiance.

Begets *passive-aggressive* "style."

Desires intimacy but is overly fearful of rejection, disappointment or abandonment, so actively avoids involvement.

Begets *avoidant* "style."

AMBIVALENT ←→ **DETACHED**

Desires autonomy but fears defaulting on social expectations.

Perpetuates *obsessive-compulsive* "style."

Impoverished desire to connect in meaningful emotional ways with others.

Failure to engage in any approach behaviors begets *schizoid* "style."

PASSIVE

FIGURE 4

PREDOMINATELY NEUROTIC PERSONALITIES

The Deferential Pattern

Some predisposed individuals look externally to satisfy their emotional needs. They don't find within themselves either the resources or the confidence to tackle life's challenges, and are overly reliant on others to provide necessary stimulation and support. They are notoriously *passive*, non-assertive, accommodating, and acquiescent. And, because they habitually fail to act in their own behalf, they deny themselves the opportunities for the potential successes they need to build self-confidence. They might occasionally take a chance and venture out, but if they meet with significant obstacles or resistance, they quickly retreat and are reluctant to try again. This then perpetuates their pattern of non-assertion.

Passive-dependent (or simply, *dependent*) is the label some clinicians and researchers have given to those personalities. They are all too willing to concede defeat in the face of challenge, and to turn their lives over to the care of someone else they view as more powerful, capable, and more resilient than themselves. Because they are so emotionally dependent upon others and lack the skill to function autonomously, they can be remarkably *submissive* and *deferential* in their style of relating interpersonally.

The dependent personality is driven by several fears, namely the fears of abandonment, failure, and even success. Failure signals to them that their self-doubts are justified, and reinforces their perceived need of others. Success begets fears of separation from familiar sources of support. At a very deep level, these individuals equate being "on their own" with being "alone," and this creates intense and deep-seated anxiety.

The dependent, interpersonal style of relating is both begotten and maintained primarily by what these individuals do not do (hence the *passive* component of passive-dependency). Typically, they don't assert themselves or act autonomously and independently. They experience considerable anxiety with respect to their personal safety and well-being, especially when they are not firmly tied to a reliable source of emotional support. Their anxieties about self-assertion and the potential loss of support systems fuel considerable neurosis. When they say "no," they too readily feel guilty. When they're tempted to challenge an oppressive situation or partner, their fears of potential abandonment kicks in. So instead of standing up for themselves and becoming more independent, they acquiesce and remain emotionally dependent.

The core characteristics of the Deferential Personality are:

- Over-reliance on external sources of emotional gratification and support.
- Excessive readiness to capitulate or submit in interpersonal encounters or when facing the challenges of daily living.
- A tendency to affiliate with those viewed as more powerful or capable than themselves.
- Apprehension, anxiety, and other symptoms of distress when faced with potential losses of support.

There are several factors that have been advanced as possible contributors to the development of the deferential "style":

Possible Constitutional (biological, temperamental) Factors:

- These individuals tend to have relatively pacific, retreating temperaments.
- They tend to have high needs for safety and protection.
- They tend to be highly responsive to external reward.

Possible Learning Factors:

- o These individuals might have over-learned that powerful others will nurture and protect them, possibly even better than they have learned to protect themselves.
- o They appear to lack experience in fending for themselves emotionally, behaviorally, and occupationally.
- o They appear to have failed to adequately discriminate between functioning autonomously (i.e. being "on their own") and being emotionally abandoned (i.e. totally "alone").
- o On balance, individuals with this personality type are generally much more neurotic than they are character disturbed. If there is a dimension of their personality one could regard as character deficiency, it would be their *strength* of character. These individuals are frequently seen as "weak" and ineffective. They are often the archetypal "doormats" in relationships. They lack the necessary confidence, resoluteness, and persistence necessary to fend for themselves, and for others to be able to depend on them.
- o Millon[11] suggests that there are some common variations of this personality type, depending upon which personality traits dominate. He proposes that the underdeveloped capacity of some dependent personalities to face life's challenges and meet its responsibilities begets a pattern of immaturity and inadequacy (i.e., the "inadequate" personality variant). The disquieted or avoidant dependent anticipates danger and potential abandonment, unless closely aligned with trustworthy, supportive others. The overly selfless dependent cares so little about self that any sense of personal identity or worth becomes obscured

or absorbed by another viewed as stronger or more powerful. The accommodating variation is overly agreeable, compliant, and subservient, catering to the needs of others in exchange for a sense of being valued and cared for.

The Histrionic Pattern

Another personality type also depends upon external sources for satisfying emotional needs. But individuals with this personality type are very *active* in pursuing those sources of support and stimulation. They are expert at securing the involvement of others in their lives. They have a flair for the dramatic, and a repertoire of highly seductive and superficially appealing behaviors they employ to solicit attention and lure others into relationships. This is the histrionic personality type.

Some histrionics have a marked tendency to be overly reactive and theatrical. Heightened emotionality is part of their constitutional makeup. To some degree, however, their antics are often superficial and manipulative. They tend to over-dramatize and to experience the secondary gains of securing attention from others. This often leads them to form relationships that are shallow, unsubstantial, and unstable, although they can often be quite intense.

Some histrionic personalities tend to be rather vain and self-focused, not only seeking to be the center of attention, but becoming quite unhappy when others are not doting on them. Some are preoccupied with physical beauty and other "accidental" but desirable human attributes. Others can be quite manipulative when it comes to securing the attention and involvement they seek from others.

On balance, histrionic personalities tend to be a bit more neurotic as opposed to character-disordered. But because of some of the traits just mentioned, they are not as far toward the neurotic end of the spectrum as some of the other personalities we'll be discussing; and certainly not as far toward that end as their passive-dependent counterparts. Vanity, superficiality, and excessive self-focus naturally reflect poorly on anyone's character. Exactly where a particular histrionic personality lies on the character-disorder vs. neurotic continuum can vary considerably. It depends on the various other traits that might be dominant in their personality (e.g., the craving for novelty and excitement, the tendency to be overly emotional, reactive, sensation-seeking, erratic) as well the other personality traits that might co-exist with their dominant coping style.

The core characteristics of the histrionic personality are:

- Over-reliance on external sources of emotional support, gratification, and stimulation.
- Active, often dramatic attempts to secure desired attention and involvement with others.
- Interpersonal gregariousness.
- Displays of intense and occasionally superficial emotionality.
- Tendency to form highly emotionally-charged but relatively shallow relationships.

Possible Constitutional Factors:

- These individuals tend to crave novelty and to be excitement-seeking.
- They tend to have high levels of emotionality and reactivity.
- They appear highly responsive to external sources of stimulation and reward.

Possible Learning Factors:

- These personalities might have over-learned that others can be seduced or manipulated into providing attention, support, and gratification of emotional needs.

- o They may have failed to learn that others have value that goes deeper than the accidental attributes they possess and the excitement or stimulation they can bring to a relationship.

The Asocial Pattern

Asocial personalities are individuals who simply don't connect or engage with others as most of us do. What's more, they don't experience any pressing urge to do so. They have been given all sorts of clinical labels in the past such as "schizoid" or "detached." In common parlance, they have been frequently but *erroneously* labeled "anti-social" by individuals attempting to describe their idiosyncratic aloofness or *asociality.* They are often described as "loners" or social isolates who don't appear to enjoy or desire the same kinds of social connection and involvement that give most individuals' lives meaning and richness.

Many asocial personalities appear predisposed to their style of relating as the result of biologically-based characteristics (e.g., mild autistic traits, lack of ability to respond to external stimulation and reward, and impoverished capacity for emotional responsiveness and expression) as opposed to the environmental factors that often contribute to dysfunctional personality development. Some researchers suggest a dimension of human functioning and a "spectrum" of conditions exist that include schizoid personalities as well as the disorders of Asperger's Syndrome and Autism.

Most of the difficulties these individuals experience for functioning adaptively do not appear to arise out of neurotic conflicts or deficiencies of integrity and morality. So it's not really useful to assign them a place on the continuum of neurosis vs. character disturbance. Naturally, however, if other traits associated with either neurosis or character disturbance are also present, it can further complicate the problems such personalities experience in relating to others.

Millon[12] suggests some major variations of this personality, each of which is characterized by the predominance of one or more of their typical traits. He notes that some asocial personalities are remarkably remote and live an almost hermit-like existence. Others appear to be extremely introversive, living in their own world, detached from others and things around them. Some are lethargic and energy-depressed, and appear to have a fairly chronic anhedonia (i.e. inability to experience pleasure or joy). Others are primarily characterized by their emotional aloofness and/or constriction.

The core characteristics of the Asocial Personality are:

- A marked pattern of social detachment.
- Diminished capacity to experience pleasure in typical human social activities.
- Emotional constriction.
- Diminished capacity to react and respond to others.

Possible Constitutional Factors:

- Diminished capacity to be affected by external reward.
- Emotional imperturbability and constriction.
- Intrinsic lethargy and psychomotor retardation.
- Social detachment.

Possible Learning Factors:

- It does not appear that learning failures, environmental trauma, or response to over-learning issues play significant roles in the development of this personality pattern. However, schizoid individuals generally don't experience the same types of social engagement, encouragement, reward, etc., that most of us do. So, the relative absence of such social reinforcements might play a role in the perpetuation of their interactive style.

The Avoidant Pattern

Some individuals actually want to connect with others but experience inordinate apprehension about doing so. As a result, they typically "avoid" potentially hurtful or disappointing intimate involvements. Such individuals have been often labeled "avoidant" personalities.

A few avoidant personalities are so hypersensitive to perceived rejection or disappointment that they misjudge the intentions and actions of others. So they end up denying themselves reasonable opportunities for intimacy and support. Others tend to over-react to circumstances in which they allowed themselves to be vulnerable, and to erroneously perceive that they were mistreated, ignored, or abused. Some avoidant personalities display a marked negativity and pessimism. Others have a characteristic but less than paranoid level of mistrust. Still others experience a fair degree of persistent apprehensiveness, especially in situations where intimate involvement with or trust of others is at stake.

Avoidant personalities will form close attachments when they perceive they've received unusual and unquestionable re-assurance that they will not be disappointed, criticized, or rejected. Even then, however, they are likely to continually test the loyalty of those with whom they wish to bond. When they sense they are safe, they often remain involved and loyal to the end.

Because they are so fearful of rejection or disapproval, avoidant personalities will often shy away from occupational endeavors, or other enterprises that expose them to the social spotlight, inviting the risk of being negatively evaluated. Chronically fearing to venture out, some avoidant personalities develop a marked sense of inferiority and incompetence. By persistently not taking risks, they only perpetuate their sense of personal inadequacy.

The core aspect of their personality involves a strong desire for meaningful involvements, yet anticipation of rejection, abandonment, and mistreatment. So avoidant personalities experience a considerable degree of chronic anxiety. Their inner turmoil about whether they can safely satisfy their basic need for affiliation begets many approach-avoidance conflicts. On balance, therefore, they are much more neurotic than they are character-disordered.

Avoidant Personalities display the following core characteristics:

- o Apprehensive about intimate involvements.
- o Preoccupied with approval and loyalty, and hypersensitive to perceived rejection, disappointment or betrayal.
- o Avoid intimate relationships unless given strong guarantees of acceptance, and avoid ventures that might result in disapproval.

Possible Constitutional Factors:

- o Hypersensitivity to rejection/disapproval.
- o Excessive anxiety, especially social anxiety.
- o Innate shyness.

Possible Learning Factors:

- o Social immaturity may have led to high levels of social rejection, mockery, and isolation.
- o Early bonding experiences might have led to initial intimacy followed by rejection and abandonment.
- o Chronic avoidance of risk-taking often leads to self-perceptions of ineptness and incapability.

The Obsessive-Compulsive Pattern

These individuals are distinctively and intensely ambivalent about one of the most crucial dimensions of interpersonal functioning: emotional independence vs. dependence. They want to function in an independent way, to chart their own course, and set their own rules. But they also fear potentially losing the approval, support, and reinforcement they desire from others. So, they keep their inner urges to rebel and defy in close check, leading lives of conformity, and rigid adherence to principles and expectations. Their deep-seated ambivalence is perpetuated by what they will not let themselves do, namely from time to time cut loose and act with relative indifference to the expectations of others.

Obsessive-Compulsives are the folks who are proverbially "wound too tightly." These days, it's become fashionable once again to call them "anal" personalities. This gives some recognition and credence to Freud's notion that they developed their personalities because they gained too much satisfaction, did not get sufficient satisfaction, or experienced too much trauma exercising their sphincter muscles during toilet-training, and as a result became obsessed with "control" issues. The validity of this notion (especially as a general characteristic of all such personalities), however, has never been clearly demonstrated.

There are several minor variations of this personality, some whose cardinal attribute is their high level of conscientiousness. This can easily lead to work addiction, some who tend to be miserly and non-giving, and some who tend to be so concerned about the rules that they lack imagination and appreciation for human emotional needs.

Obsessive-compulsive personalities are among the most neurotic of all the personality types. They suffer considerable, chronic anxiety, because underneath it all they so want to break free of their self-imposed chains, yet greatly fear to do so. They never fully mastered the developmental task outlined by Erikson of initiative vs. guilt.[14] Here's the main aspect of their personality that reflects negatively on their character: Their tendency to be so preoccupied with their obsessions and compulsions that they don't fully appreciate the negative impact on others of their apparent cold and controlling ways.

These personalities have an overly developed sense of guilt for doing things they think others will disapprove of. Overly guilt-sensitive would describe their core psychological dynamic. Their excessive desire to avoid pangs of guilt is what drives their obsessive and compulsive behavior. They never want others to be able to convict them of wrongdoing.

Some Obsessive-Compulsives have certain other traits that make them slightly different in their overall modus operandi. Some are conscientious to a fault, harder on themselves than on anyone else, and prone to doubting whether they can ever measure up to their own standards. Some tend to be miserly and unforgiving and prone to hoarding. Others tend to revel in bureaucracy and find security in rules and regulations. Others are overly puritanical and dogmatic, tightly controlled morally, prudish, and judgmental.

Obsessive-Compulsive personalities appear to be endowed with a high capacity to experience both fear and anger. They both reduce fear and channel anger by maintaining rigid control. Even though they are among the most neurotic personality types, some O-Cs evidence a degree of character disturbance. The thing that makes the big difference revolves around how their penchant for control is expressed. The more neurotic obsessive-compulsives cause themselves no end of grief because of the unreasonable demands they place upon themselves. Those who frequently attempt to control others and use tactics to get others to do their bidding, in total disregard for the emotional toll it can take, have additional traits in their personality (which will be discussed later) that represent a degree of character disturbance.

The core characteristics of the Obsessive-Compulsive Personality are:

- Over-conscientiousness regarding rules, propriety, etc.
- Perfectionism and orderliness.
- Hesitance to surrender control.
- Rigidity and inflexibility.

Possible Constitutional Factors:

- Hypersensitivity to feelings of guilt.
- Excessive anxiety related to initiative vs. guilt behaviors.
- High limbic arousal (heightened capacity to experience both fear and anger).

Possible Learning Factors:

- Very *conditionally*-approving, and possibly overly punitive and overly-controlling parents.
- Overly learned to reduce fear and release anger through the exercise of rigid control.

The Passive-Aggressive Pattern

This is an often misunderstood and mislabeled personality type. The official psychiatric manual doesn't even recognize this as a personality pattern anymore.[13] One of the reasons: the confusion that's always existed with respect to adequately defining this personality type. In the deepest recesses of their psyches, these individuals are every bit as ambivalent as their obsessive-compulsive counterparts about whether to function in an autonomous, independent manner or to rely on others. The difference: These personalities perpetuate this ambivalence very actively in the way they conduct their interpersonal relations.

There is no escaping the ambivalence of the passive-aggressive. They might appeal to another for support, but when the support is offered they will typically reject it or stymie it. They will ask for another to take the lead, and then resist cooperating. The label passive-aggressive was applied to these individuals early on because of the extent they displayed passive resistance to cooperation in their relationships. But over the years, the term passive-aggressive also came to be commonly, but erroneously, used by professionals and lay persons alike to describe a very different personality type.

Life with a genuinely passive-aggressive personality is always difficult and engenders considerable frustration. Consider the following example: A husband asks his wife where she wants to go for dinner. She replies, "I don't know, honey, you decide." He says: "Let's go to the Chinese place." She replies: "Why the Chinese place? You know the last time we went there I didn't like it that much." He then says: "We'll go wherever you want. Where would you like to go?" She replies: "I've got my hands full. You decide." "Okay, let's go to Smith's Steakhouse." She replies: "Now you know how that will stretch our budget, and how that would wreck our promise to eat more healthily." And on and on it goes for the passive-aggressive personality. Equally desiring to be taken care of and utterly resenting the idea of following someone else's lead, they actively vacillate between crying out to others for direction and then thwarting others' attempts to take charge and resisting the perceived demand to fall in line.

Passive-Aggressive personalities have been labeled by Millon as *negativistic*[15] because of the distinctively negative character of their ongoing internal conflict, and the whininess, poutiness, contrariness, and infuriating uncooperativeness they display in a variety of overt as well as subtle ways. There are minor variations of this personality type, and in each variation different aspects or traits tend to dominate. There are those whose: (1) characteristic fence-sitting and indecisiveness are more prominent, (2) complaining and negative mood is more pronounced, (3) negativism takes on a harsh, critical and biting edge, and (4) penchant for uncooperativeness is reflected in their not-so-accidental forgetfulness, dawdling, and foot-dragging.

Unfortunately, clinicians and lay persons alike erroneously use the term passive-aggressive when they're trying to describe deliberate (*active*) but subtle, underhanded, and otherwise *covert* attempts to dominate, exploit, manipulate and control. What's worse, there is a personality type (to be discussed later) best defined by their extraordinarily manipulative (i.e. covert-aggressive) character. Such individuals, who are not at all ambivalent about whether they want to dominate, frequently engage in crafty, hard-to-detect, "gotcha" behaviors and back-stabbing. This personality type has been also erroneously labeled passive-aggressive by many. These underhanded connivers are better labeled differently, and will be discussed at length later on. But it's important to remember that there's absolutely nothing passive about their manner of relating to others. Besides, such connivers are among the most character-disturbed of all personality types, whereas the passive-aggressive (perhaps the better descriptor would be *recalcitrant*) personality is among the most neurotic.

Passive-aggressive personalities and obsessive-compulsive personalities are similar in their deep-seated ambivalence about whether to function independently or depend upon others. They're also similar in the degree to which they are neurotic. But the ambivalence, anxiety, and neurosis they experience have different origins. The obsessive-compulsive personality is driven by a hypersensitivity to guilt and the desire to avoid at all costs doing something which might lead to feeling guilty. In contrast, the passive-aggressive personality is driven by an excessive sensitivity to shame. Passive-aggressives appear to have failed to master the developmental task, outlined by Erikson,[16] of autonomy vs. shame and doubt. These individuals are overly sensitive to what appears to be a lack of unconditional approval — not of their behavior so much — but of themselves as persons of worth. They are deeply ambivalent about taking charge of their own lives, as opposed to relying on the approval of others. They want to act in an autonomous fashion, but they also don't want to risk the potential for self-blame should they fail. Similarly, putting themselves in a position to follow the lead of others only invites them to feel weak and ineffectual. They are constantly in a real bind. They want others to take charge, but resent acceding to demands placed upon them. They can't seem to find the balance between doing as they wish and relying on others. They are proverbially and perennially caught between a rock and a hard place.

As mentioned before, passive-aggressive personalities are, on balance, more neurotic than character disordered. However, their characteristic obstinacy, deficient capacity for autonomy, and sometimes abrasive negativism all reflect poorly on their character.

The core characteristics of the passive-aggressive personality are:

- Pervasive negativism and complaining.
- Expression of anger through passive resistance (not talking, pouting, not-so-accidental "forgetting.")
- Frequent refusal to meet perceived demands of others even when self-defeating.

Possible Constitutional Factors:

- Hypersensitivity to shame. Inordinate desire for unconditional love and acceptance.
- Difficulty expressing anger openly and directly.

Possible Learning Factors:

- Mixed messages about self-worth in childhood. Sometimes "schismatic" families in which some members are overly doting and unconditionally regarding while others are critical, demanding, shaming, and rejecting.
- Mixed messages about whether greater reinforcement comes from functioning primarily on their own vs. relying on others for direction, approval, and support.

The Assertive Pattern

Generally, this personality is fairly balanced with respect to the neurotic vs. character-disturbed dimension. This is an "actively independent" personality type. That is, this personality actively seeks to maintain control over his/her life and actively attends to getting his/her needs met without reliance on others. Whereas most healthy personalities have achieved an adaptive balance between the degree to which they need and depend on others and the degree to which they rely solely upon themselves, this personality is unabashedly self-reliant. But unlike their aggressive-personality counterparts (to be discussed a bit later), these personalities are not driven toward independence by a fierce desire to dominate or exert power over others. Rather, they simply appreciate the benefits of not depending on others. Further, in their pursuit of self-advancement, they impose limits and boundaries upon themselves, taking care not to impinge upon or violate the rights of others. Sometimes, this is out of a neurotic sense of undue guilt or shame for doing otherwise. Sometimes the motivations are more altruistic. Most of the times, the motivation is purely pragmatic because the last thing the independent personality wants is to be at others' mercy (which they would be if caught and sanctioned for injurious acts to others). On balance, the assertive personality is arguably among the most psychologically healthy of all personality types.

Predominately Character-Disordered Personalities

These personality types tend to lie much further toward the character-disturbed as opposed to neurotic end of the spectrum. So it's appropriate to examine them with greater depths than the other types we have discussed. Although instances occur in which their dysfunctional interpersonal "style" outwardly manifest underlying neurosis, for the most part these personalities are not the way they are primarily because of their unconscious fears, insecurities, and defenses. Rather it's mostly because of their conscious yet dysfunctional and irresponsible choices, as well as their innate predispositions about how to view the world and interact with it. While the various character-disordered personality types have some unique characteristics, they also have some features in common. Those are:

- **Problematic Attitudes and Thinking Patterns.** Predominantly character-disturbed personalities tend to think in ways that impair healthy interpersonal relations. Sometimes, their thinking reflects deeply-rooted but erroneous and dysfunctional beliefs about the nature of the world, their place in society, and requirements for conducting healthy human relationships. Such erroneous core beliefs and thinking patterns foster markedly antisocial attitudes. These in turn predispose them to engage in some of the most problematic social behaviors. At other times, the problematic ways they think reflect their persistent disdain for the truth (more about this later), their refusal to reckon honestly with themselves, and their resistance to conform their thinking (as well as their behavior) to society's expectations.

- **Problematic sense of regard for self and others**. Whether they are inordinately egocentric, harbor attitudes of entitlement, or have complete disdain for others, disturbed characters possess a distorted and dysfunctional sense of both their own worth and other people's value and dignity. Because of this, their relationships tend to be shallow and superficial at best, and abusive and exploitive at worst.

- **Disregard for the Truth.** Disturbed characters often ignore the reality of circumstances. They act in indifference to the truth about themselves and their behaviors. Some engage in such expansive and unbridled fantasy that truth for them is only what they imagine it to be. Others are at outright war with the truth. They know the truth, but because it might challenge their core beliefs or interfere with their various agendas, they refuse to acknowledge or accept it. Their disregard for the truth predisposes the most disturbed characters to lie to themselves as well as others. To a great degree, it also predisposes them to engage in deceitful impression management (more about this later). The truth could potentially "level the playing field" in their relations with others, exposing character features that might give others pause. The more disordered characters so disregard truth — with a penchant for lying so deeply ingrained and habitual — that they lie even when telling the truth would have no perceivable adverse consequence (i.e. the truth would do just fine).

- **Responsibility-Resistance Behaviors and Manipulation Tactics**. The more character-disturbed personalities frequently engage in fairly "automatic" behaviors that, by their nature, obstruct internalization of pro-social values, principles, and inner controls. These same behaviors often serve as "tactics" to help the disturbed character manipulate and gain advantage over others. The tactics also reinforce the disturbed character's attempts to manage the impressions of others. We'll be exploring these responsibility-resistance behaviors and power tactics in substantial detail.

- **Impression Management**. Some disturbed characters frequently engage in managing the impression others might form of them. For some, it's a matter of keeping an unrealistically inflated self-image. For others, it's more a matter of keeping others in the dark about the kind of person they're dealing with. Without exception, however, impression management primarily serves to help the disordered character maintain a position of advantage over others. If you don't really know exactly who you're dealing with, and what their real intentions are, in their relationship with you, you're at a distinct disadvantage and ripe for their exploitation.

- **Impaired Capacity for Empathy and Contrition**. There is a big difference between regretting adverse consequences to oneself for bad behavior (e.g., getting "caught," paying fines, receiving other social sanctions), and experiencing genuine, empathy-based remorse for injury caused to others. For a person to experience any degree of genuine "contrition," prompting them to change their ways, two things must occur: (1) they not only have to feel genuinely bad about what they have done (i.e. guilty), but (2) they must also be internally unnerved about the kind of persons they've become (i.e. shameful) through acting so irresponsibly. Their shame and guilt can propel them to make amends to the best of their ability, to work very hard not to engage in the same misconduct again, and to make themselves better persons. True contrition also always involves what the Greek philosophers termed "metanoia" or a "change of heart." And a true change of heart always involves correcting prior dysfunctional beliefs, attitudes, and ways of doing things.

  Disturbed characters will often scream loudly how sorry they are; but their behavior patterns rarely reflect any genuine remorse. Sure, they can feel sorry for themselves, especially when they're caught, and have to pay the occasional very high price for a serious misdeed. They will often protest something akin to: "I have to live with my mistake every day," inviting you to pity them, view them as a victim in some way, and imagine that they must be experiencing all sorts of inner emotional pain. Meanwhile, their tightly-held attitudes, thinking and behavior patterns give few indications that they either appreciate or feel badly about the impact of their irresponsible conduct on others.

  Three real-life examples of the most disordered characters' deficient capacity for genuine empathy-based remorse remain seared into my mind. All three examples come from counseling sessions with sexual offenders:

1. A young man who had sexually molested his younger sister finally decided he wanted to talk about the abuse. As he began to describe in detail the things he had done to force his victim's compliance, tears began rolling down his cheeks. As a young and naïve therapist, I prepared myself for what I anticipated would be an emotional flood of regret and remorse for the pain he had inflicted. My co-therapist (herself also crying) wanted to interrupt the session, assuming the shame he was undoubtedly feeling might be "too much" for him to bear. But what eventually became clear was that he was feeling sorry only for himself. You see, it turned out that his tears were all about this fact: His victim had put up much less overt resistance to other (older and physically stronger) members of her extended family who had also abused her. The resistance she put up invited him to feel like he wasn't as "worthy" as the others, and this made him feel rejected and inferior. He didn't even regret the intense brutality he used to get her to comply, but only that her "rejection" of him drove him to take her by such force, and made him "look like a bad guy." He admitted he was still angry with her for this.
2. A middle-aged man convicted of participating in a brutal gang-rape sobbed uncontrollably when telling me about the crime. When talking about the source of his pain, he revealed he still believed he was the least culpable of his accomplices. He only "went along with" the caper whereas others had done the initial planning. He further complained that he was the last to assault his victim, barely penetrating her at the very moment police burst in on the scene, so he "didn't even get a chance to bust a nut." Not only did this upset him, but he also cast himself as a "victim" of a corrupt system: The court had ordered him to serve the same amount of time as his comrades.
3. A white-collar rapist used date-rape drugs to facilitate his victimizations of several women. He expressed outrage at

> the fact that I didn't appear to believe he was sorry for what he had done. He protested that "not a day goes by" that he doesn't have to "live with the consequences" of what he did. His later enumeration of these consequences centered mostly on three losses: his freedom, his very profitable business, and his stature in the community. He never expressed any appreciation for the nature of the injury he inflicted on his victims, or one iota of genuine sorrow for the pain he inflicted on them and their families.

Now, we can spend a lot of time examining all of the disturbingly pathological thinking at work here, but I'm trying to make two main points with these illustrations. First, not everything is as it outwardly appears. We err greatly when we assume that words of regret or even crocodile tears are necessarily prompted by genuine remorse. Some characters are so deeply disturbed that they can even feign remorse. So, when it comes to disturbed characters, you must be careful not to assume anything. And we have to be particularly careful about traditional assumptions we've tended to make (most promoted by classical psychology paradigms) about the kind of wounded soul we've long believed must lie beneath disturbed characters. Second, a huge difference exists between the pain of self-pity and genuine, empathy-based contrition. In the end, actions speak louder than words or even emotional expressions. It's so easy to say you're sorry. It's another thing to act like you're sorry and be willing to make amends. All of us have transgressed in one way or another. But when people have true contrition, their greatest pain is for the injury they caused someone else; and their actions reflect a sincere effort, not only to repair the damage, but also to change their ways. So, when people show some sign of emotion related to a terrible event, it's wrong to jump to the conclusion that they must necessarily be experiencing genuine remorse or empathy for the injury caused another. It's also important to remember that, in the case of the most severely disordered characters, the very capacity for empathy is non-existent.

- **Problematic temperament, mood, and disposition**. Generally speaking, disturbed characters have abnormal and problematic aspects of their temperament, mood, and general disposition. These play key roles in their dysfunctional interpersonal styles. The more disordered characters possess irascible temperaments, low frustration tolerance, and high reactivity, making them "walking time bombs." Others are so emotionally labile that living with them is like riding a roller coaster of passions and sentiments. Still others are so disagreeable that working or living with them is often an exasperating experience. But all of the most disordered characters have aspects of their temperament, mood, and general disposition that not only contribute to the habitual ways they tend to interact, but also to the difficulty they have maintaining stable, healthy relationships.

- **Deficient Impulse Control**. Disturbed characters notoriously lack self-control. They act without thinking or with indifference to the potential consequences. They do things that hurt people and (sometimes) feel bad about it afterward. They don't stop to think first how their actions might impact others or what consequences might occur. They have a deficient capacity to delay gratification and lack internal "brakes." Sometimes, their aggressive predispositions are so strong that they overwhelm their weak braking system and cause a multitude of problems.

- **Failure to Suitably Profit From Experience**. Disturbed characters are not incapable of learning, but they frequently fail to learn what most of us hope they might from their experiences. That is, most of us hope they would stop and reconsider their ways of doing things, since those ways seem to invite so many problems. Instead, disturbed characters not only persist in their ways, but often solidify or even intensify them. This occurs despite ample, obvious evidence that their manner of doing things is tragically flawed.

- **Impaired Conscience**. Disturbed characters' consciences are not sufficiently developed to either "push" them to do what they should, or "restrain" them from doing what they shouldn't. In some of the most seriously disordered characters, conscience is virtually non-existent or absent altogether.

Although the various disturbed characters have traits in common, certain traits cluster together in some very distinct ways. This allows us to differentiate some major disturbed character types. Sometimes, the distinctions can become a little blurred when a particular disturbed character shares more than a few of the traits. But it's nonetheless helpful to categorize these personalities. So let's call attention to the primary traits they possess that cause problems in their interpersonal relations.

The Egotistic Pattern

Some individuals simply cannot see themselves as anything else but the very center of the universe. Preoccupied with their own desires, concerns, and image, their self-focus makes it difficult to give attention to or even recognize others' rights, needs, or concerns. They harbor a completely unrealistic sense of self-worth. These egotistic or narcissistic characters see themselves as inherently superior to others, and believe they rightfully enjoy "special" status and privilege. As a result, they easily come to feel *entitled* to things they want and to do whatever they wish. After all, in their minds, others and their needs don't really count. Only they — and what they desire — matters.

There are some prevailing notions about the underlying dynamics associated with this personality type. Many of these notions are not as well-founded on traditional principles as they purport to be, and some are totally without foundation. The most popular prevailing notion: The ego-inflation that characterizes narcissism is a "compensation" for underlying feelings of low self-worth. This idea is generally attributed to Alfred Adler,[17] whose individual psychology was heavily dominated by this theory: People are in natural competition with one another for social status, and compensate for their natural deficiencies by various mechanisms which produce "complexes."

I have come across a few narcissistic personalities whose apparent ego-inflation was rooted in an unresolved neurosis. For these few — and I do mean *few* — their displays of grandiosity and haughtiness represented a true false self-presentation or façade, masking deep feelings of inferiority and fears of rejection. One theorist[18] categorizes this type of individual as a narcissistic personality subtype: the *compensatory* narcissist. So, neurotic narcissists do indeed exist. But *the vast majority of egotistic individuals I've counseled over the years have been far more character disturbed than neurotic.* As such these individuals have displayed a sincere and deep conviction about their superiority to others, whether or not such a belief is based on any kind of rational or solid foundation. They're not compensating for anything. They ***really do think*** "they're all that!" Stanton Samenow has written about this[19] and sometimes described these individuals as "legends in their own minds." In fact, the shaky foundation sometimes seen for their inflated opinion of self is precisely *because* they chronically overestimate their power and worth. So, it's not that they start out with a weak foundation and compensate for it. Rather, they spend their lives constructing the "house" of their self-image "out of a deck of cards," unrealistically assessed regarding their strength and integrity.

The histories of character-disturbed and disordered narcissists are often quite different from those of neurotics, too. Sometimes they had good reason to believe they were the most powerful, important or capable persons in their immediate environment. Their mothers may have doted on them from day one. Their fathers may have abandoned them or abdicated all responsibility early on. Their principal caretakers might have been so inadequate that they were led to feel like the "masters" of their home. They may have been, in fact, the most functional and capable person in their extended family system, with every reason to feel special or superior. If they were blessed with abundant natural gifts (e.g., physical attractiveness, technical or artistic talent, high intellectual capacity, etc.) — and *most especially if they received much praise, adulation, and social reinforcement from others* ***simply because they possessed these gifts*** — they might have easily come by the notion that they were indeed "special" individuals, and by right should have the world by the tail.

The narcissistic character is defined by the following traits:

- **Inflated self-image and sense of self-worth**. The narcissistic character sees himself as "special" and more important than others. The neurotic narcissist might "compensate" for an impaired sense of self-worth, and a "fear" of rejection for being anything less than perfect, by putting forth a false pretentiousness. But the narcissistic disturbed character genuinely believes (sometimes despite ample evidence to the contrary) that he is a most unique and *superior* creature. In one of the most seriously disordered character types (the psychopath), this trait is magnified to a chillingly pathological level (more about this later).

  The narcissistic character's self-appraisal is almost always out of whack with reality. This doesn't mean the indivdual's necessarily compensating for feelings of inferiority. It simply means the person's opinion of self often exceeds the situation's objective reality. Sometimes, these individuals possess very few genuine talents and few remarkable accomplishments in their histories. Folks can be strongly tempted to erroneously presume that their inflated self-perceptions are a form of compensation. But many times they've been blessed with positives that contribute to very strong self-esteem or appraisal (e.g., talent, looks, brains, etc.). Sometimes, they've also experienced a fair degree of occupational and vocational success. Still, it's not unusual for them to overplay and overstate their accomplishments, and overvalue their own worth.

Sometimes professionals working with narcissistic characters — whose histories of accomplishment are relatively lacking — simply assume that their ego inflation must be a compensation for underlying low self-esteem. But they fail to consider this: There is a very significant difference between *self-esteem* and *self-respect*. Sometimes these terms are used interchangeably. However, I find it crucial to distinguish between these very important concepts, especially because issues related to a healthy balance of self-esteem and self-respect play pivotal roles in shaping several character types.

Self-esteem literally means to estimate worth. It arises out of a person's intuitive assessment of what he has going for himself in the way of talents, abilities, etc. Self-respect, on the other hand, comes from the Latin *respectere* (spectere being the root of the word spectacles) which means to look back. It arises from a retrospective assessment a person makes about what he has done with the gifts he has been given. In healthy societies, the most favorable retrospective assessments belong to those who have made meritorious efforts and attained achievements that benefit the common good.

All disturbed characters, but most especially narcissists, chronically overvalue and claim "ownership" of the desirable but accidental attributes (i.e. gifts of nature or blessings of God) that foster a sense of high self-esteem. What's more, many times they get reinforcing messages from others like: "You're so smart," or "You're so talented." In short, they both receive and are readily willing to claim credit for things they can't genuinely attribute to their own doing. They know what they have going for themselves, and they equate their endowments with their identity. This inflates their egos.

Narcissists and the other disturbed characters often lack self-respect. That's because they know that, with their gifts, they haven't done enough good for others to merit a positive appraisal of social worth. In short, they lack respect because they haven't earned it. Many societies and cultures inadequately recognize and reward *meritorious* conduct. Even some of our major religions and philosophical schools of thought unwittingly downplay the value or even existence of human merit. Merit has to do with the manner in which a human being exercises the ultimate human power, the power to choose. Human beings are endowed with a free will. Making the meritorious choice is never easy, yet it is the essence of character. When a soldier enters a minefield knowing full well he could die, but seeks to rescue a fallen comrade, he commits a meritorious act. A father and husband turns down a flagrant offer to engage in a tryst with an attractive co-worker. He does so out of concern for the solidity of his marital commitment, the stability of his family, and the welfare of his children. He performs an equally meritorious act. Doing the right thing is never easy. The problem: Within modern culture, and even within major schools of religious and philosophical belief, the value placed on such conduct is minimal. Often we expect good people to do right. Teachers and parents rarely "catch" and reward children for making the right choices, but we're quick to chastise when they choose wrongly. Jesus said: "Render to Caesar the things that are Caesar's and to God the things that are God's." If we ever want to reverse our cultural nightmare of inflated self-esteem and deficient self-respect, we're going to have to do much better. We need to stop reinforcing people for the things which only God (or nature, if you will) can rightfully claim credit, such as their looks, their brains, their talents and abilities; and we must reinforce people for the truly meritorious, principled exercising of their wills, and their willingness to subordinate their baser instincts in the service of the common good.

Sometimes professionals, as well as others, are acutely aware of the disturbed character's deficiencies of self-respect. However, they often then confuse this with "underlying feelings of low self-worth" that they presume are being "compensated for" with the disturbed character's displays of grandiosity. They need to be more mindful of the distinction between self-esteem and self-respect. A person can have too much of one and not enough of the other. They also need to be more acutely aware of the factors that contribute to both, so they can help the person achieve a better balance. Most importantly, they need to avoid automatic presumptions about "compensations" that neurotic personalities engage in when they're dealing with disturbed characters.

Narcissists' lack of humility with respect to both their natural endowments and their success resulting from their endowments, as well as good fortune, inflates their sense of self-worth. They don't have room in their heart to acknowledge the roles of any outside factors or a higher power. They don't consider their native talents and abilities as gifts, but rather as their defining characteristics. Humble, religious persons attribute their talents and abilities to God or "grace." Humble, non-religious persons attribute those things to a fortuitous accident of nature. The humble person also recognizes that all the raw talent in the world can't guarantee success. That, too, is dependent upon the "grace" of God, a certain amount of "luck," opportunity, personal effort, and working with others. Narcissists think that every blessing in their lives is the logical result of their own greatness. Even when they engage in acts of philanthropy or "giving back" to the community, it's generally done with a lot of fanfare. They want to further aggrandize themselves and receive adulation. They lack the humble perspective that might foster the creed: "To whom much is given, much is expected."

- **Attitudes of entitlement**. Narcissistic characters' belief that they are *entitled* to have the things they want derives from their credence that they are special and superior individuals. Preoccupied with fantasies of unbridled success and prestige, they believe they deserve by natural *right* all the valuable things in life that most of us have to *earn*. They think that, because of who they are and their natural endowments, the world *owes* them; and they expect to be showered with recognition, adulation, and reward. Because they believe the world owes them everything in the first place, they easily justify taking what they want, without feeling obligated to really pay for it through some kind of pro-social labor. They believe they have a right to anything they want simply because *they* want it, and their special nature and status entitle them to it.

- **No concept of a higher power**. Narcissistic characters can't conceive of anything more important, more capable, or more potent than themselves. This leaves no room in their hearts for any concept of a higher power or authority. Now, I'm not necessarily talking about the concept of a God in a Judeo-Christian sense. As adherents to A.A. precepts know, there are many ways to conceive of a higher power. For the humanist, one needs to respect the collective "greater good" of society. For the non-deist scientist it might be recognizing the nature and complexity of the physical universe that leads to humbly identifying oneself as a relatively insignificant character in a grand cosmic drama. Most of us have a deep, abiding sense that there is *something* bigger than us.

  In the social world, most of us both recognize and feel the need at times to pay deference to authority figures. Most of us recognize that there are people who know more than we do, possess competencies we don't, and have been entrusted with decision-making authority over us. Narcissists have a hard time with this. They might *feign* paying some deference for practical reasons, but in their heart of hearts they can't make themselves believe that anyone is in any way their superior. Lacking the humility to see themselves as inferior to anything or anyone, they don't recognize that any powers or entities exist; nor that these powers not only play a role in their success, but also place demands on them for gratitude and a felt obligation to give back. They might give lip-service to the notion of a higher power, but they almost always leave its consideration absent from their hearts when they reflect on their lives and their successes.

As was discussed earlier, true core beliefs naturally beget certain kinds of actions. It's impossible to really believe in a higher power, subordinate your will to that power, and then act in exploitive and entitled ways towards others. For most of us, a belief in something that is not only greater than us, but also puts ethical demands on us, keeps us morally grounded.

- **Expansive fantasy**. The narcissistic character sees no reason to place limits on his abilities, or even his thoughts or desires. For him, imagining that he is something, or that he can have or do something, is akin to making it so. He finds no limits on what he can conceive or do. Similarly, he passively disregards the limitations of objective reality or truth. Reality is what the narcissistic character says it is. He is not influenced or swayed by others' judgments or opinions. The more character disturbed he is, the more he does not seek consensual validation. Rather, he finds validation in his own beliefs. As Samenow has commented, such individuals harbor the sincere belief that "thinking makes it so." If they want something to be, in their mind, it is.

  These days, it's fairly common for some clinicians to attribute this characteristic of narcissists to a tendency toward bipolar disorder, hypomania, or mania. They then attempt to validate this view by pointing out that sometimes giving such an individual mood stabilizing medication will dampen the tendency to engage in this unrealistic thinking. However, this could also be argued: The tendency of narcissists to repeatedly engage in their unbridled fantasies and passive disregard for objective reality might put them at increased risk for eventually developing more serious conditions such as hypomania, mania, or a bipolar disturbance.

Now, I know that what I just said is likely to be quite controversial. But I don't think it's a notion that should be summarily dismissed. Ample research suggests that the link between biochemistry and behavior is not just a one-way street. We know, for example, that a person who repetitively eats foods with a high glycemic index puts himself at increased risk for developing type II diabetes. We've also long known that strictly behavioral and cognitive-behavioral treatments for obsessive-compulsive disorder result in the same types of biochemical changes in the brain's same areas as do purely medication-based treatments. Now, I'm not insinuating that true Bipolar Disorder isn't a genuine condition in its own right with its own etiological factors. It can occur at times without warning in almost any personality type. What I am saying, however, is that certain personalities appear to have developed a style of relating that includes habitual ego-inflation. It's entirely possible (and should be subjected to empirical test) that, when the pattern goes unchecked, it can eventually provide a segue into a much more serious condition.

- **Pathological desire for adulation and admiration**. A narcissist can never get people to fawn over him or praise him enough. This character thrives on people being enamored with him. It's not so much that he values their opinions or that he *depends* on them for a solid sense of self. Rather, he seeks to use others to fuel his massive appetite for self-aggrandizement by manipulating their attention and praise.

  I had a conversation with a college classmate in which he told me of a disappointing sexual experience with a woman he had dated. Sexual conquest was a very big interest for this individual. Here was his main complaint about the particular experience he shared with me: He couldn't really enjoy himself because the woman didn't seem to be "really getting off on" being in bed with him. To add insult to narcissistic injury, she appeared to be merely using him to gratify herself. She was, in fact, very beautiful; but even an encounter with such an attractive person didn't really excite him. He wanted her to be enthralled with *him*. *That* would have excited him. So, despite her stunning beauty, he couldn't perform. The frequency of his sexual exploits, the shallowness of those liaisons, and the nature of what he was really looking for in those encounters — these revealed just about everything one needed to know to understand his character.

- ***Passive disregard* for the rights, needs, or concerns of others**. No one else really matters. It's all about the narcissist. It is a truly malignant egocentrism that makes it virtually impossible for the narcissistic character to develop or maintain genuine empathy. He is often completely oblivious to the emotional injury he inflicts on others. He doesn't set out to do harm, but so lacks conscientiousness about anyone else's welfare that he doesn't stop to consider the potential impact of what he says or does. The narcissist is so self-centered and so self-absorbed, he doesn't really recognize others as independent entities with their own, wants, needs, desires, and concerns. Sometimes he views others merely as extensions of himself. He can also view them as objects to bring him pleasure. He doesn't view them as persons of value in themselves to be respected or cherished.

The core characteristics of the Narcissistic Personality can be summarized as follows:

- o Unrealistic (grandiose) sense of self-worth.
- o Preoccupation with power, brilliance, or appearance.
- o Excessive desire for admiration.
- o Impaired empathy and regard for others.
- o Excessive self-focus.
- o Sense of entitlement.
- o Oblivious to the wants or need of others — exploitive.
- o Haughtiness, arrogance toward those regarded as inferior.

Possible Constitutional Factors:

- o Imperturbability. Doesn't get shaken by adverse events or challenges to perceived power and greatness.
- o Active imagination and penchant for fantasy. Not constrained by the demands or confines of reality.
- o These individuals appear to be moderately responsive to external praise but highly unresponsive to external condemnation.

Possible Learning Factors:

- o Received too much unconditional positive regard from others.
- o Got too much praise for what they accidentally *are* (e.g., talented, smart, physically attractive) and not enough contingent attention or reinforcement for what they voluntarily *did* to earn respect or admiration.
- o Raised in an environment in which they were arguably the most powerful, capable, or reliable procurer of their wants and needs.

CHAPTER 3

The Aggressive Pattern

Some individuals are inherently warriors. They have a "me against the world" mentality, and often pit themselves against others and society's major rules and authority structures. They don't passively disregard or place themselves above the rules like narcissists do; they actively challenge and defy them. They have a pathological level of disgust for *submissive* behavior of any kind. It riles them to think of themselves as weak or powerless, having to acquiesce or *subordinate* themselves and their wills to a higher authority. They strive to be "on top" and "in control" (i.e. in a position of *dominance*) at all times. They want to define the rules and call the shots. They're also willing to do whatever it takes to satisfy their desires, even step all over the rights, boundaries, and feelings of others. These are *the aggressive personalities.* We'll soon be examining several subtypes of these individuals in greater detail. But before taking an in-depth look at the various aggressive personality subtypes, it will be necessary to introduce some concepts and define some terms, especially with regard to the nature of aggression in humans.

The Nature of Human Aggression

Aggression in human beings is not synonymous with violence. Human aggression is the forceful energy we all expend to survive, prosper, and secure the things we want or need. We reflect a deep-seated awareness of this fact in our linguistics: We say things like, "If you want something, you have to *fight* for it." We encourage those who are sick or infirmed to rally their resources and *do battle* with their cancers, infections, other diseases. As a society, we launched a "war on poverty."

Humans have always done a lot of fighting. Although for years both mental health professionals and lay persons have engaged in much denial about this most important fact, fighting is a huge part of life. It's fair to say that in the arena of human relations, when we're not making some kind of love, we're waging some kind of war (and sometimes the distinction between the two activities is not all that clear). *How* we fight is another matter entirely. The following diagram helps illustrate the difference between necessary, disciplined, and potentially *constructive, assertion,* and undisciplined, *destructive aggression.*

ASSERTION VS. AGGRESSION

ASSERTIVE BEHAVIOR	AGGRESSIVE BEHAVIOR
• Fair fighting (i.e. without putting the other at a disadvantage).	• Seeking unfair advantage – attempting to victimize another.
• Fighting for a legitimate purpose.	• Fighting for a self-serving and possibly immoral purpose.
• Fighting disciplined by self-imposed limits designed to prevent undue harm to another.	• Fighting without limits or with poor limits on what you're willing to say and/or do.
• Always non-violent.	• Sometimes violent.
• Fighting constructively (i.e. with the goal of improving a situation for all concerned).	• Fighting in a destructive manner (i.e. in a manner that destroys opportunities to improve a situation for all concerned).

There are also several major subtypes of aggression. Two of the more important subtypes, *reactive* and *predatory* (some theorists prefer *instrumental*) aggression are contrasted in the next diagram.

TYPES OF AGGRESSION

REACTIVE	PREDATORY
• Spontaneous.	• Premeditated, calculated.
• Prompted by fear.	• Prompted by *desire.*
• Mostly *defensive* character.	• Strictly *offensive* character.
• Goal is self-preservation.	• Goal is *victimization*.

Reactive Aggression

All creatures display reactive aggression in response to a perceived threat to life or well-being. It's the kind of aggression a cat displays when it sits on the front porch and witnesses a pit bull rounding the corner, slowly approaching, and licking its chops. Frightened that the pit bull might be planning to make it his lunch, the cat is likely to engage in several characteristic behaviors. Its hair will stand on end. It may arch its back. It may hiss. It will brandish its claws. In a variety of ways and in an obvious manner, it will signal its readiness to aggress. Does it want to aggress? No. Was its original intention to victimize? No. Is it primarily angry and looking to pick a fight? No. In fact, it's primarily frightened. The last thing it wants to do is fight. Besides, it's no match for the pit bull and would probably lose the contest. It might engage in some aggression-threatening behavior such as reaching out with its claw-displayed paws in a motion to scratch or slash. But it will only do so in response to threatening moves on the pit bull's part. All of its actions are of a strictly *defensive* character, and its sincerest hope is that its potential adversary will change its mind and move on. If the dog appears to be considering backing off, the cat will not antagonize it or otherwise provoke it into a more combative stance.

Reactive aggression is a purely *spontaneous*, unplanned response to an unanticipated and potentially serious threat to life and well-being. It's prompted by *fear*. That fear then triggers a very innate and basic flight or fight response. The response is mostly *defensive* in character, and the purpose of any aggression-like behavior displayed is strictly to ward off or diminish the likelihood of any potential victimization.

Predatory (Instrumental) Aggression

Contrast the above scenario with that of another cat that spots a mouse in a room's corner and fancies the rodent for lunch. It probably will not arch its back, but instead might put its belly low to the ground. Its hair does not stand on end out of fright. Instead, its hair lies normally. The cat is not terrified but both calm and calculating. It won't hiss or make noise. And it won't signal potential aggression by showing claws or making clawing motions. It will instead stealthily, and as unobtrusively as possible, sneak up on the mouse and pounce when reasonably sure of success. Its goal is not the avoidance of its own victimization but successful victimization of the mouse. It isn't praying that the mouse will react to signals and go away. In fact, it wants the mouse to be right where it is, or in a hard-to-escape situation. Most importantly, it's not prompted to act because it's frightened. Its aggression is neither spontaneous nor based in fear, but rather carefully premeditated, prompted primarily by *desire*. It's also *not motivated by anger*. It's not mad at the mouse; it just wants to have it for lunch, an act that necessarily involves the mouse's destruction.

It's fairly common for mental health professionals and lay persons alike to lack awareness about predatory aggression and the many ways people can display it. Unfortunately, *it's a common but erroneous belief that all aggression is always a defensive response to a perceived threat.* Some folks simply can't imagine why someone would aggress unless they felt threatened in some way. Other folks presume that people only aggress when they're angry. The presumption that anger is always the precipitant of aggression is the guiding philosophy behind many of the anger management programs so popular these days. Let's not go into all of the many misconceptions about aggression, and especially the misconceptions about predatory or instrumental aggression. Instead, let's go back to the example of the cat and the mouse. I'll ask some questions to exemplify the absurdity of some of the most widely-held notions about why and how humans aggress. Would you say that if the cat chose to eat the mouse, the cat must have felt "threatened" in some way? Would you say that the cat probably had "anger issues," simply didn't know how to manage and express its anger appropriately, and ended up taking out its anger on the mouse? Would you say that the cat probably had a very traumatic history involving mice, probably in childhood, leading it to have "trust issues" with mice in general? That the cat anticipated maltreatment by mice, thus justifying a "get them before they get you philosophy?" Hopefully, by now you're having a bit of a laugh. What's not funny, however, is this: Often folks make assumptions very similar to the ones described above when trying to understand the motivations for human aggression, especially aggression of the predatory or instrumental variety.

Predatory aggression is motivated by desire. It's as simple as that. At one of my workshops, an attendee posed the question: "Well, couldn't you still say that the cat was fearful that if it didn't eat the mouse it might have to go hungry? So, isn't it really still *fear* after all — the fear of not being able to satisfy this most basic need — that motivates the cat? My reply was that one certainly *could* frame things in that manner. And such a perspective would once again reinforce the notion that fear is always the motivation for aggression. But what benefit is derived from such a perspective? Why stretch an inadequate metaphor to such an absurd degree that it finally fits when an alternative one better describes the situation's reality? Sometimes I think we get so married to our preferred ways of understanding the nature of the world around us that we simply cannot entertain a more sensible perspective. Reasonable scientists have long accepted the law of parsimony (also sometimes referred to as "Occam's Razor"). The simplest adequate explanation of a phenomenon most often turns out to be the best explanation.

Other Major Types of Aggression

In addition to the reactive or predatory (instrumental) variety, there are some other major types of aggression (see figure on next page). People display *overt* aggression when their bid for dominance is open and obvious. A prize fighter in the ring attempting to knock out an opponent is displaying overt aggression. So is a corporate CEO when he openly lays out a plan to "destroy" the competition and emerge as the dominant player in a particular sector of the economy.

Aggression can also be *covert.* That is, a person can do his or her best to conceal any aggressive intent toward another. Keeping aggression under cover serves a dual purpose: (1) possibly being more successful in the aggressive quest (by catching the other person unaware); (2) effectively managing others' impressions and preserving a positive image (thus keeping others from rightly discerning the aggressor's character). Besides, persons who intuitively sense the aggression, but can't objectively verify it, are quite prone to being manipulated and controlled.

Aggression can also be *active* or *passive.* People *actively* aggress when they *do* some things deliberately to get the better of another, or to forcefully take the things they want. Conversely, they aggress *passively* when they won't do things that others want them to do. Persons using the technique of a sit-down strike to protest against injustice employ passive aggression or resistance. So does a partner in a relationship when he or she won't answer, pouts, or resists cooperation with the other partner. There are still more types of aggression, several of which will become apparent as we discuss the various attributes of the aggressive personality subtypes.

OTHER TYPES OF AGGRESSION

- Overt Aggression – Open attempts to win, dominate or control.
- Covert Aggression – Subtle or concealed attempts to win, dominate or control.
- Active Aggression – Trying to get something you want by actively doing things and employing tactics to victimize others.
- Passive Aggression – Trying to avoid things you don't want by resisting cooperation with others.

Understanding the Aggressive Personality "Styles"

As mentioned earlier, some personalities tend to view the world as a combat stage. Every situation they encounter is a contest in which they must emerge as the victor. We best describe such personalities as fundamentally *aggressive* in their styles of interpersonal interaction. They are among the most disturbed in character of all the various personality types. Some aggressive characters are so wanton in their disregard for society's dictates that they frequently run afoul of the law, engage in criminal conduct, and spend a fair portion of their lives incarcerated. These "criminal personalities"[20] have been the subject of much study over the years. They have often been given the label "antisocial personality." But it's important to recognize that many other aggressive personalities exist other than the career criminal. Most of us have encountered one or more of these types in our daily lives. Extremely difficult to deal with, they are among the most character-disordered personalities you will ever encounter.

The various aggressive personality subtypes have many characteristics in common. They all display a pervasive style of doing battle with others and the world at large. All the aggressive personalities also share traits common to the narcissistic personality. Some theorists tend to view the aggressive personalities as merely an aggressive variant of the narcissistic personality. What's more, one of the aggressive personalities is principally defined by the term *malignant narcissism* (all the attributes of the narcissist carried to the most pathological extreme.) The principal distinguishing characteristic of the aggressive personalities, however, is not their narcissism. It's their penchant for aggression.

The various aggressive personality sub-types have more in common than they have differences. But there are several major aggressive personality subtypes, each defined by some fairly unique traits. Before we take a look at the major subtypes, let's outline what the aggressive personalities have in common:

All of the aggressive personalities:

- **Actively seek the superior or dominant position in any relationship or interpersonal encounter**. There's a saying in the real estate business that three things really matter: location, location, and...location. With aggressive personalities, three things really matter (see figure X): position, position, and, of course, position! The determination to seek this position cuts across a wide variety of situations and circumstances.

PRIMARY INTERPERSONAL AGENDA

FOR AGGRESSIVE AND OTHER CHARACTER-DISORDERED PERSONALITIES

1) **Position** (seek the upper hand/advantage/superior location.
2) **Position** (seek to dominate, control, or win).
3) **Position** (doesn't recognize or actively resists submission/subordination to a higher power.)

Aggressive personalities strive for the dominant position at all times and in all circumstances. This premise is very hard for the average person and especially the neurotic individual to understand, let alone accept. It's incomprehensible for most of us to conceive that in every situation, every encounter, every engagement, the aggressive personality is predisposed to jockey with us for the superior position, even in situations with no recognizable need to do so. The failure to understand and accept this, however, is how aggressive personalities so often succeed in their quest to gain advantage over others.

More than once I've attended professional workshops in which the presenter advised that a therapist should refrain from asking probing, intimidating, or challenging questions. Why? Because that would necessarily put the client "on the defensive" and prompt him to engage in acts of resistance, as opposed to allaying his "anxieties," thus making it safe for him to "open up." Of course, such concerns come from the notion that people simply won't fight unless they have to or feel threatened in some way. I used to observe the caveat when working with aggressive characters, until I realized it was unnecessary and often even counterproductive. I eventually came to realize that, whether I wanted to admit it or not, aggressive personality clients had begun resisting any intervention efforts long before my first encounter with them. As mentioned before, neurotics troubled by their circumstances both seek and appreciate therapeutic "help." Disturbed characters are most often reluctantly pressured into the therapeutic process by an outside agent. They don't want any part of it from the beginning. They're happy with who they are and their way of doing things. They might be superficially cordial, but make no mistake, if they're dragged into therapy, they plan from early on to fight any efforts encouraging them to change. So, the "fight" starts long before they first arrive at the office. If a therapist is not inclined to confront it directly and set limits and contingencies immediately, he or she is wasting the person's as well as his or her own time.

My eyes were really opened to shortcomings of traditional therapeutic approaches as soon as I began confronting character-disturbed clients. Firstly, they seemed to show at least a superficial level of interest and rudimentary respect for the challenge they knew they faced, trying to manipulate my impressions of them. Secondly, they seemed to appreciate the cut-to-the-chase approach in which all the cards were on the table and everything was out in the open. Lastly, I implicitly conveyed messages in my benign but firm confrontation of the issues, especially messages like: (a) "It's my opinion that no matter what tactics you use to convince me of the contrary, you *do* have a problem with your character"; (b) "I have some techniques you can use to change the kind of person you are for the better"; and (c) "I'm not going to waste time listening to you blame others, justify your way of doing things, or trivializing the wreck you've made of your life and the lives of others; but I will only engage with you if you are at least to some degree willing to be open to guidance and accepting of the need for change." These emerged as very powerful messages to send. Such messages led them eventually to conclude that: (1) I could not be manipulated; (2) I actually had principles (i.e. willingly subordinated myself to a higher authority) and was willing to adhere to them; (3) I could be trusted (this is so critical because it takes away the most common excuse aggressive personalities give for their conduct). The main reason they eventually knew they could trust me is because I didn't *need* them to need me or like me. I wasn't going to prostitute myself to the person or entity that referred them to me. I wasn't going to try and manipulate these aggressive clients into tolerating me, or even eventually liking me a little through subtle seduction and attempts to curry favor. And I certainly wasn't going to "frame" their serious psychological issues in more palatable or politically correct terms to avoid confronting character concerns head-on.

Many of my colleagues do not share my belief in focusing on the person himself, as opposed to solely the behaviors displayed. They think, of course, that confronting the person about his or her character instead of simply the behaviors is potentially damaging to self-esteem and necessarily invites resistance. These critics would have a valid point if it were really true that *everyone* struggles with low self-esteem like neurotics do, and that people fight and resist only when they feel attacked. But I have not found these assumptions to be valid. While disturbed characters' behaviors are problematic, equally if not more problematic is this sobering fact: They have chosen to define themselves as being comfortable with their negative behavior patterns, at peace with their antisocial attitudes, and unashamed of their repeated abdications of responsibility. Not only that, but they also choose to define themselves as retaining an unwarrantedly high opinion of themselves (ego inflation) despite the big mess these patterns have created. So, who they *are* — not just what they do — is a major issue needing attention and confrontation. Their *character* needs to be a center of focus. I also don't pretend that I'm their unconditional friend or ally. If they want my respect and support, they'll soon learn that they earn it only by making some pretty hard choices with respect to changing their usual ways.

- **Abhorrence of submission to any entity viewed as a higher power or authority**. The aggressive personalities are fundamentally at war with anything blocking unrestrained pursuit of their desires. Unfortunately, this often means society's rules, dictates, and moral obligations, and the expectations imposed by authority. Some aggressive personalities will accede to, or give *assent* to, demands placed on them when it is expedient or self-serving to do so; but in their heart of hearts they never truly submit or subordinate themselves to a higher power or authority. It is anathema to think of themselves as under anyone else's influence, power, or control. So, they resist subordinating themselves. Their innate aversion to any kind of submissive behavior plays a critical role in their problems with forming consciences in their early development, and profiting from experience. (We'll take a closer look at this aspect of the aggressive character a bit later.)

- **Ruthless self-advancement, most often at others' expense**. The aggressive character is an unscrupulous competitor. He will lie, cheat, steal, "con," manipulate, or do whatever he must to seek the position he wants over someone else. The end almost always justifies the means. Actively and deliberately, aggressive personalities seek to exploit and victimize others. Whereas the narcissist simply doesn't pay attention to others' rights or needs (because he doesn't consider them important), the aggressive character tramples their rights and needs to satisfy his own desires. When the aggressive character wants something from you, he will take it by whatever means he finds necessary.

- **A pathological disdain and disregard for truth**. Aggressive characters don't just disregard the truth, they're at war with it. Truth is the great equalizer, and aggressive personalities always want to maintain a position of advantage. So, they deliberately play very fast and loose with the truth when they're not flat out lying. They don't want you to "have their number." That upsets the balance of power. So, they're usually about the business of conning and duping you. And because they want to have advantage over you, they often lie in subtle and sophisticated ways, carefully managing your impression of them and manipulating you through deception. Their lying is so pervasive and automatic, they will lie even when the truth would do just fine; except lying keeps the con game going, which they perceive as maintaining the position of advantage. Also, the lying takes so many forms it's almost impossible to count them all. Nonetheless, we'll take a look at some of the major ways when we talk about manipulation tactics later on.

- **Defective internal "brakes" (lack of inhibitory controls)**. Aggressive personalities are like a runaway train with no means to stop. When they're on a mission, they can't or won't put on the brakes, even when it's in the best interest of all to do so. They appear to have a constitutionally-based deficiency in their neurological inhibitory networks. But since they are also hardwired to fight so intensively and frequently, installing such controls presents an almost insurmountable challenge during their development.

  When most of us are fed up with someone and have the urge to punch their lights out, we exercise restraint, contemplating the possible negative consequences. In short, we think first and act later, usually with some moderation. Because they lack inhibitory control, aggressive characters act first and think or reflect later. They might even have some genuine after-the-fact regret (although the most severely disordered of these personalities lack regret or remorse); but such regret is usually too little and too late in coming. Their lack of inhibitory control, as well as their overly aggressive predisposition, leads to their *impaired ability to delay gratification*. They want what they want, and they usually want it NOW.

- **Irascible Temperament**. Aggressive characters are often quick to react to any environmental event, and their reactions are often quite intense. Someone will say something that most people would simply ignore, whereas they overreact. They have a remarkably low frustration tolerance, and become easily upset when things don't go as they want them to go. As a result, in their development they cultivated little will to bear discomfort. It doesn't take much to set them off. They might become enraged at the slightest provocation. Say just the wrong thing, or look at them in the wrong way, and you might find yourself facing their wrath.

- **Lack of Adaptive Fearfulness**. Although this characteristic is common to other disturbed characters, aggressive personalities are the most lacking in what researchers sometimes call adaptive fearfulness. They lack the squeamishness or apprehension a person should ideally have when contemplating doing something they probably shouldn't do. They neither weigh nor fear the potential consequences. They frequently engage in unhealthy risk-taking, daredevil-type behavior, and are notoriously sensation-seeking.

  When most folks experience a negative consequence of their behavior, they at least consider modifying that behavior. But aggressive personalities' imperturbability allows them to remain unshaken, and therefore undeterred with respect to their destructive behavior patterns. In fact, adversity often prompts them to solidify their combative stance against the world. They tend to view adverse consequences as proof that the world is a cold, cruel place in which they must fight to survive. They tend to regard their tenacious facing of adversity as a noble character trait. They not only value it, but also sometimes try to intensify it with every adverse consequence they experience.

The World According To Aggressive Characters

Aggressive personalities believe every situation has only four possible outcomes:

1. I win, you lose.
2. You win, I lose.
3. I win, you win.
4. I lose, you lose.

Naturally, they prefer the first possible outcome. They like it best when they win and you lose. For them, this is the clearest indication they've emerged the victor in a contest, securing the dominant position. Contrarily, they abhor the notion that you might win and they will lose. They resist this potential outcome with passion. It casts them in the inferior or subordinate position, which they detest. Aggressive personalities will reluctantly (although not usually graciously) accept win-win outcomes. That is, they'll stop warring with you if they think they've secured at least some modicum of victory, even if you also end up with something you want. Tragically, if it becomes clear they're certainly headed for defeat, aggressive characters often won't go down easily. They want to take someone else with them, lessening the sting of defeat. Sadly, this scenario sometimes plays out in the tragic murder-suicides that occasionally make headlines.

To summarize, the following are the core characteristics of the aggressive personality:

- Problems with authority and societal expectations.
- Reckless trampling of the rights/needs of others.
- High-risk behaviors and sensation-seeking.
- Problems with self-control and delay of gratification.
- Frequent, sometimes flagrant, lying.

Possible Constitutional Factors:

- o High reactivity and aggressive predisposition.
- o Low anger threshold and frustration tolerance.
- o Deficient inhibitory capacity.
- o Lack of adaptive fearfulness.
- o Innate revulsion to submissive behavior modalities.

Possible Learning Factors:

- *o* *Sometimes* raised in hostile, abusive, severely neglecting environments.
- o Experienced excessive success (reinforcement) in securing goals aggressively.
- o Insufficient experience with correctly administered punishment.
- o Failed to learn the long-term benefits of short-term self-denial.

Traditional Paradigms' Failure to Accurately Understand and Address Aggressive Personalities' Problems

Traditional thinking about antisocial characters has always been this: Abuse and neglect in their histories led them to deeply mistrust the world and others' motivations. As a result, Traditionalists thought disturbed characters found it too anxiety-evoking to "bond" emotionally with their primary caretakers as well as others. Within this model, aggressors' offensive postures are perceived to be an underlying and rational "defense" against anticipated injury. They are seen as having adopted an "I'll get you before you get me" style of coping with life's challenges. Traditionalists have adhered to the notion that all human beings would naturally bond with others, behaving in pro-social ways unless severely traumatized and conditioned to believe that others are untrustworthy. So traditional theories propose that, when they engage in their hostile acts, antisocial personalities are "acting-out" deeply unconscious conflicts about their safety. They perceive a cold, hostile, and rejecting world. As a result, they reduce their internal pain and anxiety with antisocial conduct, minimizing feelings of guilt or shame through unconscious mechanisms such as denial, projection, and rationalization. Traditional beliefs about antisocial personalities have often been viewed as validated by the fact that such individuals frequently cast themselves as victims of mistreatment. They claim that they rightfully don't trust others, and insist that their behavior was a matter of self-defense. Traditional perspectives have some value if, in fact, the aggressive personality is mostly neurotic. But this is actually fairly rare. The aggressive personalities are among the most frequently and severely character-disordered individuals.

In my work over the years with disturbed characters, I have found that *most* of the time, when aggressive personalities cast themselves as victims, they don't really believe they are the injured party. Rather, they want *you* to believe that they think that way. They know full well that *they* are the victimizers who injured others for no other reason than wanting to take something, regardless of the damage they inflicted on others. But if they can convince you that their actions weren't purely maliciously motivated, they can possibly evoke some sympathy from you, keeping you in the dark about their true character. Knowing what they're really all about would put them in a position of disadvantage with those they seek to manipulate (Remember: position, position, position!). A "level playing field" is something they always seek to avoid. So, they engage in deceitful games of impression management, working hard to have you see them as a victim in some way.

A few of the many aggressive personalities I've counseled over the years actually experienced significant abuse, neglect, and trauma. But I've encountered many more who greatly exaggerated how badly they were victimized while simultaneously minimizing their history of victimizing others. I've also encountered many personalities whose childhood environments were unremarkable or as nurturing and supportive as any — sometimes even better than most. Yet, these individuals appear to have been "fighters" from the start, actively resisting the socialization process during their formative years, and showing an inherent lack of empathy and capacity to bond with others.

Any reasonable theory of personality formation simply has to take this into account: Countless individuals have experienced great hardship, abuse, and trauma in their formative years; but they did not become aggressive personalities or any other type of disturbed characters. It's dangerous to make blanket assumptions about what must underlie the aggressive predispositions of these personalities. It's also dangerous to accept their stories without scrutiny, skepticism, and objective verification. My experience with these individuals has shown me how problematic it can be to blindly accept traditional perspectives on what makes these disturbed individuals "tick."

In recent years, research has pointed to errors of many traditional assumptions about aggressive character formation. For many years, therapists generally accepted that "bullies" were in fact cowards who "compensated" for feelings of insecurity and low self-esteem. They were seen as displaying bravado to mask feelings of inadequacy. They often picked on those weaker, which was regarded as "proof" that they inwardly felt incompetent. But some solid research has demonstrated that most bullies aren't cowards at all. They're not struggling with low self-esteem. They're merely brutes with outrageously inflated egos and a huge sense of entitlement. We also now know that starting off as an egomaniacal brute early in life very strongly predicts all kinds of social maladjustment later in life, including possibly becoming a full-fledged antisocial personality.

Contrary to popular belief, substantial evidence shows that a history of trauma, especially abuse and neglect, does not necessarily predispose a person toward antisocial personality characteristics. In fact, many individuals who lead antisocial lifestyles were raised in supportive and nurturing environments. Evidence also exists that genetic factors play a significant role in whether someone will eventually display antisocial characteristics. Yet myths persist that such characters simply must have been subjected to abuse and neglect, and that their early trauma explains why they behave as they do.

Disturbed characters understand keenly what kinds of attitudes, beliefs, and biases most people hold. They know full well that neurotics are quick to believe no one would engage in aggressive conduct unless they come from a disadvantaged or traumatic background. They often use this knowledge to play on others' sympathies, avoiding responsibility for their choices and actions. But when one carefully examines their entire history and seeks corroboration from reliable sources, here's what generally emerges: Antisocial characters (especially psychopaths) over-represent their degree of being victimized by others, and under-represent how seriously they have intentionally and wantonly victimized others. I usually treat their initial claims with some healthy skepticism, or possess contradictory documentation. Then such characters will often admit a much more lengthy history of doing horrible things to others. They'll also acknowledge that very few, if any, horrible things ever really happened to themselves. But I've also observed just the opposite in two situations: (1) when such individuals are questioned by a naïve interviewer; or (2) when the disordered character senses the interviewer believes that people only do bad things because of traumas they've experienced in the past.

With all disordered characters, here's one very important thing to remember: Mounting evidence shows it isn't so much what bad events happened early on in their lives that shaped them. It's what *didn't happen* with respect to the kinds of influences people need to adequately shape their characters. In some cases, the shaping influences were simply inadequate (i.e., discipline was absent, inconsistent, or improperly administered). Or the child's constitutional predispositions overwhelmed or stymied caretakers' attempts at providing and promoting positive-shaping influences.

Major Aggressive Personality Subtypes

Both Simon[21] and Millon[22] suggest several major variations of the aggressive personality type exist. Although they share many traits in common, some important characteristics differentiate some of the aggressive personalities. As a result of my experience working with such individuals over the years, I find the patterns described below to represent the major aggressive personality subtypes:

Unbridled Aggressive (Antisocial) Pattern — This aggressive personality is best distinguished by frequent, wanton violations of major societal norms and refusal to subordinate his will in service of the greater good. When the unbridled aggressive sees something he wants, he takes it, regardless of whether his actions run afoul of the law or otherwise transgress others' rights. Unbridled aggressive personalities often have a lengthy history of criminal conduct. Many have spent a considerable amount of their lives incarcerated (repeat incarcerations are also common).

The unbridled aggressive has often traditionally been labeled the *antisocial* personality. As the term implies (literally, "against society"), this personality makes himself the adversary of the prevailing social order, engaging in a perpetual contest with others and the world at large, seeking personal gain no matter the cost or impact on others. Some individuals use the term "antisocial" inappropriately to describe the social aloofness and loner status of shy individuals, as well as the avoidant and asocial (schizoid) personalities. But such personality types differ radically in character from the unbridled aggressive. Unbridled aggressive personalities are not afraid to engage you; they're not at all shy or lacking in the normal human urge to interact with others (although they might at times deliberately act indifferent and aloof). Make no mistake. These folks want to engage you, but usually to get something from you, taking advantage of you, defeating you, exerting power and dominance over you, or inflicting injury upon you.

The core characteristics of the Unbridled Aggressive Pattern are:

- Brazen defiance of major social norms of conduct.
- Frequent engagement in behaviors that could result in social sanction if detected.
- Frequent brushes with the law/history of criminal offenses/convictions.
- History of overtly aggressive and sometimes violent conduct toward others.

- Persistence in an aggressive pattern of conduct despite adverse consequences.
- Emboldened in the aggressive behavior pattern when they manage to "beat the system."
- Frequent parasitic lifestyle.

The Channeled-Aggressive Pattern — Not all aggressive personalities are flagrant lawbreakers. One aggressive personality type generally refrains from allowing his overtly aggressive interpersonal style to lead to frequent and brazen violations of the major rules. Channeled-Aggressive personalities place some limits on their obtrusive modus operandi. They generally confine their aggression to social pursuits in which others not only tolerate but often highly value the will to win at all costs. We've all encountered these tough-minded, callous, *driven* people. They're determined to prosper, generally at someone else's expense. For them, all that matters is taking care of themselves. Stay out of their way, and you might never have a problem with them. Get in their way, and you're probably "toast." Insensitivity, disregard for boundaries, extreme competitiveness, and intolerance for weakness are their core characteristics. These personalities want to win at all costs, and don't mind others knowing it. They display their aggressive tendencies openly and proudly. They want all to know, see, and respect their willingness to do whatever it takes to get what they want, and to deal resolutely with those who would oppose them. They don't mind if others fear them or are intimidated by them. In fact, they might regard it a perverted indication of respect that they are a force with which to be contended. They are proud of their tenacity and lack of apprehension when tackling the challenges of life. They rigidly adhere to the belief that the spoils of life's conflicts rightfully belong to those willing to fight for and take them.

Several personality theorists have long equated aggressive personality disturbance with severe anti-sociality and a history of criminal conduct. Indeed, the mental health community's official diagnostic manual pretty much defines the antisocial personality as a career criminal. Some researchers, however, have always recognized that only a certain sub-group of aggressive personalities can be defined by their habitual criminal lifestyle.[23] Channeled-aggressive personalities are very much like their antisocial (i.e. unbridled aggressive) counterparts, except they don't habitually lead lives of crime.

Channeled-aggressive personalities gravitate toward situations in which they can amass power, exert control, and satisfy their insatiable appetites to dominate or win. They are often found in the ranks of law enforcement, military command, and professional sports. They sometimes become heads of corporations, policy makers, administrators, and leaders of various types. Some have the manipulative skill to favorably manage others' impressions, appearing less ruthless or even as team players. In reality, however, they are a team unto themselves, always looking out for number one. Many times, they are respected for their ambition, drive, capability, and tenacity.

Natural leaders, these personalities know how to get any job done. They are radically different from assertive personalities, however, because they don't pay much heed to how their actions might negatively affect others. And they don't temper their actions to display care for others' rights, needs, boundaries, and concerns. They are individuals who are hell to work with and work for.

Channeled-aggressive personalities generally adhere to major social norms, but not out of a neurotic sense of guilt or shame, nor a truly altruistic regard for the greater good. A well-developed conscience is not what holds them back. Rather, it's the practical reality that they run the risk of social sanction, potentially restricting their freedom if they violate major rules. Not wanting to be hampered, they take some pains to see that nothing interferes with their quests for power and success. They don't willingly subordinate their wills to a "higher power" or authority. They detest the notion that "the man" or "the system" might actually exert power over them if they're caught and sanctioned for antisocial acts. So they do their best to avoid that possibility. But, like all aggressive personalities, they lack mature conscience and a sense of moral obligation. So they won't hesitate to engage in minor transgressions unlikely to be discovered; or which, if discovered might result in significant social sanction. Nor will they refrain from major transgressions, including criminal behavior, when reasonably convinced (through the use of power, money, or influence) that they can get away with it.

The character deficiencies of the Channeled-Aggressive Personality become all too evident when they're convinced they won't be caught or sanctioned for breaking the rules. Believing their latest laser and radar detectors are the best on the market, they take to the highway with reckless abandon, weave between cars, and prove to the world they can shave at least four minutes off the time other hapless commuters spend getting to work. Assured that their corporate books have been "cooked" well enough that no oversight agency could possibly detect deception, they'll raid their company's coffers, line their pockets, and swindle their investors. Confident they can successfully buy off corrupt officials, they'll engage in shady business deals. They're as much at odds with the rules as any other aggressive personality. And it's not devotion to the greater good that leads them to avoid the life of the common criminal.

The principal features of the Channeled-Aggressive personality are:

- Interpersonal ruthlessness and heartlessness. Channeled-Aggressives are as disregarding of others' rights and needs as any aggressive personality. This trait differentiates them from another actively "independent" type: the "assertive" personality.
- General confinement and channeling of aggressive interpersonal conduct to non-criminal activity and relatively socially acceptable outlets.
- Abdication of all controls when they're convinced they can successfully avoid detection or sanction.

Covert-Aggressive Pattern — Covert-Aggressive Personalities are the archetypal manipulators I first described in my book, *In Sheep's Clothing,*[24] which, after almost 16 years in print, has been revised a third time and re-released. These personalities are not openly aggressive in their interpersonal style. In fact, they do their best to keep their aggressive intentions and behaviors carefully cloaked. They can appear charming and amiable on the surface, but are just as ruthless as any other aggressive personality underneath their façade. They are devious, underhanded, and subtle in the ways they abuse and exploit others. They are power-oriented individuals who do their best to look anyway but overtly power- and dominance-seeking. They are generally equipped with an arsenal of interpersonal maneuvers and tactics to manipulate, exert power over, and control others in relationships. Their tactics are generally effective because they simultaneously accomplish two objectives:

1. The tactics effectively play on the sensitivities, vulnerabilities, and conscientiousness of others (especially neurotic individuals). The other persons then go unconsciously on the defensive (i.e. retreating mode). This quashes all potential resistance.
2. The tactics conceal obvious aggressive intent. The other persons have little *objective* evidence that the covert-aggressive is intending to take advantage of them. Instead of trusting their "gut" instincts, the other persons question themselves and get hoodwinked.

Covert-Aggressive personalities don't proudly broadcast their combative style as do their unbridled and channeled-aggressive counterparts. They have found that the most effective way to advance their self-serving agendas is to keep them, as well as the nature of their true characters, carefully veiled. They gain advantage over others and catch them unaware. They've learned from experience that overtly self-serving acts are likely to invite resistance. They'd rather not have to "fight" openly, fairly, or constructively, because they might actually lose. So, they fight surreptitiously, hoping that by the time their victims realize they've been taken advantage of, it will be too late. They're also confident in their ability to craftily "reframe" the nature of events, looking good despite the damage they're doing. This makes others feel like the bad guys for doubting them, and "justifies" a whole host of behaviors that negatively impact the others' lives. This manipulative skill (sometimes referred to as "impression management") is developed to its most pathological extreme in one of the other aggressive personalities, which we'll discuss later.

Also, many of the tactics covert-aggressives use are also employed by other disturbed characters. We'll present these in a later chapter.

Some covert-aggressive personalities are remarkably skilled at hiding their quests for dominance while simultaneously wielding incredible power and influence over others. Some cult leaders, as well as masterminds of radical religious and political movements who occasionally make headlines have this personality type. While their devoted minions might truly believe the ideology they espouse, the master-manipulators know full well that their true agenda is power only. They know all combinations of tactics to bring others under their influence.

The cardinal characteristics of the covert-aggressive personality are:

- Distinctly *active* yet carefully *veiled* aggressive style of interpersonal relating, resulting in the abuse, exploitation, and victimization of others.
- Frequent use of a variety of tactics that simultaneously conceal their aggressive intent while putting conscientious others on the defensive, thus manipulating them.
- Skilled at impression management. Covert-aggressives "frame" events to maintain a favorable image, making others doubt their own intuitive mistrust of motives.

The Sadistic Pattern — Any aggressive personality is capable of causing great harm to others. However, for most of the aggressive personalities, inflicting injury or pain upon others is not their primary objective. Aggressive personalities simply want what they want and fight tenaciously to get it. If they have to run roughshod over others to reach their goals, they will. They'll do whatever it takes to emerge victorious in an interpersonal encounter or secure the dominant or controlling position. When others either deliberately or inadvertently interfere with their quests, they attempt to remove or obliterate that interference. Sometimes their effort is violent in character, but most of the time it is simply forceful yet non-violent. They generally don't inflict any pain on others for its own sake. Rather, it's most often a secondary by-product or consequence of the overly aggressive quest to win.

Sadistic personalities differ from the other aggressive personality subtypes because inflicting pain is a primary objective of their interpersonal modus operandi. The sadist relishes hurting others, and derives genuine pleasure (sometimes even sexual pleasure) from others' suffering and humiliation. The sadist especially seeks to put or keep others in a degrading and humiliating position. He wants to feel in such total control that his victims are truly helpless and at his mercy. Sadistic personalities take the aggressive personality's quest for domination to its most pathological extreme.

Now, traditional thinking has often postulated that no one would inflict such cruelty unless they themselves had been subjected to such treatment; and they were "acting-out" some sort of psychological "payback" against the world, or seeking a perverted sense of redress. But there's no solid, reliable, and objective evidence for it. In fact, some studies have shown that although some highly disturbed characters *report* mistreatment and abuse in their early histories (i.e. give the "abuse excuse") to justify their cruel actions, such claims are often exaggerated and sometimes bogus.

Sadistic personalities are often found in the most extreme examples of abusive relationships. Such individuals delight in physically, emotionally, and psychologically battering and demeaning those unfortunate souls involved with them. And, contrary to popular belief, their victims don't usually stay with them because they are "weak" and emotionally "dependent." Rather, they often stay because they realize the perverted reality that they are actually safer caving into the abuser's wishes (to feel powerful and dominant) than they might be if they were to declare their independence.

The core characteristics of the Sadistic Personality are:

- Sadists actively and intensely seek positions of dominance and control over others.
- Sadists derive satisfaction (and in some bizarre instances even experience sexual arousal) from exerting a level of control over others, leaving the victim cowering in fear, feeling helpless, utterly dependent, degraded, and humiliated.
- Sadists view those perceived as weak with callousness and disdain.

The Predatory Aggressive Pattern — Among all the aggressive personalities, by far the most pathological subtype is the one I prefer to label the predatory aggressive personality. These individuals are capable of the most heinous acts. The seemingly senseless brutality they engage in sometimes makes headlines. They are the true predators among us.

This personality type has been given many different labels in the past. The term *psychopathic* was one of the first labels given to this deeply disordered character. The dominant thinking at the time was that every aspect of the human personality (including antisocial characteristics) could be explained by the theory of neurosis. That theory also proposed that when neurosis became extreme, or the inner conflicts underlying it were so intense that they caused a breakdown of the more common and sophisticated "defenses" that made "normal" neurotic functioning impossible, the result was "psychosis." Cleckley[24] and others conceptualized the psychopath as a personality who appeared to be sane on the surface, but whose level of sociopathic neurosis bordered on insanity. Psychopathy, therefore, was conceptualized as a nearly insane level of antisociality.

Cleckley noted that psychopaths could be superficially charming, and appear to the casual observer as quite benign and ordinary characters. But they could also entertain almost unthinkable beliefs and attitudes (while not being truly delusional), and were prone to the vilest and seemingly senseless antisocial acts. These characteristics would lead almost anyone to question their sanity. He also incorporated into his thinking Pinnel's observations in the early 19th Century and even some of the ancient philosophers such as Aristotle. Cleckley determined that these individuals *know* their behavior would be rightfully regarded by almost anyone as irrational, yet they persist in it. This fact appeared even more irrational and, therefore, nearly insane. But, although they know well the vileness of their behavior, psychopaths persist in it *voluntarily*. So, by current definition, they are not insane. People who are *psychotic* (this term is still confused by some with the term *psychopathic*) are indeed sometimes capable of heinous behavior, but it is not voluntary because their brain dysfunction impairs their capacity to reason logically and deduce right from wrong.

The term *sociopath* has also been used to describe this personality type, and has recently again come into vogue.[26] The psychopath label focuses more on the uniquely abnormal mental processes of this disordered personality, whereas the sociopath label focuses more on the pattern of severe social dysfunction. Over the past several decades, the terms psychopath and sociopath have alternately enjoyed varying degrees of popularity among clinicians and researchers.

Some suggest that the terms psychopath and sociopath should not be used synonymously; that each term describes a slightly different and uniquely extreme pathological variation of the antisocial personality. In my experience, I find some merit to this notion. I have met individuals who justify their unconscionable behavior by espousing beliefs that are truly chilling but seem crazy. Although such individuals are rarely truly delusional, they appear to really hold deeply troubling beliefs and attitudes that make them a constant danger to others. This contrasts with other equally dangerous persons who espouse beliefs that they really don't hold; but they want others to believe that they believe, thus conferring a certain degree of bizarre rationality or justification to their heinous acts. So, even though they don't believe the "B.S." they sling, they *say* they do. It's their way of manipulating others and conducting their con game of impression management.

In recent times, the eminent Canadian psychologist Robert Hare has re-popularized the label of psychopathy, and defined its characteristics with a good deal of clarity. His arduous research also helped identify the two principal traits (i.e. factors) that accompany this severe disturbance of character: (1) Hare indicates this is a *necessary condition* for someone to be considered a psychopath. It's what others have called a viciously *malignant narcissism* exemplified by the psychopath's callous, senseless, and remorseless use and abuse of others.[27] Their callousness as well as their lack of capacity for remorse is, within Hare's model, due to the absence of any conscience. This results from the psychopath's non-existent capacity to bond emotionally to the human race and to have *empathy* for others. (2) This often accompanying trait is not an essential feature. It's the socially parasitic lifestyle (e.g., criminal activity, checkered work history, abusive, and exploitive relationships) common to antisocial personalities.

The nature of the first factor Hare describes, and what gives rise to it in the very disordered characters, has always intrigued me. I've strived to better understand this factor in my work over the years with individuals in the prison population. There, estimates of the percentage of persons who score highly on "psychopathy" rating instruments range as high as approximately one in four or five. Such individuals are also found among the ranks of true sexual predators. I have long observed these personalities to consider themselves superior creatures in comparison to "common" human beings. As they see it, amoebae, plankton, and paramecia are at the bottom of the "food chain"; ordinary humans are higher up, to be sure; but those like themselves are definitely at the top. Viewing themselves so pathologically superior, they tend to regard every creature "beneath" them (in status as well as worth) as *rightful prey.* So, their seriously malignant narcissism reveals an extremely pathological kind of grandiosity, as well as an extraordinary attitude of entitlement. Just as most humans don't consider it a particularly heinous act to pluck an apple off a tree and devour it, psychopaths don't even think twice when they use, abuse, or exploit "ordinary" humans in whatever ways they see fit to gratify their desires. For them, *ordinary* humans — those unfortunate creatures with fears, insecurities, emotional vulnerabilities and sensitivities, and especially compunctions about their actions that arise from their consciences — are innately weak, inferior, defective, and relatively worthless beings. They're not as entitled to survival as are those like themselves, whom they regard as the *fittest* of all creation. So they prey at will on those they see as beneath them, and with great self-edifying pleasure. That's why I think the label "predatory aggressive" more fully and accurately captures the pathology of these highly disordered characters.

It's natural to wonder what factors could possibly make a person become so disordered in the first place. And, of course traditional frameworks have always assumed that such individuals must necessarily have been exposed to the most extreme cruelty and neglect; that failure to bond with others and their hostile style of relating to the world resulted from the kinds of "defenses" they had to mount to deal with their cold and hostile environment. But there's no solid evidence that any of these traditional notions are valid. Ever-mounting evidence shows that the backgrounds of these individuals do not differ all that significantly from those of other personalities, including "normal" or relatively well-adjusted personalities. Also, there appears to be some very unique constitutionally-based differences in these individuals that predispose their unusual character development, regardless of the environments to which they've been exposed.

Some research studies have indicated that the brains of psychopaths operate differently from those of normal individuals. The differences are most striking in the brain regions that integrate our emotions with our experiences. Such findings might help explain how psychopaths are able to carry out the most heinous acts without any apparent emotion or later remorse. A constitutional predisposition to lack genuine empathy also helps explain why individuals like Scott Peterson, Ted Bundy, Bernie Madoff and countless others have made headlines over the years. They could be so superficially charming and normal-appearing, could come from such relatively benign backgrounds, and yet be capable of such predatory and heartless behavior toward others.

In my work with predatory aggressive personalities, I have encountered many who, as Hare notes, lack any modicum of conscience or empathy for others. Such individuals are truly incapable of what psychologists call "emotional bonding" in a relationship. They experience absolutely no remorse when they commit acts of unspeakable horror against others. But a few that I've encountered actually appear to have *some* capacity for these things. Unfortunately, they also have an extraordinary capacity to mentally wall-off or "compartmentalize" feelings they might have — emotions which might otherwise unnerve them or interfere with their predatory agendas. This explains, for example, why a psychopathic child sexual predator can feel genuine hurt when his own child is injured in an accident, or bristle at the thought of sexually offending one of his own, yet be capable of the completely cold and heartless kidnapping, brutal rape, and murder of a child across town when he feels the need to satisfy his craving. In my experience, this capacity for compartmentalization is more disturbing. Those individuals can appear so normal much of the time that, when others get a clue about just how dangerous they might be, it's far too late.

Some people report that just being in the presence of this kind of personality makes the hair on the back of their necks stand up. A few researchers regard this intuitive sense of danger as a "gift" from our ancestors, letting us know we're in the presence of a predator.[28] But not all predators give off warning "signals," and not everyone has the intuitive capacity to pick up on those signals. Some predatory aggressives appear to have an uncanny ability to charm and manage the impressions of others, a trait that goes beyond their typical superficial glibness. Such individuals could be considered a more extreme and predatory variation of the covert-aggressive or manipulative personality.

As a result of my work over the years with both predatory aggressives and their victims, I have concluded the main reason these predators are so successful in manipulating others: It lies not so much in their highly effective knowledge and use of manipulation tactics; but rather in the reluctance of normal "neurotic" individuals to make harsh judgments about others, or to trust their gut instincts about the kind of person they're probably dealing with. They don't attach enough significance to the "gift of fear," and mistrust their instincts. On top of it all, they're also often blinded by the notion promoted by traditional psychology theories over the years that everyone is basically good (and most especially, just like them underneath their wall of "defenses"). So they allow themselves to believe that a person will only behave badly when hurting, frightened, or in some kind of inner pain. Such beliefs allow them to be easily victimized by the truly heartless. By now it should be evident that entertaining traditional notions about human behavior can easily be *fatal* when it comes to dealing with a psychopath.

Like all the other aggressive personalities, predatory aggressives share some characteristics of the other aggressive personality subtypes. Predatory aggressives who have significant sadistic traits are among the most notorious serial killers you've ever read or heard about. In addition to callously preying on others, they often delight in watching their victims suffer, squirm, beg for mercy, or grovel in abject humiliation. And predatory aggressives are often noted for having incredible manipulation skills. As the most pathological variation of the aggressive personality, it's no surprise that these individuals can often have other aggressive personality traits, each of which might exist at a disturbingly pathological level of intensity.

Some researchers say that these severely disordered personalities are untreatable; that exposing them to the kinds of treatment most commonly employed actually enables them to become more skilled as predators. Why? Because in typical treatment modalities where feelings and unconscious conflicts are still given prominence, these predators gain greater and more intimate knowledge of others' emotional concerns and vulnerabilities. Presently, it's rare for treatment programs or providers to actually employ models that have a genuine chance of impacting severely disordered characters. So it will be some time before reliable data emerges on whether psychopaths can, in fact, be effectively treated. The emerging new models need much more development, and must be more widely employed before the research becomes clear.

Through my years of experience, I believe I have witnessed significant changes take place in some predatory aggressive personalities who were confined long enough, exposed to sufficient ongoing "corrective emotional and behavioral experience," and who showed some degree of "internalization" of appropriate values and standards. More work and research need to be done. But it is becoming increasingly evident that traditional interventions are virtually useless, and may actually make matters worse.

To summarize, the core characteristics of the predatory aggressive personality are:

- Lack of empathy that severely impairs conscience formation, begetting a callous disregard and remorseless use and abuse of others.
- Persistent "conning" and predatory behavior.
- Glibness and capacity for charm, often superficial, but sometimes quite convincing impression management.
- Sometimes parasitic lifestyle.

The Mistrusting (Paranoid) Pattern — Again, contrary to traditional notions, most aggressive personalities aren't motivated to take their power-oriented stance toward the world because of a deep-rooted mistrust of others, nor because they want to "pay back" the world for mistreatment they once suffered. Although they might claim so as a manipulation tactic, most don't really anticipate mistreatment by others nor believe the best "defense" is a strong "offense." Rather, their offensive posture is simply a preferred way of doing things. And often, their experience successfully rolling over others has convinced them that their strategy works. However, one aggressive personality "style" *is* primarily influenced by a deep and irrational mistrust of others.

Mistrusting Aggressive Personalities (alt. Paranoid Personalities) have a pervasive sense of wariness about others' intentions and motivations. They are innately cynical and vigilant, respecting others only for their perceived capacity to do harm if one's guard is dropped. They ardently strive to amass as much power as possible, concerned that others' power will inevitably be used against them. They can be extraordinarily spiteful and vengeful; but their aggression is most often muted, subtly expressed, or carefully channeled. Fortunately, it's rarely expressed in violent ways.

Traditionalists view this "paranoid" personality style as deeply neurotic and bordering on "psychotic." The suspicious character of their cognitions, though not technically psychotic delusions, are most often quite irrational. On the dimension of neurosis vs. character disturbance, these individuals are equally neurotic and character disordered. They're in part neurotic because their style of coping is truly fueled by deep inner conflicts of which they are largely unaware. But they are also very comfortable with their approach to dealing with the world. They're undeterred in their style by the adverse consequences of their typical behaviors, have distorted thinking processes and an inflated sense of self. So they are also by definition to a great extent character-disordered.

Constitutional factors appear to play a significant role in this personality style. Their maladaptive wariness appears much less chosen as opposed to hardwired. Further, this trait appears to play a significant role in how the personality style develops in the first place.

The core characteristics of this personality style are:

- o Persistent, pervasive mistrust of others' intentions and motivations.
- o Absence of truly delusional (psychotic) thinking.
- o Intensely hostile feelings, most often controlled, leading to holding grudges, unrealistic jealousy or suspiciousness, and excessive vigilance.

Constitutional factors:

- o Excessive wariness, vigilance, and suspiciousness.
- o Tendency to interpret the nature of events, circumstances, and others' behavior in a manner that easily ascribes malevolent, hostile intent to them.

Learning factors:

- o Provocative behaviors toward others invite hostile responses, thus reinforcing distorted perceptions.
- o Hostile responses to others prompt hostile, defensive reactions from others, thus reinforcing distorted perceptions.

Borderline Styles

Probably no personality pattern has been the focus of as much study and debate as the Borderline Personality. Originally the term "borderline" was intended to describe personalities held together with fragile, primitive, and ineffective ego defenses. They literally straddled the border between extreme neurosis and outright psychosis. Indeed, some borderline personalities do experience brief but reversible psychotic episodes.

As the The Diagnostic and Statistical Manual of Mental Disorders (DSM) notes, some clinicians tend to view the borderline style as a distinctive personality pattern (i.e. the "unstable" pattern). Others tend to view the phenomenon as basically representing degrees of deficiency in personality organization and solidification. Still others assert that at heart, the borderline pattern represents a disturbance or disorder of the "self": The individual was never able to master the principle task of adolescence. He never developed a stable, functional identity. (Indeed one of the previous editions of the official diagnostic manual required that the label "identity disorder" be given to individuals under age 18 showing borderline characteristics unless their symptoms far exceeded the criteria for an identity disturbance.) This is compatible with the notion that the resulting instability can easily become a "style" of its own.

We can view the borderline personality's disturbance as a failure of varying degrees to arrive at an integrated and stable sense of self. This helps explain the wide variety of experience people have with borderline personalities, and how any two borderlines can be so very different in character. That's because all of us have a variety of different personality *traits* in us. Most of us form personalities that are fairly balanced, even though some of our tendencies or traits tend to be more dominant. In the case of disordered personalities, dysfunctional traits are so intensely present, unyielding, or overly dominant that they predispose a person to problems with functioning in an adaptive manner. In the case of disturbances of character, dysfunctional traits predispose individuals to chronic problems with functioning in a socially responsible manner. In the borderline personality, part of the disturbance's nature is this: Overall personality organization is so weak that we see behavior patterns associated with many different personality styles glaringly present in the same person. So, the defining overall "style" of interaction for the borderline is often a multitude of shifting styles (and some propose that, in the most extreme form, it's a multiple personality). Nonetheless, some traits tend to be more dominant than others, making for a wide degree of variability in borderline personalities. A borderline personality with prominent passive-dependent traits is a remarkably different individual from a borderline personality with prominent antisocial traits. And a borderline personality with prominent histrionic traits is very different from one with prominent obsessive-compulsive traits, etc.

Some borderline personalities had problems successfully mastering crucial psychosocial developmental stages. They experienced so much chaos, instability, abuse, and trauma that safe, reliable role-models were not available to them. They endured such high levels of anxiety that the all-important task of identity solidification was overwhelmingly difficult, if not impossible for them to resolve adaptively. Other borderlines seemed naturally predisposed to personality difficulty in solidifying a stable sense of self. This seems due to their inherent and chronic instability of mood, their legendary capacity for dialectical thinking (and therefore considerable ambivalence with respect to "resolving" any developmental conflict), and their gross deficiencies for managing anger.

Their lack of a stable sense of self and balanced management of various traits and tendencies cause a pattern of instability, impulsivity, and severely self-defeating behavior. Not knowing how to cope, and lacking internal controls, borderline personalities are notorious for attention-seeking, reckless, and self-damaging acts when under duress. The more dependent borderlines are inordinately clingy and have an almost irrational fear of abandonment. The more antisocial borderlines tend to enter numerous intensely-charged but remarkably shallow, volatile, and short-lived relationships. In some borderlines, the lack of a stable sense of self leads to a lifetime of sexual-identity confusion and fluidity. In others, the marked tendency toward dialectical thinking creates such intense ambivalence about almost every life issue, so emotional growth and maturation is chronically impaired. In recent years, Dialectical Behavior Therapy has demonstrated some efficacy in the treatment of this personality disturbance.

The core characteristics of the borderline personality style are:

- o Extreme emotional instability or lability.
- o Intense uncertainty, instability, and variability with respect to personal identity and style of inter-relating.
- o Intense and contrary (dialectical) urges, impulses, thinking patterns.
- o Erratic and impulsive patterns of behavior including episodic acts of self-harm and irrational displays of anger toward others.

Possible Constitutional Factors:

- o Deficient emotional self-regulation.
- o Excessive tendency toward dialectical thinking.
- o Deficient impulse control capacity.

Possible Learning Factors:

- o Experience of severe trauma, chaos, instability, and chronic anxiety during formative years hampering many aspects of development.
- o Absence of stable, reliable role models sometimes a factor impairing identity formation.

Borderlines whose dominant personality traits are more closely associated with neurosis (e.g., dependent, avoidant) tend to be more neurotic than character-disturbed. Borderlines whose dominant personality traits are more closely associated with character disturbance (e.g., narcissistic, antisocial) tend to be more character-disturbed than neurotic.

The Eccentric Style — Many labels have been applied to individuals whose interpersonal style of relating is best described as "odd" or eccentric. These individuals appear to have such an unconventional view of the world, entertain such unusual beliefs about themselves, and behave in such a "weird" or peculiar manner that they appear nearly insane. However, by definition, they are not psychotic. They do not suffer from the kind of brain dysfunction that makes rational thought impossible. They don't dysfunction in a truly "psychotic" manner. Their thinking is organized and *logical* in the strict sense of the word, even if it is *unconventional*. They are also not plagued by hallucinations or true delusions. The term "schizoid" was once used to describe such individuals, but we now associate that label with the "asocial" or socially aloof style. In more recent times, the label "schizotypal" has been applied to these rare and strangely interesting personalities.

I was once asked to interview a woman who spoke with a distinctly British accent. She carried herself in a manner that suggested she came from a long line of aristocrats. She spoke of her delight at inviting her fashionable neighbors for tea, and was very prim and proper in her manner. In fact, this woman was of humble origin, raised in the back woods of a southern American state. She was a perfectly delightful conversationalist and displayed none of the cardinal signs of psychosis. She did not operate under any true delusions. Her eccentricities did not rise to the level of intensity, pervasiveness, or inflexibility to significantly impair her ability to function socially or occupationally, or cause anyone any appreciable distress. Therefore, she would not have even qualified for a diagnosis of a personality disorder. Still, she displayed many prominent traits of the schizotypal personality.

On balance, such personalities are much more neurotic than they are character disturbed. Here's one of the few similarities they share with disturbed characters: They are usually quite comfortable with their style of inter-relating (i.e. their traits are ego-syntonic). However, their comfort with their personality characteristics does not fly in the face of extreme discomfort caused to others, as is the case with disturbed characters.

The core characteristics of the eccentric or schizotypal personality are:

- Odd or unusual patterns of thinking, speaking, and behavior.
- Impaired intimate relations except with close family members.

Possible Constitutional Factors:

- Predisposed to thinking that is bizarre or seemingly irrational.
- Impaired ability to experience and express normal emotions.

Possible Learning Factors:

- Odd beliefs and manner alienate others, thus reinforcing social interaction deficits.
- Difficulty relating normally increases anxiety which in turn fuels increased social avoidance.

CHAPTER 4

The Process of Character Development

Conscience and Character Development

I use a catchy little rhyming saying at workshops. It sums up what must happen for values and standards to become firmly embedded in a person's psyche. It also explains why so many disordered characters (especially the aggressive and narcissistic personalities) don't form good consciences. The ditty goes like this: "Internalizing a societal prohibition is at heart an act of submission." That's right. *Internalizing* a *prohibition* is most fundamentally an act of *submission* to a higher power or authority. A person who truly accepts a principle of conduct, and actively incorporates it into their conscience, willingly subordinates his or her individual will to serve the greater good. This is the very essence of healthy conscience formation.

Of all the disturbed characters, those with narcissistic and/or aggressive personality traits have the hardest time developing a healthy conscience. Narcissists struggle with forming good consciences because they find it difficult to even conceive of a power or cause greater than themselves. Further, their excessive sense of self-importance and attitude of entitlement make it difficult for them to entertain the notion that anything besides what they want has any real value or importance. So, they pay little attention or heed to the wants and needs of others.

The aggressive personalities despise the idea that anyone or anything might exert power, influence, or authority over them. They experience an innate revulsion to engaging in behaviors that even resemble acts of submission. So they wage a constant war with the potentially civilizing influences they encounter in their lives. It's not that they don't know what values and principles others want them to adopt. They know these very well. But even though they know what society wants and expects from them, they simply won't allow themselves to serve any master other than themselves.

Predatory aggressive (psychopathic) personalities are distinguished by their extreme lack of conscience. Their severely impaired capacity for empathy and their extraordinary capacity to compartmentalize any sensitivity they might have make it virtually impossible for them to identify with and care about others in the ways most of us can. Their malignant narcissism (i.e. extreme sense of superiority) prevents them from recognizing any higher power and allows them to feel entitled to dominate and prey upon those they view as inferior. Their deficient capacity for empathy, ability to wall-off emotion, pathological sense of superiority, and extreme predisposition to aggressively prey all combine to make it virtually impossible to form a normal, healthy conscience.

Socialization is a *Process*

Let's boil down traditional schools' underlying assumptions about how people become disturbed, and how you help them heal: People are inherently good and geared toward health. They become unhealthy because bad or "traumatic" things happen to them. They develop fears and insecurities in response to their traumas. They learn to protect themselves, cope with stress or "defend" themselves against emotional pain in less than optimal ways. With unconditional positive regard, empathy, and support, they can heal their wounds, lower their defenses, overcome their fears, and become naturally inclined once again to lead healthy, loving, compassionate lives. These principles lie at the heart of traditional psychotherapy.

Some schools of philosophical and religious thought adopt an opposing view: Man is basically a "fallen" or evil creature, inherently defective. Without sufficient guidance from a higher power, and left to his own devices, man will naturally tend to descend into all types of decadence, indecency, and depravity. His greatest need is to be "saved," especially from himself. Such views are at the heart of much religious fundamentalism.

There is also the "nature vs. nurture" argument. For a long time, behavioral scientists argued that we'd all be the same if we weren't subjected to very different environmental influences and contingencies. Strict "behaviorists" in psychology believe that our attitudes and actions are entirely dictated by environmental contingencies. But plenty of evidence is emerging these days showing that certain behavioral tendencies are strongly influenced by genetic, biochemical, hormonal, and other constitutional factors.

In my work over the years with various personality types, I've encountered individuals whose early environments were so full of chaos, pain, loss, and other trauma that they had good reason to form dysfunctional coping styles. But I have also known individuals who blossomed into unbelievably noble characters despite having endured the most horrendous upbringing and history of trauma. I have also encountered many who, despite being reared in the most nurturing environments, having ample opportunity, and being afforded the best of academic as well as character education, became the most disordered personalities.

So, as is almost always the case, it appears the truth about human nature lies somewhere in the middle of these various extremes. Man is neither inherently good nor evil. And he is neither at the mercy of his genes and biochemistry nor is he fated to behave solely as his environment has "programmed" him to respond. He is neither inherently defective nor saintly. And although he's basically an animal endowed by nature with some very primitive instincts, he has the remarkable capacity to become ever so much more than a mere animal. That's what the processes of socialization and character development are all about. Character development is a difficult, painful, complex, ongoing process.

In my book *In Sheep's Clothing,*[29] I define the process of character development this way:

Character-building is the lifelong process by which we instill self-discipline and develop the capacities to live responsibly among others, to do productive work, and above all, to love. ... [And] loving is not a feeling, an art, or a state of mind. It's a behavior, and precisely the behavior to which the two Great Commandments exhort us to commit ourselves.

Similarly, I define a philosophy for responsible living:

Even though a person might begin life as a prisoner of the natural endowments he was given and the circumstances under which he was raised, he cannot remain a "victim" of his environment forever. Eventually, every person must come to terms with him or herself. To know oneself, to fairly judge one's strengths and weaknesses, and to attain true mastery over one's most basic instincts and inclinations are among life's greatest challenges. But ultimately, anyone's rise to a life of integrity and merit can only come as the result of a full self-awakening. A person must come to know himself as well as others without deceit or denial. He must honestly face and reckon with all aspects of his character. Only then can he freely take on the burden of disciplining himself for the sake of himself as well as for the sake of others. It is the free choice to take up this burden or "cross" that defines love. And it is the willingness and commitment of a person to carry this cross even to death that opens the door to a higher plane of existence.

None of us is born civilized. We are not naturally predisposed to be socially conscientious or responsible beings. Rather, we are inherently brutes with the capacity to develop dignity, integrity, and communal awareness. Socialization is a *process*: We transform ourselves from self-serving impulse-ridden creatures into the "civilized," responsible beings we can become. This process of socialization takes many years and an incredible amount of investment on the part of others. Other than humans, no creatures require 20 or so years of 24/7 education, monitoring, guidance, and discipline to function in an adaptive, independent fashion.

Some very critical factors play key roles in developing traits that most regard as distinctive marks of a healthy and responsible character. Biology and temperamental factors play a role, to be sure. So do environmental circumstances and experiences (e.g., the prevailing atmosphere in the home, and dominant cultural values). But no matter how one is biologically predisposed, and regardless of one's environment, certain crucial lessons must be learned at various life stages if one is to develop a balanced personality and healthy character. What's more, individuals prone to developing certain personality styles will find it quite challenging to learn some of these lessons.

Regardless of the challenge, humans must teach these important lessons that shape character. They must be taught primarily by the most influential teachers (i.e., parents or primary caretakers), and affirmed and reinforced by significant others in social environment and culture. Then it's up to the individual to take the lessons to heart, incorporating the principles of responsible living into one's character structure (i.e. to *internalize* these values).

Over the years, I've come to believe in what I call the "Ten Commandments" of sound character formation. The most fundamental principles associated with character development have been known and debated for centuries. Socrates and Plato mused about the various human "virtues," and religious scholars throughout the years have attempted to delineate and codify the most essential (i.e. "cardinal") ones. So, there's nothing really new in the perspective I offer. But I find it helpful to incorporate time-honored principles into this framework. It lays out the most essential caveats a person must observe in learning the life lessons essential to forming good character.

The Ten Commandments of Character

- **You are not the center of the universe**. Rather, you are but a small part of a greater reality more vast, complex, and wondrous than you can even imagine. You inhabit space with many other persons, creatures, and objects of creation. So, despite your tendency to think otherwise, it's definitely not all about you. **Be mindful of how you, your wishes, desires, and especially your behavior impact everyone and everything else that exists.** Conduct yourself with both caution and concern for the consequences of your very presence on the rest of creation.
- **Remember, you are NOT ENTITLED to *anything*.** Your very life is an *unearned gift.* **Strive to be truly *grateful*** for the many gifts you've received. Regard life and the miracle of creation with appropriate awe and appreciation. Gratitude will enable you to develop a sense of obligation to value, preserve, and promote life and to respect all aspects of creation. Knowing how inherently indebted you really are will keep you from feeling entitled.
- **You are neither an insignificant speck nor are you so precious or essential to the universe that it simply cannot do without you**. Know where you fit in the grand scheme of things and **keep a *balanced* perspective on your sense of worth**. Thinking too much of yourself is as dangerous as thinking too little of yourself. Do not dismiss your accomplishments, but don't laud yourself or lord over others any position or good fortune you've managed to secure. Avoid pretense. Keeping a balanced sense of self and being genuine will help you stay humble and avoid false pride.

  Remember, you are not synonymous with your talents, abilities, or physical attributes. They are all endowments (i.e. fortunate accidents of nature, "gifts" of God, the universe) entrusted to you. **Recognize where things really come from and give credit and recognition where credit and**

recognition are truly due. Who you are and how you are defined as a character are in large measure determined by what you do with what you've been given. The credit for your life and innate capabilities belongs to nature or, ultimately the creative force behind nature. The credit for what you *do* with all you've been given goes to you. This is the essence of *merit*. Honor the life force within you as well as all who might have nurtured your potential by using your gifts for the good of all. It's not so much the outcome of your actions that matter either, for that's also not entirely in your hands. It's the effort you make that matters most. Judge yourself on your merits. Having appropriate reverence for what you've been given and honoring the creative force through your actions is the essence of both genuine humility and healthy self-respect.

- **To know, pursue, speak, and display the truth to the best of your ability, have the utmost reverence for the truth**. Unnecessary and brutal full disclosure is never required of you, nor is sharing every ugly thing you know to be true. But you must **be ever mindful of man's incredible capacity to deceive** himself as well as others, and the temptation we all face to secure what we want and avoid what we don't want through deception, cheating, and conniving. Avoid short-cuts and the temptation to manipulate. **Honestly and humbly acknowledge and reckon with your mistakes**. Always take the honest and sincere course.
- **Be the master of your appetites and dislikes**. You were meant to survive and prosper, but you were never meant to be pampered or indulged. Your ability to experience pleasure and pain is meant to help guide you through life, not govern your life. Taking pleasure for its own sake is almost always a pathway to destruction. Avoid greed and excess. Be willing to endure necessary discomfort. Sometimes, one has to embrace hardship in order to grow and love. There are two great drives within us all: the pleasure-seeking drive, and the drive to thrive

(i.e. to live and prosper). We are born aligned with the pleasure principle, and the vast majority of us remain aligned with it for most if not all of our lives. We leave the comfort of the womb in fear of life until we get our first taste of pleasure, and then live in fear of death unless our pain becomes too great. But we have the power to subordinate our will to gratify ourselves to life's greater cause. No man can serve two masters. One of our two great drives must always be subordinate to the other. The unbridled pursuit of pleasure for its own sake (hedonism) is always the pathway to psychological ill-health and spiritual death. Most of us need to be reborn in spirit or to remake our lives on a different operating principle. Cherishing and advancing life (i.e. *loving*) and placing the call to love above all that might please or displease us is the surest mark of good character.

- **Be the master of your impulses**. Be "mindful" of both your inclinations and behavior. Temper your urges with reason and foresight. Neither rush into action nor into judgment. *Think* before you act. Think not only about what you're about to do but also about the consequences. You need not be paralyzed into inaction simply by taking time to contemplate the soundness and rightfulness of the choices you might make. And remember, you do not have to act on every urge.
- **Perseverance, patience, and endurance are not really virtues in themselves**. A man intent on robbing a large bank may spend hours or days meticulously planning and executing his caper as well as waiting for the best time to strike. And even some criminals remain of solid resolve in dealing with life no matter how many incarcerations or life losses they've experienced. Daring is not the same as courage or forbearance. Nor is obstinacy the same as strength of will. Still, **it is imperative that you develop solidity and strength, as well as rightness of purpose, with respect to your will**. Your *will* says "yes" or "no" to every temptation

you face, and that will can be strengthened with practice. But merely exercising and strengthening will is insufficient. It's important to adhere to principles of rightful conduct. That way, when the time comes, you can "put on the brakes" when you're tempted to run pell-mell into trouble or "push" yourself to take a difficult but correct path.

Willfulness in the service of justice and righteousness is indeed a virtue. To accept moral and social obligation, to work, and to persevere in service of the welfare of others, to pursue justice and live righteously (i.e. to love), are indeed the most noble ways to exercise your will. So, pledge yourself to principled living and stay the course. Faith in something bigger than you really helps. And faith and commitment are the antidotes to fear.

- **Neither your tendency to anger nor your instinct to aggress is inherently evil, although wrath is a "deadly sin."** Anger is nature's way of prompting you to take action to remedy a disquieting situation. You have the right to look out for your welfare. But you also have an obligation to consider the welfare of others. Some things in life really do have to be fought for. It's important to learn when and how to fight. When you must, **fight *fairly*.** Above all, fight constructively and for a truly just cause. Do not strive simply to win, injure, or to gain advantage over others. Expend your aggressive energy in a manner that *builds* instead of destroys. Take care to respect the rights, needs, and boundaries of those with whom you might struggle. Most especially, appreciate when it's in your best interest as well as the interest of others to back-down, back-off, concede, or capitulate. Managing your aggressive urges thoughtfully and effectively is the task of a lifetime. Yet it is a task that, when well-done — perhaps more than any other task you face in life — defines your character.

- **Treat others with *civility* and *generosity*.** Behave responsibly and with positive regard, even to those who do otherwise to you. While respect should rightfully be earned, treating others in the decent and genuinely loving manner that you would want for yourself — this is the most important of all virtues. It should be done freely and without reservation. You don't have to condone or embrace everything someone else does to behave nobly yourself. Nor do you have to make yourself a victim by subjecting yourself to constant mistreatment. Rather, you need only remember that your character is defined not so much by how others regard you but rather how you treat them. And it takes a strong sense of generosity and a deep abiding faith to treat others with the kind of positive regard we wish for ourselves.

  Most of us are plagued with anxiety about whether we will have enough, be supported enough, be valued enough, or prosper to the degree that we would like. But we need to remember that our very existence is not an entitlement but a gift. And despite the way it might appear at times, no one in this life has really been "cheated" or denied. Despite whatever hardships we might have been dealt, we have also been blessed with abundant gifts and resources. So, we need not envy others or greedily pursue our own welfare to the detriment of others. And from those to whom much has been given, much is expected. So, for the sake of our own well being, we must bring generosity and free giving into all our relationships. We must treat others not necessarily as we think they deserve but with the level of care, regard, concern, and love that we truly wish for ourselves.

- **To the best of your ability, *have sincerity of heart and purpose*.** Be honest with yourself about whatever you do and the reasons you're doing it. And be straightforward with others. Let your intentions be noble and transparent. Harbor no hidden agendas. Avoid hypocrisy and the tendency to cast yourself as someone or something you are not. Although you need not broadcast your every desire, sincerity is a prerequisite for developing integrity of character.

Teaching children the ten essential commandments of character is a difficult and lengthy process, even in the best of circumstances. But there is little doubt in my mind that the disintegration of the archetypical, nuclear family is one of the main reasons for the extent of character pathology we see today. Kids do best when they have stable, committed caretakers, upon whom they can rely for support as well as direction. When parents are committed and reliable, strong emotional bonds form between them and their children, who are inherently "dependent" upon them for almost everything for many years. That bond is essential to guiding children through the inevitable power struggles and conflicts that ensue when parents attempt to enforce discipline, rules, and structure. Children will only subordinate their wills and internalize principles promoted by their parents if they can truly come to believe and trust that it's in their best interest to do so and when they experience a healthy degree of anxiety about possibly losing the support or approval of their parents when they misbehave. When children are fortunate enough to have loving and responsible parents, as well as siblings with whom they can experience the essential dynamics of living in a social world, most will eventually learn to be responsible.

Abusive and neglectful families have always been capable of inflicting significant emotional scars on children. But no amount of alternative social structure and support can match a healthy, intact family when it comes to learning all the basic social tasks like respect for authority, social give-and-take, and the principles of right and wrong. Here's an ever-increasing problem for teachers in schools today: Many of their students are so under-socialized that they are completely "unprepared" mentally, emotionally, and spiritually to learn. This unpreparedness is in large measure because of their impoverished home environments. One can argue that this impoverishment is material in nature. But the fact is that most economically poor homes in the western world are infinitely richer than many places in the "third world," and the impoverishment of which I speak is common in affluent homes as well. In the character-impoverished home, children don't get a sense of what it means for people to care for one another — to be faithful to one another — to sacrifice for one another — and to commit to rightful conduct, even under difficult circumstances. So, some schools have taken it upon themselves to teach such things as *character education.* Educators then try to help a child learn what it means to be human and responsible, as well as how to read and write.

Coming to adhere to the first commandment is a difficult process. Very young children are inherently narcissistic. They're not only in their own universe; they also tend to view everything around them as extensions of themselves. Some children don't move past this primitive perspective. It can happen for a lot of reasons. Sometimes parents and caregivers have an unhealthy *need* for the children in their care. They dote on them, sending them constant messages that they are the very center of things. Sometimes a child can be so utterly disconnected from support, the only reality they know is that of their own making. In order to become a more mature, less egocentric being, every child eventually has to learn that he's a part of something greater than himself alone. All children must learn that they have an inextricable relationship to the rest of the world, and that the nature of that relationship largely defines their character.

The second commandment is also difficult to learn. We live in an age of extraordinary entitlement. We have reached a remarkable level of technological development and material prosperity. As a result, it's easy to take almost everything we have for granted. And, we are pretty full of ourselves for having achieved the high standard of living that many enjoy.

It's really hard to instill a sense of gratitude in our children. They grow up thinking their possessions are nothing special because most of their friends have the same things. They don't naturally have any concept of value or sacrifice. Even those without material things often grow up thinking that the rest of the world owes them. Children must be taught the value of things as well as to appreciate them.

In most western cultures, almost everything once seen as a privilege is now considered a right. The neurotics among us are largely responsible for this. In their well-intentioned desire to better the human condition, they have worked tirelessly to bring us to a point where people can and do take almost everything good for granted. One of the reasons disordered characters have a characteristic sense of entitlement is because they never "learned to earn" the good things they want in life. They somehow came to believe that they were "owed" these things, and either expected them to be handed to them or learned how to con or manipulate their way to securing them.

Children need to be taught that everything in life of any real value comes with a very real price tag in terms of human effort, endurance, and sacrifice. Instead of growing up with expectations about what the world will give them, they need to cultivate a sense of obligation to give of themselves and to make a meaningful contribution, thereby making the world a better place. Appreciation and gratitude are prerequisite virtues to developing a healthy sense of moral obligation.

The third commandment is crucial for character development. Almost nothing is as important as developing a right and balanced sense of self-worth. For years, well-intentioned authors in various mental health fields wrote many articles and books on self-esteem. They basically asserted that no one can have too much self-esteem, and that almost all psychological problems stemmed from low self-esteem. The truth is that just as many problems develop when people think too much of themselves as when they think too little of themselves. And, as mentioned earlier, it's ludicrous to think that people only display ego-inflation as a compensation for underlying low self-esteem. In truth, some people don't value themselves enough, whereas some value themselves entirely too much. Teaching children the balance is absolutely crucial to their character development. A parent must be a fair and careful monitor of their child's ego development. They must be attuned to when an unsure child really needs to be built-up. They also must judge when a child has become entirely too big for his or her britches, needing a reality check and some life lessons in humility to knock him or her down a peg or two.

There is a very dominant trend in most western cultures to lavish praise, recognition, and even financial reward on people blessed with remarkable gifts or talents and those who have managed to achieve great things. Yet, there's virtually no real recognition or reward given to those who display true integrity of character in their various pursuits or interactions. We give massive attention to and heap huge financial rewards on sports figures because of their talent and what they can do to help us satisfy our insatiable appetite for winning. But when they engage in all sorts of misconduct that reflects serious defects in their character, we are surprised. Sometimes, even when their character deficiencies become all too obvious, they are still honored, praised, or even idolized. Gone are the days when a public figure needed to display integrity of character and serve as a positive role model in order to receive respect and admiration of others. They also endured significant shame and rejection from the public when they engaged in conduct unbecoming their status. We live in a culture that heaps affirmation on people for what they have been given (e.g., looks, talent, intelligence, or charm) instead of how they conduct themselves. This is a surefire way to bend an ego completely out of shape.

Parents often make the same mistake with their children. Kids need to learn what belongs to them and what belongs to God (or a pure accident of nature, if one insists on a purely secular perspective). Kids blessed with good looks, intelligence, and talents are used to getting frequent messages of affirmation from a wide variety of sources. What they often don't get is a lot of praise, recognition, or reward for making the tough choices in life about how to behave. In the end, they equate their value as persons with the gifts they know they possess as opposed to the caring humans they might have made of themselves. Until we recognize and reward what matters, we'll continue to get what we've been getting: a society full of individuals with a very distorted and unhealthy sense of self-worth.

The different varieties of religious practice have also impacted our poor understanding and appreciation of *merit*. Some faiths promote the notion that a person basically has no choice but to follow a script already laid out for them. Others preach that a person can earn paradise by behaving righteously on earth. Still others overly emphasize that the Savior's sacrifice alone opens heaven's doors for us, and that nothing we could possibly do will earn salvation. Yet, paradoxically, advocates of this position insist that a person must engage in at least one act (the leap of faith acknowledgement that Christ is Savior) to be personally rescued. Even the first apostles debated the role and importance of meritorious conduct. Paul, of course, claimed that faith in Christ is the singular vehicle of salvation. James and Peter insisted that one cannot say they "believe" without corresponding action. It seems they had a very early understanding of the intimate and inextricable connection between one's thinking and core beliefs and one's actions, as well as the principle that actions speak much louder than words. It's easy to "profess" with one's lips a belief in a person or principle. It's quite another to demonstrate with one's actions that faith truly abides in one's heart. Jesus himself spoke of this when citing the false righteousness and hypocrisy of the elders and scholars in his religion.

Not only do talents and abilities belong to "God," but so do outcomes and circumstances. Although we can frequently and safely predict likely outcomes of our actions, this leads us to falsely believe we are in control of outcomes. In fact, we only have power over our actions. True, most often there will be predictable results. But there are no guarantees. Sometimes, despite our best and most conscientious efforts, we do not realize anticipated or desired outcomes. Ultimately, the results of our actions are in the hands of God (fate, if you will). Thinking that we're solely responsible for what happens can lead us to despair if things don't go well or to overconfidence and ego-inflation if things turn out just as we planned. Whenever we leave our "higher power" out of the equation, we run the risk of getting our egos bent out of shape.

The fourth commandment addresses one of the difficult challenges facing individuals as they try to develop good character: It's always been easier to cheat, lie, and steal than to take the honest path. Judeo-Christian tradition prohibits bearing false witness (intentional misrepresentation to injure someone else). Theologians differ as to whether this commandment also forbids other forms of lying. In my experience working with disturbed characters, *all* the lying they do is damaging, including the lies they tell to themselves.

Human beings have an incredible capacity to deceive. Traditionally-oriented theorists have frequently advanced the notion that people desire to avoid feelings of shame and guilt, which lies at the heart of why they lie. But I have witnessed people who lie for a vast number of reasons other than merely avoiding pangs of guilt or shame.

For the most part, lying is simply *easier* than accepting and dealing with the truth. It's a quick way to prevent something we don't want, or to secure something we want but might require more than we're prepared to give.

We live in a world full of lies and liars. Companies will promote a food product as "thicker and richer" when what they've really done is add more filler, cut costs, and improved profits. News programs and political pundits put various "spins" on the day's events or actions of others to advance their agendas and hide their biases. Being honest is a difficult task almost any time, but being honest with ourselves is especially hard. Reckoning with our shortcomings, the reality of our circumstances, and striving to better ourselves is very hard work. We are not creatures naturally attracted to the idea of work. And some personalities have a virulent aversion to work.

Jesus reportedly said that the truth shall make a person free because, ultimately, the very personification of evil and slavery to sin is the lie. In the book of Malachi there is a saying that "truth is mightier than all things." In my work with disturbed characters, I have found incredible power in the truth. It's the basis of trust and ultimately of the genuine human connection that facilitates positive change. Some therapists make the mistake of placing their own desire to be liked and to appear affirming above everything else. I think the truth must take precedence. Now, delivering the truth in a manner that is truly *benign* (i.e. loving), is an incredible challenge and a genuine art. It requires that the therapist be simultaneously accepting, of pure intention, and genuinely (i.e. "brutally") honest without being brutal at all. I have worked with many young persons struggling with character development issues who shared a smile, gave a wink, nodded in acceptance, or verbalized the greatest appreciation for being unreservedly confronted about their issues. They instinctively trust and respond to those who tell the unvarnished truth, but who their gut tells them mean no harm.

Truth not only sets us free and enables us to trust, but also carries with it a significant burden. Truth forces us to acknowledge our frailty. It then challenges us to reckon with that frailty and rise above it. The truth is rarely pretty, but it is almost always redemptive and transformative.

Parents trying to instill good consciences in their children can follow the same basic guidelines: honesty and truth, not to produce shame and guilt, but to develop an understanding of reality. Shame and guilt are powerful instruments of shaping behavior, but some children don't respond to shame or guilt very well, and some don't respond to shaming or guilting at all. Children (and adults) are better off when confronted with truth that is both "inescapable" and non-distortable, so they don't develop a pattern of self-deception. Children are much more likely to acquiesce and acknowledge the truth when confronted about their behavior in a frank but totally benign manner, devoid of denigration or condemnation.

The fifth commandment flies straight in the face of the values promoted by our age of greed and sensual license. We are a society of gluttons, sex "addicts," and coveters of various sorts. We want to indulge every craving we have, and we are forever raising the thresholds of satiation. Here's what it has gotten us: a glut of Wall Street swindlers, behavioral addicts of all persuasions, and a populace out of control physically, emotionally, psychologically, and spiritually. At the heart of these problems is a failure to subordinate the pleasure-seeking principle upon which most of us have operated since birth. From a psychological perspective, if there's any way a person of character needs to be "born again" it's with respect to the most fundamental governing principle upon which we operate. Folks who don't transcend or subordinate the pleasure principle are doomed to be enslaved by it, causing many problems for themselves and society.

The sixth commandment goes to the heart of cognitive-behavioral techniques for helping people change patterns that impair their character development. For the most part, disturbed characters act first and think later. This pattern starts early in their development. Constitutional predispositions affect this, too. As mentioned before, some personalities appear to have a constitutionally-based lack of adaptive fearfulness. And when a person lacks apprehension about what he's about to do, he's less likely to engage in any meaningful contemplation before he acts. For a variety of reasons, some influenced by constitution, some arising out of learned experience, the actions of disturbed characters are often not tempered by sound advance reasoning.

When raising kids, we want them not only to think before they act, but to think rightly and with due respect for the principles of moral conduct. Inevitably, doing the wrong thing is the easier path. What we want them to do, however, is to display the strength of will and character to make the harder, more responsible choice. The mistake most parents make is that children make right decisions all the time and barely get noticed for it. It's important to build up a high potential for right-acting by routinely reinforcing the little things they do correctly. Then kids will have sufficient strength and soundness of will to face greater temptations as they come along.

The seventh commandment addresses the development of strength of purpose and will. I owe a profound debt of gratitude to a very early pioneer in cognitive-behavioral therapy, Abraham Low. These days, some of his techniques might be regarded as antiquated, even evoking laughter from mental health professionals. But Low founded a program to help individuals who had suffered from what used to be called "nervous breakdowns" (i.e. intense levels of anxiety, depression, and other syndromes causing a person's usual coping ability to collapse). Such persons were often hospitalized. Because very few medications existed for them at that time, they had to learn techniques to manage their symptoms. These included any "residual" symptoms such as anxiety or depression, once they were able to leave the hospital. His program focused on the thinking patterns of individuals, as well as the behaviors they engaged in that perpetuated their problems. So, he was pioneer in the realm of cognitive-behavioral therapy (without really knowing it). He wrote a few books and put out some audiotapes of lectures that participants in a self-help group called "Recovery, Inc." used to change their lives and prevent "relapses." One of his lectures was entitled "The Will Says 'Yes' or 'No.' " This concept literally saved my life. By practicing the principles it advocated, I discovered that the human will, like any other natural endowment, can be *developed and strengthened* through appropriate exercise. Wow! What a concept! There are ways for a person to strengthen the will! And to top it off, it's the will that determines whether or not we do something we're tempted to do (i.e. the will says "yes" or "no" to an urge). Within a matter of months, I was transformed from a person almost enslaved by my needs, desires, urges, and fears to a person who could direct the course of his own life through the exercise of his will. I will forever be grateful.

Will-training is a fundamental job of parenting. Appropriate development of will is crucial to delaying gratification, persisting on difficult tasks, enduring hardships, and having the courage to meet and overcome challenges. As parents, we want our children to have strength of will, but we also want to shape and temper their willfulness without breaking their spirit. Some naturally willful children must learn to bend more, and some naturally passive children must learn to assert themselves more. In the end, how the will is shaped greatly affects the kind of character that will form.

The eighth commandment involves learning to manage our anger and aggressive impulses. Although not all aggression is rooted in anger, there is a relationship between anger and aggression. Everyone must learn to moderate both the emotion of anger as well as temper their urge to aggress. This is how a solid character forms.

Generally speaking, anger is an adaptive emotion that prompts us to take action to remove a threat to life or well-being. Anger that is chronic or excessive has been linked to a host of problems, including heart disease. So the emotion does need to be regulated. We also need to learn when our anger is righteous versus when it serves no purpose or has gotten out of control. I am not of the belief that kids should be allowed to throw their temper tantrums until they "run out of gas." Such a tact only reinforces the notion in the child that it's okay to pitch a protracted snit; it puts no limits on emotional expression. Nor do I believe that every outburst should be stifled precipitously, leading the child to believe he has no right to protest; that only builds resentment. A healthy balance must be struck here.

When it comes to aggression, the stakes could not be higher. People naturally do a tremendous amount of fighting in life. Humans are the only creatures to do so much of their fighting against and among themselves. Children have to learn why, when, and how to fight, as well as why, when, and how to back down, concede, or acquiesce. Perhaps no lessons are as crucial to character development as these.

Among the most disturbed characters, the aggressive personalities are notoriously undisciplined and unscrupulous fighters. From early in their development, individuals with aggressive personality traits appear to have been overly ready to lash out, significantly lacking in "internal brakes." For that reason, their aggressive behavior usually needs to be confronted early on in their cycles of escalation. This gives them a fair chance at developing the mechanisms of self-control they so desperately need.

The ninth commandment embraces true charity. The word is often misunderstood. It comes from a Greek word "caritas," which describes a particular type of loving behavior: an abiding respect for and kindness toward other human beings. It is not synonymous with giving aid to the poor, which has become one of its most popular meanings. Rather, it is basic regard for the value of human life, which can inspire acts of almsgiving (merely giving to the poor need not be rooted in genuine *caritas*) as well as other acts of human kindness. Charity requires empathy, which is why individuals with an impaired capacity for empathy (i.e. psychopaths) find this behavior so foreign.

St. Paul put charity in the spotlight in one of his most famous letters to Christian converts living in ancient Corinth, extolling it even over the other timeless virtues of faith and hope. He also pointed out how empty a life can be without it. Perhaps there is no command more constructive in the development of character than the call to "do everything with love (caritas)."

Teaching children to love in this way is relatively simple (i.e. straightforward) yet as difficult as any parental task can be. That's because parents are required to model this behavior fairly consistently through example, large and small. Parents need to remember to do everything — from setting limits and expectations to saying "no" and withdrawing support — not with resentment for the ordeal, but with love.

The tenth commandment, teaching sincerity of heart and purpose, is a difficult task, also. If one is not surrounded by others of solid character (often the case), sincerity receives a poor welcome. So it's easy to learn how to present a false face. Neurotics hide their true feelings and intentions for fear of rejection. Disturbed characters sometimes hide their true selves and their real agendas for more nefarious purposes. The sincere course, however, is most often the best course, if not in the short run, then in the long run. Our entire social environment would take on a marvelous, productive character if more of us were willing to risk sincerity, and to engage in honest, open communication and debate. Many of our most pressing social problems have lingered far longer than necessary because of our impaired ability to have an honest, open, sincere discussion and debate on the issues.

CHAPTER 5

Thinking Patterns and Attitudes Predisposing Character Disturbance

Here's one of the central tenets of the cognitive-behavioral paradigm: An inextricable relationship exists between a person's core beliefs, the attitudes those beliefs engender, the patterns of thinking various beliefs and attitudes predispose, and the ways the person will tend to behave as a result of his thinking. For example, a husband may believe that women are naturally inferior to men and should therefore be subservient. Then he might tend to think his wife is "getting way too big for her britches" whenever she asserts her point of view or tries to stand up for herself. He may engage in all sorts of problematic actions in an effort to "keep her in her place." How we think greatly influences how we act. The major premise of cognitive-behaviorally-oriented therapy is that we can change the way we think — and when we do, it will necessarily impact the way we behave.

Disturbed characters don't act the way most people do largely because they generally don't think the way others do. They often don't hold the same values, harbor the same attitudes, share the same core beliefs, as most folks. Their way of thinking is marked by a "distorted" view of reality and an impoverished sense of accountability.

How disturbed characters think is always reflected in the ways they act. Their ways of thinking can also be discerned from the things they say, but to a much lesser extent. That's because the things they say don't necessarily reflect beliefs they hold with genuine conviction. This is a very important fact to remember.

For some time, most clinicians and researchers using the cognitive-behavioral model have known that the "cognitive distortions" of disordered characters can represent *actual* but *erroneous* beliefs. Sometimes, they have developed these beliefs with total obliviousness to the ways that most other people think about things. But my experience has taught me that disturbed characters can also entertain their twisted views with full awareness of how most people might think about the same situation. I'm also struck by how often the research literature will categorize the types of thinking errors disturbed characters engage in based simply on the things they frequently say. This is problematic because what they say does not necessarily reveal how they really think. Sometimes they say things to make other people believe that they think a certain way, as a manipulation technique. In reality, their *behavior* is a much more reliable indicator of their true thoughts and attitudes. So, corrective treatment programs largely based on "challenging" strictly verbally espoused beliefs, and then "teaching" alternative ways of thinking, are not likely to be successful.

In my work with disturbed characters, I have found that some disordered characters were truly raised in environments so impoverished in multiple dimensions that their beliefs about the nature of the world, and how to operate within it, understandably became quite skewed. So, they developed patterns of thinking and attitudes that most responsible people don't share. Ask such people what they were thinking when they engaged in some troublesome behavior, and what they tell you is actually what they believe, as irrational as it might sound. But with many disordered characters, the things they tell you, as well as the things they tell themselves, are nothing more than part of an elaborate "con game." Such folks are very aware of how most people tend to think, and how out of step their purported way of thinking is. But they tenaciously protest their contrary point of view to justify themselves and their actions. They try to manipulate others into the notion that their behavior had some rational basis other than the simple intent to victimize. Sometimes, after lying so often they might even succeed in duping themselves about the distorted perspectives they advance; but they will often back off their ridiculous contentions when firmly challenged. For example, a repeat wife beater might very well know how society at large feels about abusive spouses' violence toward women. Nonetheless, he might try to justify his behavior by constantly complaining that his wife is a vindictive "bitch" who constantly eggs him on. So she rightfully "had it coming" when she finally heaped more "disrespect" on him than anyone could possibly stand. This type of offender might very well know how most people would look at his situation. And he probably also knows full well who the victimizer is and who is the real victim. Nevertheless, such a person might do all he could to convince another to adopt the point of view that he was a victim of sorts and therefore "justified" in his actions; not so much because he needs or wants validation, but because if he can get you to buy into at least part of his argument, he succeeds in casting himself in a slightly more favorable light. You might then see him as an ignorant and perhaps misguided soul who simply "doesn't get" how to view women; he needs only to learn better. He's not really a person who already "gets it" just fine yet vehemently resists adopting the standards he knows society wants him to accept. In reality, he doesn't want to be correctly pegged by others for the dangerous person such an attitude makes him.

I can't overstate the importance of being skeptical about what disordered characters say. Remember, a great deal of the time they're engaged in a game of manipulation and impression management. Early in my work, I interviewed several child molesters who tried to advance the notion that their inappropriate touching of their victim was not motivated by aberrant sexual desire; rather it was a foolish or misguided attempt to "teach" the child about sexual behavior. I asked myself, "Do they really believe what they're saying?" The treatment manuals I had read seemed to regard this type of thinking as a truly held belief, needing correction by "illuminating" the offender. Adopting this perspective, the goal of treatment became to educate him about the damage caused the child and help him overcome the "denial" he was experiencing about other motives, such as his deviant urges. But I eventually learned that *most* of the time, child molesters that said such things didn't really believe what they were saying. They hoped that I would believe they did, so that I would neither ascribe the appropriate degree of malevolence nor the correct motivation (e.g., sexual interest in a child) to their behavior. If I bought their excuse, I might, for example, see them as an undereducated, poorly guided soul who made a stupid mistake, instead of as a predatory pedophile or a heartless psychopath. So, the thinking they reflected with their talk was not truly a belief. More importantly, their misrepresentations weren't based in "denial," shame, or guilt. In fact, genuine guilt or shame would likely have kept them from offending in the first place. Rather, the "twisted" justification they were providing was merely an attempt to manipulate and impression-manage others.

A child molester enrolled in a required treatment program readily volunteered to me that he knew his thinking process was "twisted." He told me that prior to treatment, he had the erroneous belief that his actions were actually okay. Incestuous behavior, he said, was so common throughout his extended family that he truly believed it was "normal." This made some rational sense. But being the skeptic I've learned to be, I did some digging. I learned that not only was such behavior not "normal" in his family, but, because of the outrage and suspicion of family members, he'd gone to great and elaborate lengths to keep his actions under the radar. After I confronted him, he reluctantly reported that he knew very well that it "sounded better" to cast himself as the product of an abnormal environment who simply didn't know better. Once again, his actions (the things he did to guard against discovery) were the more reliable indicator of his true thinking.

Some Major Thinking Errors

Stanton Samenow[30] was among the early researchers to catalogue the more common distorted thinking patterns or *errors in thinking* that some of the most severely disturbed characters display. Over the years, I've adapted and modified several of these problematic thinking patterns, adding some of my own that I believe played a crucial role in relationship problems of disordered characters I have treated. In the various character-disturbed personalities, some thinking errors are more common than others and some tend to cluster with others. The major problematic thinking patterns are:

Egocentric Thinking — The disturbed character is almost always concerned with and for himself. Whatever the situation, it's always about *him*. He frequently finds himself thinking about things that *he* wants, because that's what's important to him. He hardly ever thinks about what someone else might want or need, because he attaches so little importance to that. Because he thinks the entire world revolves around him, he believes it's the duty of others to place what he desires or what interests him above everything else.

When he wants something, the disordered character also doesn't consider whether it's right, good, legal, or if his pursuit of it might adversely affect anyone; he only cares that he wants it. His constant concern for himself and the things he desires promotes an ***attitude of indifference*** to the rights, needs, wants, or expectations of others. Such an attitude fosters a complete ***disregard for social obligation***. In some cases, as Samenow notes, there's an ardent distain for and total ***refusal to accept obligation***. As self-centered as he is, the disturbed character believes the world owes him everything and that he owes the world nothing. Such thinking is the reason the disturbed character develops an attitude of entitlement. He has extremely high expectations for everyone else, but feels no sense that he should submit himself to the expectations of others or society in general. His egocentric thinking patterns, attitudes, and their resultant behaviors prompt him to lead an extremely *self-centered lifestyle*.

Possessive Thinking — Disturbed characters tend to view their relationships as possessions that they rightfully *own*; they should be able to do as they wish with these people. This type of thinking frequently accompanies **Heartless Thinking:** The disturbed character tends to *objectify* others (i.e. view them as mere *objects* or pawns to manipulate as opposed to individuals of worth with whom one has to form a co-equal relationship). Possessive and heartless thinking promote a *dehumanizing attitude*. This makes it more likely that the disturbed character will view others, not as human beings, but as objects of pleasure, vehicles to get things he wants, or simply potential obstacles in his path that must be removed.

Possessive and heartless thinking make it all but impossible for the disturbed character to view others as individuals with rights, needs, boundaries, or desires of their own, and beings of dignity worthy of respect and consideration. Such thinking is carried to a most pathological extreme in the Predatory Aggressive or "Psychopathic" personality.

Extreme (All-or-None) Thinking — Disturbed characters frequently see things in terms of black and white, all-or-none. They might take the position that, if they can't have all that they ask for, they won't accept anything. If someone doesn't agree with everything they say, they will frame it as not being valued or listened to at all. If they don't see themselves completely on top and in total control, they will cast themselves as being on the bottom and under someone else's thumb. This erroneous way of thinking makes it virtually impossible for them to develop a reasonable sense of give and take in their relationships. It promotes an *uncompromising attitude* that impairs their ability to develop any sense of moderation in their behavior patterns.

Inattentive Thinking — Some researchers describe this thinking error as the "mental filter"[31] because disturbed characters selectively "filter" what goes on around them, paying attention to and heeding only the things they want to, and disregarding all the rest. They hear what they want to hear, remember what they want to remember, and learn what they want to learn. They invest themselves intensely in the things that interest them; but they actively disregard the things they don't care about, even though they may be quite aware that others want them to pay more attention to these things. They use the responsibility-avoidance tactic of *selective attention* (discussed later): They "tune out" someone who's trying to teach them a lesson, or only half-listen whenever they hear something they don't like. They do this most often when others are urging them to submit themselves to pro-social values and standards of conduct. So this erroneous way of thinking is a major reason they develop both *lackadaisical antisocial attitudes.* In turn, their devil-may-care and antisocial attitudes predispose them to chronic and unyielding behaviors that conflict with major social norms.

Deceptive (Wishful) Thinking — Disturbed characters are prone to seeing things as they want instead of as they really are. Two of their core characteristics — the ease with which they lie, and their resistance to demands placed on them by their environments — prompt them to distort the reality of most situations. It's not that they don't know the truth, but they simply don't want reality to get in the way of what they want. They lie to themselves with the same ease that they lie to others. They alter their perceptions and distort the reality of situations so they don't have to alter their stance, change their point of view, or question their usual way of doing things. Sometimes they live in a world of their own fantasy, adhering to the belief that "thinking makes it so." Their determination to make reality what they want it to be breeds a pervasive attitude of disregard for the truth.

Self-Deceptive thinking is not the same thing as the "defense mechanism" of Denial. The latter is an unconscious defense against unbearable emotional pain. Deliberate, self-serving twisting of facts and misrepresentations are bad habits for sure, as well as ways to avoid responsibility; but they're not the result of an altered psychological state. Many times, self-deceptive thinking accompanies the responsibility-avoidance and manipulation "tactic" of denial (i.e. deliberate denial of responsibility or malevolent intent for the purpose of manipulating or impression-managing others). We'll discuss this in the next chapter. But again, that's an entirely different kind of denial.

When doing the research for my first book, *In Sheep's Clothing,* I counseled many individuals of disturbed character who initially balked at the notion that they had any real problems. For example, a person referred for Anger Management Training (which, by the way, I always translate into aggression-replacement training) might assert, "I've really thought about this, doc. If you want to know the absolute truth, I really don't think there's a problem here." He might make this assertion despite a virtual mountain of evidence to the contrary presented by those who pushed him to seek counseling in the first place. He might even maintain the assertion despite a litany of problems in relationships dating back many years that testify to his lack of emotional self-control. This kind of thing always raises the question in the minds of others: "Does he simply not see the problem?" Actually, most of the time he *sees* it just fine; but he isn't really motivated to deal with it or change it, so he tries to justify himself and get others off his back by suggesting there is no problem. Other times, he's lied to himself so long and so often that he has begun to believe his own lies. Then again at other times, he has so twisted and so distorted so many aspects of life's realities, it's become hard for him to tell what's real anymore.

Here's one of the benefits of counseling disturbed characters within the Cognitive-Behavior Therapy paradigm: By focusing on behaviors that can be objectively verified as issues of concern, a person's distorted beliefs automatically become evident. Once the problem behaviors are identified and out in the open, attention can be given to the erroneous ways of thinking that led to those behaviors in the first place.

Impulsive Thinking — Disturbed characters think primarily about what they want at the moment. They don't bother to think long-range or about the likely eventual consequences of their behavior. They don't think before they act. They act first and sometimes think afterwards. Some disturbed characters never regret their impulsive acts. Some, however, do experience some after-the-fact regret. They might even know from past experience that they'll end up regretting making an impulsive choice; but that's never a serious consideration at the time they want something. They don't spend time thinking about the potential impact of their behavior before they act. They think only of what they want and how to get it *now*. This type of thinking predisposes them to think short-range and to ignore potential long-term consequences. It also promotes a "*devil-may-care*," lackadaisical attitude, and attitudes of *indifference, uncaring, or nonchalance.*

Egomaniacal Thinking — Disturbed characters think far too much of themselves. At times they think they're so smart, clever, or "special" that they can do what most others wouldn't even dream of trying and somehow get away with it. They tend to think of themselves as so important or superior that they deserve things others don't deserve. They often consider it a testament to their greatness if they can use their wits or manipulative skill to take things as opposed to really earning them. This erroneous way of thinking about themselves, along with their pathologically grandiose sense of self-importance, inevitably engenders attitudes of *arrogance, superiority,* and most especially, *entitlement.* In some extreme cases, their sense of entitlement can predispose them to commit acts of unspeakable cruelty toward others.

In recent years, big changes in cultural norms have reinforced the tendency toward egomaniacal thinking. It's not uncommon for young persons to be bombarded with messages that they're "special" simply because they have a heartbeat. That's because well-meaning individuals (e.g., teachers, parents, and even mental health professionals), steeped in old-school psychology, thought it simply wasn't possible for a person to have too much self-esteem, and that everyone would be emotionally healthier if they got frequent messages of validation. But what these well-intentioned folks probably haven't considered is this: When we heap praises upon people for what they *are* as opposed to what they *do*, we do them a great disservice insofar as developing a healthy sense of self-worth.

Prideful Thinking — A television commercial some years ago featured a flashy sports personality hawking a fancy camera, and touting its superior picture-taking qualities with the slogan: "After all, *image* is *everything*." Disturbed characters adopt this axiom as a core belief, and often carry it to a most pathological extreme. Disturbed characters tend to think that there's nothing worse than admitting a mistake, backing down, or giving-in because it makes them look inadequate or "weak." They place their image above everything else. They think in such prideful ways that their ability to develop relationships based on mutual regard is extremely impaired. Instead of acknowledging shortcomings or errors and correcting course, they resist change while engaging in a wide variety of behaviors designed to manage the impression others have of them. They often won't concede, even when they know full well that they're off base.

Here's one important reason they engage in this relentless impression management: They don't want anyone to really know who they are or to "have their number." This would level the interpersonal playing field, taking them out of the position of advantage they always seek to maintain in their relationships. They think they will not only lose leverage but also prestige if they honestly self-reveal, or if they admit normal human shortcomings or failures.

Habitual prideful thinking promotes the development of vanity and attitudes of haughtiness, arrogance, and pretentiousness. Thinking he can never really acknowledge a mistake prevents the disturbed character from profiting from experience, especially when life is trying to teach him a lesson. Before people can really correct problem patterns of behavior, they have to humbly admit they have the problem. And, to admit a problem is to acknowledge a shortcoming. Prideful thinking is a major barrier to recognizing or correcting any of the many problematic social behaviors common in the disturbed character.

Hedonistic Thinking — Disturbed characters place a premium on the pursuit of pleasure. They don't do things unless there's something in it for them, and they want that something to be pleasurable. They tend to crave stimulation and excitement, and have an inordinate distaste for what they regard as boring, tedious, or mundane. They value their comfort and hate being inconvenienced. They think that life owes them a good time, and that a life without a steady stream of "highs" is a life not worth living. This is a most serious error in thinking that sometimes propels them to engage in reckless, thrill-seeking behaviors. It also leads them over time to develop an attitude of extreme intolerance for any kind of potentially constructive pain or discomfort.

Unreasonable Thinking — Disturbed characters are very unrealistic in their thinking about life and the world around them. They also tend to harbor excessive expectations. But their unreasonable views and expectations are usually very one-sided. They tend to set virtually unattainable standards for everyone else, while feeling no concomitant sense of obligation to meet the general social expectations most of us would like them to accept.

Disturbed characters expect a whole lot from their government, their bosses, their spouses and children, and anyone else who has any kind of relationship with them. And those expectations are most always ridiculously irrational. They expect others to trust them long before they've established a track record that proves they might actually be trustworthy. They expect others to be attentive to their wants and needs and to cater to their whims. They expect things to go their way — all the time. They expect a lot of everyone, usually putting considerable stress on a relationship.

If the most disturbed characters expected themselves to measure up to the same standards they set for everyone else, they wouldn't be nearly as difficult to live with or work with. What's more, if they imposed the kinds of standards on themselves that they try to impose on others, they wouldn't engage in so many of the antisocial and other problem behaviors they so frequently display.

Disturbed characters have no sense of balance, fairness or compromise. Thinking so unreasonably eventually leads them to develop a rigidly *demanding* attitude. The unreasonable demands they bring to a relationship are a most frequent source of conflict and relationship distress. A partner might try to reason with them to no avail. Their thinking is too focused on their own expectations of others to be refocused on what they might do differently to get their wants and needs met.

Therapeutic interventions with disturbed characters can be a real challenge, especially when inordinate expectations are placed on the counselor. Many counselors are intimidated by the subtle challenge to their capabilities that such a stance presents. Others, especially those who see their role as one of "helper," can unconsciously feel obligated to try and meet unreasonable demands. In my work over the years, one thing I know is important to establish from the earliest moments of the therapeutic encounter: Make it absolutely clear that the burden for change rests squarely and solely on the character-deficient individual. All the expectations are on him. I also know that I'll have to confront his unreasonable thinking many times during the course of treatment. But each time I encounter it, I'm careful to confront it directly, and put the burden for change back squarely where it belongs.

Irrelevant Thinking — Disordered characters will often focus on the small, petty aspects of situations, but ignore the most important things, or the "big picture." They'll take issue with their boss, the government, or with their partners on trivialities while not paying attention to the things that really matter. When someone is confronting them on their behavior, they'll get hung-up on a "technicality" or small inaccuracy while ignoring the larger truth. For example, they might complain that a highway patrolman claimed they were exceeding the speed limit by a much greater degree than they actually were, while totally ignoring the fact that they were driving recklessly and endangering others. Their habitual attention to things not really relevant leads them to develop attitudes of pettiness and thoughtlessness. Irrelevant thinking also tends to co-occur with external and hard-luck thinking.

External Thinking — Disturbed characters will often focus on things outside of their control. They will brood about the actions or opinions of others, and invest a lot of emotional energy in things they can't realistically exercise power over. I call this kind of thinking external thinking. When things go wrong, disturbed characters don't spend nearly enough time or energy thinking about changes they can make in their own behavior to make things better. Rather, they focus on external circumstances. They make what mental health professionals call external attributions with respect to the causality of events. That is, they ascribe the causality of (i.e., blame for) events to external sources. This fuels their penchant for blaming others and circumstances — when they should be taking a hard look at themselves. This kind of thinking is frequently involved in the responsibility-avoidance tactic of blaming others (more about this in the next chapter). Focusing on external events and external factors breeds an attitude of irresponsibility as well as pessimistic and negative attitudes about the world. It also fuels a tendency toward hostile and accusatory behaviors toward others.

"Hard-Luck" Thinking — Disturbed characters often portray, and sometimes even see, themselves as victims of circumstances instead of persons responsible for their own actions and the consequences of those actions. They frequently sit on their "pity-pots," feeling sorry for themselves and the "raw deals" they imagine they have been dealt in life. This kind of thinking leads to *attitudes of bitterness and resentment*. It is one of the reasons why disturbed characters enter relationships with a fairly substantial chip already on their shoulders.

End-Game Thinking — Some disturbed characters are forever thinking about outcomes. The aggressive personalities in particular are very goal-oriented individuals. That in itself is not so bad. The problem is that they don't give much thought to how they're going about getting the things they want. They tend to feel so entitled to have whatever they desire, they believe the ends always justifies the means they employ to secure their wishes. End-game thinking is like tunnel-vision. If a person confines his thinking solely to achieving a goal or ensuring a certain outcome, he's likely to give insufficient attention to the right or wrong way to go about it.

Because of their other traits, disturbed characters will often con, cheat, steal, and manipulate to reach their objectives. The way they see it, if others are so gullible or so weak that they can be easily taken advantage of, it'd a fair victory. After all, for the disturbed character, it's all about winning. What it takes to win and what it might end up costing are not considered.

End-game thinking is just one of the mental errors that over time promote the development of an antisocial attitude. Thinking only about what one wants, and not giving enough thought to how it's best to go about getting it or who might be impacted, is a sure prescription for socially irresponsible behavior.

Quick and Easy Thinking — This is perhaps one of the most insidious yet pervasive ways of thinking that disturbed characters frequently engage in. The disordered character is forever looking for shortcuts. That's because such characters detest labor and effort, most especially the kind commonly referred to as labors of love (i.e., investing time and energy in an endeavor primarily for the benefit of someone else or the long-term benefit of all). So, when they want something, disturbed characters frequently think about how they'll get it the quick and easy way. Sometimes, they even think of it as a badge of honor if they manage to "con" somebody out of something instead of securing it legitimately through hard work. The disturbed character would much rather cheat than earn.

Always wanting something for nothing, disturbed characters expect to pay the least for the things in life that are worth the most. The most disordered characters among us will attempt to command "instant respect" at the point of a gun; but they won't lift a finger to earn others' genuine respect by developing their own characters and making a meaningful contribution to society. They want trust without being willing to habitually do the things that engender trust. In short, they want all sorts of things that have value, but they're simply not willing to pay for them.

Even though they detest work and effort, disturbed characters will sometimes expend energy, especially when they think (1) there's something in it for them, (2) the payoff will be relatively quick, or (3) their effort will allow them to take advantage of others. However, as I've stated numerous times in my workshops, in general, their attitudes toward labor and their desire for immediate reward only lead them to regard W-O-R-K as the most distasteful "four-letter word." Their habitual ways of thinking and behaving engenders a pervasive attitude of disrespect for the value of work and effort. Such attitudes allow them to view others who have worked hard and achieved as just plain "lucky" and unworthy of respect. These attitudes also make it easier for them to justify trying to take something they haven't rightfully earned.

Mistrustful Thinking — Disturbed characters often have a poor concept of how to honestly gain others' trust or judge the trustworthiness of others. Just as researchers such as Samenow have noted,[32] they have no idea about what trust is or how to earn it. They also tend to think that everybody else is as dishonest as they are. So, they think they have to outwit others before others outwit them. When others make an insignificant error or innocently misspeak, they frame it as lying. Yet when they themselves lie — even egregiously — they trivialize it, reasoning that everybody else does it. They think they shouldn't have to earn the trust of others by firmly and repeatedly demonstrating honesty, a commitment to principle, and a willingness to respect the truth. They also think if they tell the truth once, others should believe them implicitly and for all time. Yet if someone else does or says even the slightest thing that doesn't ring true for them, they'll mistrust them forever. This kind of thinking leads to attitudes of guardedness, suspiciousness, and caginess.

Opportunistic Thinking — Disturbed characters don't think about the rightness or wrongness of something when they see an opportunity for personal gain or profit. Their main concern is how they can exploit the weakness of a person or take advantage of a situation for their own gain. They are quick to recognize an opportunity whenever it presents itself. They're also adept at subtly creating opportunities to abuse or exploit others.

To be sure, we can't be successful in life unless we're prepared for and willing to take advantage of opportunity when it presents itself. But always looking for opportunities to profit personally without considering the impact on everyone else can be a very big problem. One only needs to look at how greedy Wall Street executives took advantage of opportunities to reap spectacular profits while knowing that the "bubble" would eventually burst. They left the economic well-being of the country in shambles.

Habitual, opportunistic thinking is another thinking error that promotes the development of antisocial attitudes.

Combative and Defiant Thinking — The most disturbed characters, especially the various aggressive personalities, tend to view the world as a combat stage. They see most situations as a contest they have to win. They expend a lot of mental time and energy planning battles they want to wage and stances they want to take against the demands society places on them. From the first moment they think someone wants something from them, they start thinking about how they will resist acceding to those expectations. The aggressive personalities are always thinking about ways to fight, even when it would be far more appropriate or in their best interest to cooperate. They so abhor the idea of backing-down, conceding, or giving ground, that even when it would be advantageous for them to do so, their thinking is dominated by contentiousness and intractability. Habitual combative thinking promotes unnecessarily *hostile, confrontational, and defiant attitudes.* Many a relationship has been destroyed by the "my way or the highway" stance taken by some disturbed characters.

Undaunted Thinking — Disturbed characters don't allow adversity to lead them to question how they look at things or the ways they tend to conduct themselves. Even though most of the problems they experience are the natural and logical consequences of their dysfunctional attitudes and behavior, they rarely allow themselves to think of their predicaments that way. Rather, they take pride in their determination to keep doing things as they prefer to do them, no matter what happens as a result. If a relationship falls apart, they simply blame the other person and move on. If they run afoul of the law, they fault the "corrupt system," and become more resolute in their determination to beat it. They don't allow themselves to think that maybe there's something about the way they go about viewing and handling the trials of life that needs correction. Instead, they dig in their heels and harden their stance, despite all objective evidence that their stance is ill-taken. Their habitual undaunted thinking leads to attitudes of belligerence and stubbornness.

Disordered characters think they shouldn't have to do anything they don't want to do. They want to make their own rules. They understand very well the rules most people think we should all live by. And they'll do things others want or expect them to do, but only if they agree with it. They never really subordinate their wills to a higher authority. Samenow notes[33] how some disordered characters have deep disgust for accepting obligation and possess no real sense of duty. Habitually defiant thinking breeds the disordered character's attitudes of rebelliousness, disdain for authority, and refusal to recognize or accept obligation.

Shameless Thinking — Disturbed characters generally have a deficient sense of shame. They almost never think of how some action might negatively reflect the kind of person they are. This is an important point. A key feature of the most disordered individuals is often that they neither care enough nor think enough about how their patterns of behavior reflect on their character. What's more, when disturbed characters do perceive that someone is judging them in a negative manner, instead of feeling ashamed, they go into impression-management mode; they try to convince the other person that *they* have a problem.

Some of the most severely disturbed characters might even consider it a badge of honor that they are not affected by others' opinions. They hold on to their grandiose and unrealistic self-images despite a track record of wreaking havoc in the lives of those they work or live with. Over time, their shameless thinking fosters the development of quite a brazen attitude.

Guiltless Thinking — An immature or impaired conscience is a hallmark feature of the disturbed character. Therefore, such characters have a diminished capacity to experience genuine guilt over actions or intended actions that injure others. When they're thinking about doing something, disturbed characters rarely consider how their actions might affect others or possibly transgress ethical or moral boundaries. To the degree that they might have at least some rudimentary conscience, they're able to quickly and effectively block out thoughts of right and wrong when seriously contemplating how to get something they want. Not caring enough about how their behavior might impact someone else, they simply give rightness or wrongness no serious consideration in their thought processes. They might very well know that others would view their behavior as wrong, but they can still make excuses and "justify" their wrongful acts with ease. Over time, this guiltless way of thinking promotes a pervasive attitude of social irresponsibility.

Circumstantial Thinking — Disturbed characters like to think that things in life "just happen" to them or others. They don't like to think in terms of cause and effect relationships with respect to the decisions people make about how to manage their lives. So, when people of good character manage to earn good fortune, the envious, disturbed character attributes it to "blind luck." And when the consequences of his own irresponsible conduct fall upon the disturbed character, he attributes it to "just one of those things," the corrupt system, or the ill motives of others. Disturbed characters don't like to focus on the fact that behavior has consequences, and they certainly don't like to examine their own motives. In the mind of the disturbed character, "shit happens." Among criminal personalities, there is an acronym: "OTLTA." It reflects their common protestation that **O**ne **T**hing simply **L**ed **T**o **A**nother whenever they're challenged about their motivations for committing criminal acts. Such protests reveal that they don't give much focus to the series of choices they've made, but rather see their behavior and its consequences as the inevitable result of a snowball rolling out of control, and becoming too massive to stop.

There are indeed some times when fate plays the major role in life's circumstances. Sometimes, things simply happen. Tornadoes, floods, earthquakes happen without warning. But such events are rare occurrences. Responsible people know that, for the most part, when it comes to the major issues of life, circumstances are shaped by the choices a person makes. Paying attention to those choices, and taking care to make the best possible choice regardless of the circumstances, is what sound character is all about.

Circumstantial thinking means not thinking about one's motives for engaging in behaviors, one's internal decision-making process, and the consequences of one's choices, but rather telling oneself that things simply happen. That is the thinking error most responsible for the development of a socially irresponsible attitude.

CHAPTER 6

Habitual Behavior Patterns Fostering and Perpetuating Character Disturbance

Responsibility-Avoidance Behaviors And Manipulation Tactics — Some people habitually and "automatically" engage in certain behaviors that inevitably promote and perpetuate character disturbance. These behaviors serve multiple dysfunctional purposes. When individuals engage in these behaviors they simultaneously justify their irresponsible conduct, actively resist subordinating their wills to a higher authority and internalizing pro-social controls, manipulate and control others, and manage the impressions others might form of them. As a result, these behaviors strongly reinforce their irresponsible way of doing things, and diminish any motivation to change their problematic ways of relating to others.

Some of the habitual and automatic responsibility-avoidance behaviors have been traditionally viewed as ego defense mechanisms. This is based on the erroneous but still common notion that *everyone* feels badly to some degree at some level when inclined to act on their primal urges; and as a result, they attempt to defend themselves against feelings of shame and guilt with certain *unconscious* mental behaviors or mechanisms. But, as I have pointed out before, all metaphors can be stretched beyond their capacity to adequately describe phenomena or to be useful; and traditional metaphors about why people do the things they do become greatly strained when trying to understand and deal with disturbed or disordered characters. The concept of defense mechanisms, in particular, becomes highly inaccurate when we're trying to truly understand the behavioral habits and tactics of the disturbed character. Many behaviors traditionally thought of as unconscious mental processes designed to prevent pangs of conscience are better viewed as conscious and deliberate acts. They're done so frequently and without compunction that they become routine or "automatic." They obstruct the internalization of pro-social values (i.e. enable the person to avoid responsibility), as well as provide a means to effectively manipulate and control others. The figure below helps differentiate between a true defense mechanism and a responsibility-avoidance and manipulation tactic:

DEFENSE MECHANISM VS. RESPONSIBILITY-AVOIDANCE AND MANIPULATION "TACTIC"

DEFENSE MECHANISM	RESPONSIBILITY-AVOIDANCE BEHAVIOR
• Mostly unconscious. • *Defensive* in character – ***prevents*** something *feared* from happening. • Reduces inner tension/ anxiety – assuages guilt/shame.	• Conscious and deliberate but can be so habitual it becomes *automatic.* • Strictly *offensive* in character – employed to *ensure* that something *desired* happens. • Obstructs adaptive. anxiety/ development of healthy guilt and shame.

Responsibility-avoidance behaviors and manipulation tactics are fundamentally rooted in distortions of the truth. When disturbed characters engage in these behaviors, they're lying to themselves as well as others about the nature of their actions and intentions. Sometimes, they've told the same lies so many times they come to half-heartedly believe them. But most of the time, they know very well they're kidding themselves and trying to pull the wool over the eyes of others.

Over the years, several professionals attending my workshops, and who still adhere to traditional perspectives, have challenged what I advance by posing this question: Why would anyone engage in such behaviors if, in fact, underneath it all they weren't trying to "protect" a self-image badly "threatened" by a sense of deep shame or guilt? I always point out to them the disordered character's main revulsion — that most disgusting of four-letter words: W – O – R – K! Disordered characters want what they want no matter how wrong it might be; and they also want to feel okay about themselves no matter how they behave. So, they want what most of us want without paying the "price" most of us are willing to pay for it by behaving responsibly.

It's always easiest to achieve a goal through lying, conning, cheating, and stealing. Our young delinquents learn this early. They know full well the kind of character society wants them to have. But developing it takes the most arduous kind of work, especially if both your constitutional predispositions and your early learning environment pit you solidly against it. So, it's much easier to simply tell yourself lies, deceive others, manage impressions, and stay the same as you are as opposed to solidly confronting your defects of character and developing yourself into a more respect-worthy human being. To put it simply, disturbed characters stay broken because it's much *easier* that way. Change is always hard, and changing yourself for the benefit of others — even if it would benefit you in the long run — is particularly hard. For the disordered character, that kind of work represents the most distasteful of enterprises. So, they try to salvage a self-image they can live with through lies, distortions, cheating, and conning.

Possibly the most important point I need to stress about the use of the tactics to be outlined shortly is this: the *mode* of behavior the disordered character is in (i.e. his "mind set" and emotional state) when he's in the process of displaying these behaviors. He is *not* in the *defensive* mode of functioning. It may appear so, especially to someone who has been indoctrinated with traditional notions about the motivations of behavior, and especially when some of the tactics can make a good neurotic confronting the disturbed character's negative behavior feel like an attacker. But at the very moment the disturbed character is making excuses (rationalizing), blaming others (scape-goating), it is absolutely essential to remember that he is primarily *fighting*. When you confront a disordered character about a harmful behavior, he is fully aware of the pro-social principle at stake. He's likely heard the principle espoused several times and from several sources. For example, when you call to his attention that he struck his wife, he understands very well that society frowns on this kind of behavior. So he starts with these tactics: "She is always pushing my buttons" (blaming others); "I didn't really hurt her" (minimizing); and "Am I supposed to always just take it when she harps on me without mercy?" (playing the victim). He is well aware that society wants him to accept and submit to the principle that it's not okay to strike your spouse. He's also aware how most civilized persons tend to view those who, despite accepted standards, engage in such behavior. But he doesn't want to accept this principle. He's still actively *fighting submission* to such a notion and resisting internalization of this value. He also doesn't want you to be on his case or to see him for the uncivilized sort that he is. He wants you to back off and to buy his justifications so he doesn't look as badly. So, whenever a disturbed character uses these tactics, you know one thing for absolute certain: **He will engage in the problem behavior again**. He'll do it again because the very fact that he uses the tactic indicates he's still at war with the principle society wants him to accept and internalize. At the very moment he's engaged in his tactics, he's *fighting* the very socialization process that could make a better character out of him. You could say that he's *defending* his ego, but that would be a relatively insignificant point and a distortion of the bigger picture. Seeing him in any way as in the defensive mode of functioning could easily lead a person to misperceive the character of his actions, and to be taken advantage of very easily. Besides, a person in the defensive mode of functioning is primarily trying to *prevent* something they fear might happen from happening. But when someone is in the offensive mode, they're primarily fighting to *ensure* that something they want to happen actually occurs. So, it's crucial to remember that when the disordered character engages in these behaviors, he is *primarily fighting* submission to the principles that serve the greater good, and simultaneously trying to manipulate others.

We're about to take a look at the responsibility-avoidance behaviors and manipulation tactics used most frequently by disordered characters. They use these tactics primarily because they generally work. They work particularly well when the disturbed character is dealing with an individual who is neurotic to some degree. *Nobody* knows neurotics as well as disordered characters do. They know how neurotics think and most especially how their consciences work. They know that neurotics like to see the best in people, tend to be self-doubting, and are apprehensive about making harsh judgments. Every one of the tactics we'll be looking at effectively taps into the vulnerabilities of neurotics.

Neurotic individuals' main vulnerability is that they simply can't imagine that everyone isn't at least to some degree like them. They also can't imagine that people aren't motivated in their actions by the same kinds of issues that motivate them. If they're familiar with the basic tenets of traditional psychology, they're at an even greater disadvantage because they might assume that problem behavior is always motivated by feeling threatened or insecure. So, when the disordered character starts blaming others or "acting wounded," they'll easily buy into the notion that they must be "feeling attacked" and are "defending" their fragile egos, instead of merely trying to get the better of them and avoid responsibility.

Not only do disturbed characters generally know how neurotics think, but they also know how traditionally-oriented therapists tend to think. Depending on how "couch-broken" they are (professional slang for someone who's been exposed to many helping professionals, programs, and other traditional forms of intervention), they're usually quite familiar with common therapeutic jargon or "psychobabble." They have heard all of the terms and explanations before, know the theories of underlying causes, etc., and are happy to repeat them. This way they make it appear to the therapist that they both understand and go along with the tenets of the program, but all the while they're thinking in their hearts what a sham the entire therapeutic exercise is. Helping professionals must keep this carefully in mind, in addition to the tactics disturbed characters are likely to use.

Many of the responsibility-avoidance behaviors and manipulation tactics listed below also work because they carry with them one of the most powerful psychological one-two punches imaginable. First, they effectively cloak clear and obvious malevolent intent. Second, because they are inherently aggressive moves, others, especially neurotics, are put unconsciously on the defensive whenever the disturbed character uses them. A person on the defensive is much more likely to become unnerved and confused and to back-off, back-down, or be swayed.

The responsibility-avoidance and manipulation tactics disordered characters employ are far too numerous to list completely. In fact, almost *any* behavior can and has been used at one time or another by a disturbed character as a means to avoid responsibility and manipulate others. However, some tactics are used with much greater frequency than others. Also, some of the various character-disturbed personality types tend to prefer certain tactics over others. Many of the tactics go hand in hand with some of the distorted thinking patterns outlined earlier. The principal responsibility-avoidance and manipulation tactics are:

1. **Rationalization (making excuses)**. The disordered character attempts to ***justify*** a wrong behavior or make an ***excuse*** for something he knows very well is regarded as wrong. Disturbed characters always have an answer for everything. Challenge them and they'll come up with a litany of reasons why their behavior was justified. In my work with disordered characters, I've heard literally thousands of preposterous excuses for irresponsible behavior.

Now, the traditional thinking on rationalization, of course, is that it is an *unconscious* process and a defense mechanism. The theory behind this is that persons unwittingly alleviate deep-seated and intense pangs of guilt by conferring some kind of legitimacy on their behavior. They don't consciously know what they're doing. If the true nature of their wrongful act were allowed to become conscious, they'd be overwhelmed by anxiety and guilt. So, an *internal* and unconscious process takes place to spare them such emotional pain.

When disturbed characters use the responsibility-avoidance of rationalization (i.e. excuse-making), they're not primarily and unconsciously trying to justify their conduct to themselves. Rather they're consciously and deliberately trying to manipulate others into legitimizing what they know to be bad behavior. Sure, depending on how severe their disturbance of character is, they might be experiencing some qualms of conscience; but, for the most part, their rationalizations are designed to convince others that they were not acting out of pure malevolence, and to persuade others that they are not as deficient in character as others might think they are. It's all part of the game of responsibility avoidance and impression management. By habitually "excusing" behaviors they know most people regard as wrong or harmful, they continue ***resisting*** the internalization of pro-social values and standards of conduct. This makes it much more likely they will do the same kind of wrongful behavior again.

2. **Externalizing the Blame (Blaming others or scapegoating)**. The disturbed character often blames his or her misbehavior on someone or something else. They will claim that some person or circumstance *made* them do what they did instead of accepting responsibility for making a bad *choice* about how to respond. Sometimes this tactic is call **projecting** the blame. Projection is a term that comes from traditional psychology. It refers to one of those automatic mental behaviors traditionally thought of as a "defense mechanism." Here's the rationale behind that notion: Sometimes individuals "project" onto other people and situations the motivations, intentions, or actions that they actually harbor themselves, but which they feel far too unnerved or guilty about to acknowledge as their own. So, they supposedly *unconsciously* ascribe to others the feelings they themselves possess. But disturbed

characters generally know what they are doing and are very comfortable with it. They are fully conscious about what others would see as the wrongfulness of their behavior, but don't have enough guilt or shame to change course. They attempt to *justify* their behavior by casting themselves as being put in a position with simply no other choice; they had to respond as they did because of someone else's wrongdoing. In truth, they're mainly engaged in a game of impression management as well as an act of defiance. They know what standards others want them to adopt, but they are not of a mind to capitulate. So, they simultaneously evade responsibility as well as manipulate others by using this tactic of blaming others. It goes hand in hand with the tactic of portraying oneself as a victim. It's typically an effective tactic that gets others to pay attention to everyone or everything else except the disordered character, and his wrongful behavior, as the source of a problem.

A person who won't acknowledge bad choices and bad habits, and who repeatedly blames others for his own shortcomings, will never correct his erroneous thinking or behavior. Whenever you hear an excuse, you know the disturbed character has no intentions of changing his ways. Habitually blaming others is a principal way the disturbed character resists modifying his problematic attitudes and behavior patterns.

3. **Denial**. As we've mentioned, this tactic has also traditionally been conceptualized as a defense mechanism. But when disturbed characters engage in denial, they're not generally in a state of psychological unawareness prompted by a deep inner pain about who they are or their actions. Rather, disordered characters more frequently use denial (i.e., an unwillingness to admit they've done anything wrong) as one way of feigning innocence, and to manipulate others who might otherwise have their number. If the denial is strong enough, a good neurotic might be successfully manipulated into second-guessing himself. Disordered characters often won't admit when they've done something wrong. They resist looking at any role their behavior patterns have played in creating

problems in their lives. They lie to themselves and others about their malevolent acts and intentions as a tactic to get others off their back. Because they don't admit their wrongs in the first place, they don't feel any inclination to correct them.

Recent research has yielded some surprising findings with respect to the role so-called denial plays in the success of treatment. Some of this research suggests that denial is not a predictor of whether or not treatment will lead to reduced rates of the problem behavior. Many clinicians have a hard time accepting this. Their rationale is that, if persons truly aren't aware of and willing to acknowledge their problems, how can they seriously address those problems in treatment? And if they don't address the problem in treatment, why should we believe that there's any reduced risk that they'll engage in the problem behavior again? I think the answer lies in this fact: Clinicians fail to consider that the type of denial they're most concerned about (i.e., truly unconscious defense against realizing a reality too horrifying to accept) is a relatively rare occurrence, and is even rarer among the disturbed characters they treat. Clients simply refusing to admit they did something everyone else knows they did is not necessarily that type of denial. Rather, it's lying, pure and simple. Primarily, it's tactical lying. The person knows very well what they did, but for various practical reasons (usually to avoid adverse consequence or to succeed in the task of impression management), they don't want to admit it. So, when we do research and lump every kind of failure to admit into the broad construct of "denial," we're bound to get mixed results. Perhaps clinicians are still correct in their concerns over genuine denial (the defense mechanism). The problem is, however, it's not very common, especially among disturbed characters. So we'd have to define it much more carefully in order to study it reliably.

4. **Minimizing**. The disturbed character is forever trying to trivialize important matters. He wants to convince folks that the wrongful thing he did wasn't really that bad or harmful. He might admit part of what he did was wrong, and usually not the most

serious part. The disordered character uses the tactic of minimizing primarily to manipulate others into thinking he's not such a bad person. But minimizing serious transgressions is also the way the disturbed character lies to himself about the full extent of his character deficiencies and behavioral problems. As long as he continues to minimize, he won't take seriously the problems he needs to correct.

Minimization is a hallmark tactic of the disturbed character. It's one of the main behaviors that differentiate a disordered character from a neurotic. Generally speaking, neurotics have a tendency to catastrophize, whereas disturbed characters tend to minimize. A good neurotic will berate himself or herself for the most insignificant of shortcomings. The disordered character will commit the most egregious acts and then try to characterize them as relatively insignificant.

Making a mountain out of a molehill (i.e. "catastrophizing") can, however, be used as a manipulation tactic. So, on occasion, disordered characters will engage in ***deliberate exaggeration*** or ***over-generalization***. In several of his writings and thinking error-correction worksheets, Samenow points out that they will take a minor issue to an absolutely absurd level in order to play into the overly conscientious nature of a neurotic.

Minimization is a highly effective tactic. When tactfully used, it invites a conscientious person to think that he's been overly judgmental or grossly mischaracterized the actions of another. Disturbed characters love this tactic because it's so effective in manipulating neurotics.

5. **Lying**. There are many ways to lie, and the most disordered characters I've met have elevated lying to nearly an art form. They can tell you things that are simply untrue. They might also say something that's "technically" true but still doesn't tell the real story. They can "twist" key aspects of the truth just enough to make the substance of their assertions a lie. This is ***lying by distortion***. Sometimes, they don't tell the whole truth. I've known individuals

who can lie quite adeptly by reciting a lengthy litany of factual things. Such apparent truth-telling sets the listener up to believe that the disordered character is intending to be truthful. But by leaving out certain key or critical details, the disturbed character can completely misrepresent the overall reality of a situation. This is just one example of ***lying by omission***. I've known skilled con artists that can lie quite effectively by stating nothing but highly verifiable facts. This promotes an impression of credibility. But they leave out just enough essential information to take complete advantage of you.

Often, especially when you're trying to pin them down about something important, disturbed characters will be deliberately unclear, elusive, or ambiguous. As Samenow notes in many of his instructional materials, they are adept in ***using vagueness*** as a manipulative tool to keep others off track. The use of vagueness is just another weapon in their arsenal of lying tools.

Most of the time, lying or distorting is simply a tactic used to manipulate, or "con" others, and to ensure that the disturbed character is in the "one-up" position. But sometimes, the disturbed character's incapacity to be truthful can eventually lead him to believe to some degree many of his falsehoods. It's impossible for the disturbed character to adopt acceptable standards of behavior or internalize controls when he has no regard for the truth. Lying is a most serious character defect. As has been noted before, some disordered characters will lie even when there appears to be no logical need for it. The main reason for lying is to maintain the "one-up" position in any interpersonal encounter. If you're in the dark, swayed, or operating under a false assumption, you're at a disadvantage, and that's just how the disturbed character likes it.

6. **Bullying**. Disturbed characters are often so intent upon having their way that they will openly threaten or brow-beat someone else into giving up or giving in to their wishes. They will use fear as a weapon or terrorize others to get what they want.

Bullying is a favorite tactic of the aggressive personalities. Those in relationships with aggressive personalities know well that these aggressors never give up until they get what they want. So, most of the time, others know that, when the aggressors engage in bullying, even worse things might happen unless one caves in to their demands. Bullying is an effective tactic to get others, especially the overly-conscientious or overly-apprehensive, to knuckle-under. But it's also one of the principal ways the disturbed character resists any kind of submission to social standards, and therefore any internalization of principles and controls.

One of the most common forms of this ***tactic is brandishing intense anger or rage***. The aggressive personalities are adept at using deliberate displays of intense anger to instill fear in others and browbeat them into acceding to their demands. It's amazing to me how many times I've witnessed such personalities return to a normal or even jovial mood immediately after terrorizing someone else into submission.

7. **Covert Intimidation**. Sometimes disturbed characters' intimidation is overt, but at other times it can be quite subtle or covert. Disturbed characters know how to make implied or carefully veiled threats when they don't get what they want from others or if others don't see things their way. They know how to send this message: There will be some sort of hell to pay if others don't cave-in to their demands.

Mostly, covert intimidation is an effective tactic to manipulate someone who fears what else the disturbed character might do, or what might happen if they don't comply. Sometimes the veiled threat can be nothing more than a particular look or a glance. Sometimes the threat is imbedded, not so much in what someone says or does, but *how* they do or say it. Sometimes it's even in what the person doesn't say. Subtle, non-verbal gesturing, signals, or mannerisms might be all that's needed to send an unsettling message. When the disturbed character subtly implies that war will break out whenever someone else confronts his dysfunctional behavior, he refuses once again to take a good look at himself and his way of doing things. He thus blocks any chance at internalizing a standard or control.

8. **Evasion**. When they're confronted or about to be confronted about their behavior, disturbed characters will attempt to avoid the subject. They'll keep important matters from coming to light, sidestep questions raised, or otherwise dodge the issues brought to their attention. They resist giving straight answers to direct questions. It's a tactic to keep others in the dark, to maintain a position of advantage, and to avoid being exposed or put on the spot. They don't like the light of truth shining on them. It not only might reflect negatively on their character, but also it levels the interpersonal playing field and takes them out of the one-up position. As long as the disturbed character evades important issues, he will never honestly reckon with attitudes or behavior patterns he really needs to change.

9. **Diversion (deflecting or shifting focus)**. Disturbed characters often use this tactic in conjunction with evasion. Whenever the light of truth is shining on them, bringing their character deficiencies and problem behaviors to the fore, they are quick to **deflect** attention from themselves. They draw attention to someone or something else in order to keep the person potentially on their trail off-track. They will take you on a "wild goose chase" to confuse and mislead you, keeping the focus off themselves and their behavior. This tactic is a sort of emotional slight-of-hand. When your attention is focused on someone or something else, you're not going to be aware of what the disturbed character is really up to. Habitual use of this tactic is one way disturbed characters resist focusing on the behaviors they really need to change.

10. **Giving Assent**. When disturbed characters feel pretty well pinned-down and the tactics they've tried aren't working well, they might pretend to agree or to give-in on an issue or concede a point in order to get the people confronting them off their back. It's so much easier to simply *say* you'll do something as opposed to genuinely making an effort to change. When cornered, disturbed characters will say almost anything to placate others, while still harboring

defiance in their hearts. It's a tactic they use to disarm others while still actively resisting the standards or controls society wants them to take seriously and to "internalize."

11. **Posturing**. This is a frequent behavior for all disturbed characters. Remember, there's nothing more important to them than maintaining the one-up position. They are adept at throwing others on the defensive. They're quick to "challenge" the legitimacy of the outrage others feel concerning their behavior. And, if the persons being challenged are insecure, neurotic, or naïve enough, they're likely to retreat. Posturing is a powerful way to maintain the upper hand, but it also prevents the disturbed character from either accepting or benefiting from potentially helpful feedback about his behavior. It certainly stands in the way of the disturbed character accepting or valuing authoritative guidance.

12. **Playing the Victim**. Disturbed characters are good at portraying themselves as the victims of injustice. It's a means of justifying their preferred ways of dealing with the world and simultaneously eliciting sympathy from others. It's a sly tool to make someone who wants to confront them appear insensitive and heartless. A most egregious example of this remains embedded in my memory to this day. I was interviewing a prisoner who vigorously denied the crime for which he had most recently been convicted. He blamed "the system" for arresting him out of prejudice, but readily admitted a long history of antisocial conduct that included a murder in which he fully participated, but for which he was never convicted. He described a vicious assault in which he and two accomplices bludgeoned a man to death. Yet he complained, "I have to live with the image of that horrible event in my mind for the rest of my life." What impressed me the most was not the use of this tactic but what didn't accompany it — namely any signs of genuine remorse or regret. The sole purpose of the tactic was to invite me to feel sorry for him as an "emotional victim" of the crimes he did commit, and as a victim again, incarcerated for a crime he didn't

commit. Even if he is technically innocent of the crime for which he was most recently convicted, in the big picture, this individual is no victim but rather a serial victimizer. All of his troubles, including his most recent dilemma, have stemmed directly from his lengthy history of antisocial behavior. The only real victims were the persons he abused, exploited or killed. By focusing on how he might have suffered some injustice on one occasion, he plays on the sympathies of others and ignores the bigger problem of his own monumental defects of character which need to change.

13. **Feigning Ignorance or Confusion (Playing "Dumb")**. When you confront the most disturbed characters about their behavior, they'll often act like they have no idea what you're talking about. They'll pretend to be totally unaware about their behavior, or confused about what you mean. It's an effective tactic that manipulates the person confronting them into having doubts about the issue's legitimacy. Most especially, it makes others second guess whether the disturbed character *really intended* to do harm. This tactic frequently is used in tandem with *feigning innocence* (see below).

In an earlier section, I talked about never accepting "I don't know" for an answer when confronting disordered characters. That's because they're not only keenly aware of the antisocial things they do, but they also know full well what their motivation was for doing those things. Over the years, if there's one thing I've learned well when confronting these individuals, it's to stay focused on their problem behaviors no matter how unaware or clueless they act about them.

14. **Feigning Innocence**. When disturbed characters are suspected of foul play, they often act like they've done absolutely nothing wrong. If there's no way they can deny doing what they've done, then they'll at least claim that they had no malicious intent, and that any injury they inflicted was completely unintended. This tactic serves to obscure the true nature of predatory aggressive acts. If the disturbed character can make you feel bad for indicting him, he's half-way home to successfully conning and manipulating you.

15. **Playing the Servant**. Disturbed characters sometimes pretend they're only trying to help or care for you, when they really want to take advantage of you. It's a particularly cunning way they get others to trust or depend on them while they surreptitiously exploit, abuse, or wield control over those who buy into the tactic.

Predatory aggressive personalities, whose real mission is self-aggrandizement and victimization, are very adept at using this tactic to ensnare others into cults that promise safety, justice, and special status to their members. These predators play on the known needs and desires of others, and often overtly cater to these needs for the covert goal of wielding tremendous power and control over them.

16. **Seduction**. Disturbed characters can be most insincere, especially when they want something from you or are slickly trying to get the better of you. They may use flattery or "sweet talk," act congenially, or say whatever it is they think you want to hear so that they can win you over without really earning your trust.

Most of the time, when someone is praising us or giving us compliments, we don't think they're simply trying to get something from us. But disturbed characters will say and do whatever it takes to gain our favor. Once they have it, they won't hesitate to take advantage.

17. **Shaming**. This is a favorite tactic of disturbed characters because they know very well how conscientious neurotics are. As mentioned earlier, neurotics are overly prone to feeling shame or guilt. So if you can make a neurotic feel like a bad guy, you're quite likely to gain advantage over him. It's a most effective tactic of manipulation and control, second only to the one that follows below.

18. **Guilt-Tripping**. Because the conscientiousness of neurotics predisposes them to easy feelings of guilt, this is another favorite tactic of disturbed characters. In fact, it's a telltale technique with respect to identifying a person as a disturbed character or a neurotic (as is the shaming tactic). Try to shame or lay guilt upon a disordered character, and you'll find out very quickly how futile such an endeavor is. But convince a neurotic that they've committed the unpardonable sin and they'll back up, second-guess, or back down every time. The most disordered characters know well how effective shame and guilt are as manipulation tools. They know how, in stark contrast to themselves, neurotic individuals possess these qualities in abundance and regard these attributes as weaknesses that make neurotics easy to manipulate and control.

19. **Vilifying the Victim**. Neurotics never want to be the bad guy. Disordered characters know this. So they make the neurotic out to be the villain, cast him as an unjust attacker, or ascribe malevolent intent to him. Then that person will be on the defensive and fairly well disarmed when it comes to confronting the real aggressors on their behavior. By vilifying others, disturbed characters justify their own stance. It's akin to but more serious than the tactic of blaming others. It's a way to reframe events so that the true victim is cast as the attacker, and the disturbed character recasts himself as the defender instead of the predator. It's also one of the main ways disturbed characters habitually resist internalizing standards and controls regarding their own aggressive agendas.

20. **Selective Attention**. Disturbed characters see what they want to see and hear only what they want to hear. Stanton Samenow referred to their habit of paying highly selective attention as "mental filtering" or "paying attention only to what suits him." This tactic often accompanies inattentive thinking. But this behavior is a deliberate act of responsibility-avoidance. "Tuning out" someone who's trying to make a point, teach a lesson, or call attention to a problem is a principal way disturbed characters resist internalizing

the values, standards, and controls they know society wants them to adopt. One cannot be open to or accept a principle and resist paying attention to it at the same time. One cannot empathize with another's concerns and simultaneously tune out the other person at the moment they're trying to express those concerns. In short, one cannot be in the receptive/submissive mode (remember internalization is an act of submission!) and the combative mode at the same time. Most of the time, it's not that disturbed characters are struggling with attention deficiencies, but that they are very selective about where and how they will direct their focus.

21. **Hypervigilance**. Some disturbed characters are overly suspicious and critical of others' behavior. They question the motives of others, even in minor affairs. They often look for "evidence" that someone doesn't like them or is out to do them harm.

Chronically questioning the motives of others keeps the suspicious disordered character from developing a balanced sense of trust. They neither know when they would do well to place their trust in another nor do they know how to earn the trust of others.

22. **Conning and Contracting**. Disturbed characters often try to "make deals" in order to win allies, or to manipulate others into believing that they're involved in some sort of mutual support endeavor. Most of the time, the deals they cut violate generally accepted societal norms. By cutting deals in order to gain the support of others, they reject opportunities to stand on principle or to develop strength of character.

23. **Trying to escape guilt or shame on a "technicality."** The most disturbed characters are notorious for focusing attention on a few small, relatively unimportant, or unessential details. They do this especially when confronted about their behavior, while totally disregarding the bigger truth about their antisocial lifestyle. They'll focus on how you got one word wrong when you repeat something they said, but completely ignore the harsh reality of your meaning.

Sometimes they use this tactic to make people think they're more innocent than they are, or that they're "victims" of the "system." For example, they might rail for hours about how the officer who stopped them "totally exaggerated" how fast they were driving; yet they totally ignore the fact that they were speeding and endangering children in a school zone. Focusing on technicalities that are actually true, while ignoring the bigger reality and leaving out the more important facts, is also an effective way to lie and con others. Disturbed characters use this tactic to keep themselves and others from focusing on their wrongdoing, and also to resist the standards and controls they need to internalize.

24. **False concessioning**. This is somewhat like giving assent. When using this tactic, disturbed characters make some small admissions or grant a minor point to some confronting them. This way they appear contrite, open, honest, or forthcoming, at least to some degree, while actually still resisting genuine acceptance of the important issues. They often combine this tactic with other tactics, including distortion, evasion, or various forms of lying, to obscure and solidify their resolve against the principles and standards with which they are still at war.

25. **Leveling**. This is a tactic by which the disturbed character tries to "level the playing field" or "field of contest" and bolster his position with someone else when he finds himself in the "one-down" position. The tactic generally takes two forms: (1) setting oneself up as a person of equal stature to a person in authority; and (2) trying to equate one's own character, personal values, integrity, etc., with someone else's, especially one of a more mature or developed character.

Once, I witnessed a woman confronting her husband about his frequent displays of verbal abuse. She stated: "I'd like you to simply ask me for what you need instead of launching into me, cursing, and berating me. When I want something from you, I ask for it." He retorted, in a very provocative tone: "Are you saying you're better than me?" The implied message he was sending was that the two of them were of equal character standing — just two human beings of equal worth but that the wife was being "uppity" and casting herself as superior by challenging him to do things differently (and insinuating that her way of asking for things was better than his way). Being a good neurotic, she was effectively swayed by his comment, despite the reality that her character is clearly better developed than his and her proposed way of communicating her desires a more healthy way of doing things.

26. Manipulation by Insinuation. Disturbed characters will parse their words in a calculated manner, believing it's a fair bet that others might be misled or draw a false conclusion if they drop subtle suggestions about what they want others to think. If others recognize the game, and confront them on what they were implying, they might quickly deny manipulative intent, and assert something like "I didn't say that." This throws the other person on the defensive, casting them as someone who totally misrepresented things.

The Cognitive-Behavioral Triad. As we discussed in Chapter 2, the psychological problems of neurotics are mostly related to their unconscious fears, insecurities, and conflicted emotions; but the problems of disturbed characters are mostly the result of the erroneous ways they tend to think, and the habitually irresponsible ways in which they act. In Chapter 5, we took a look at the disturbed character's most common thinking errors and the dysfunctional attitudes they engender. And we have just finished taking a look at most common responsibility-avoidance and manipulation tactics, actions that often accompany the disturbed character's distorted ways of thinking. The erroneous thinking patterns, the problematic attitudes they spawn — and the irresponsible behaviors that accompany both — constitute what I describe in my workshops as the "Cognitive-Behavioral Triad." An inextricable and dynamic relationship exists among the components of this triad. Certain *ways of thinking* lead to the development of *attitudes and beliefs* that predispose the disordered character to engage in *irresponsible social behaviors.* These behaviors (and their perceived success at manipulating others) reinforce problematic thinking patterns. So, each part of the triad impacts the others in a way that creates a vicious cycle (as illustrated in the figure below) of social dysfunction.

COGNITIVE-BEHAVIORAL TRIAD

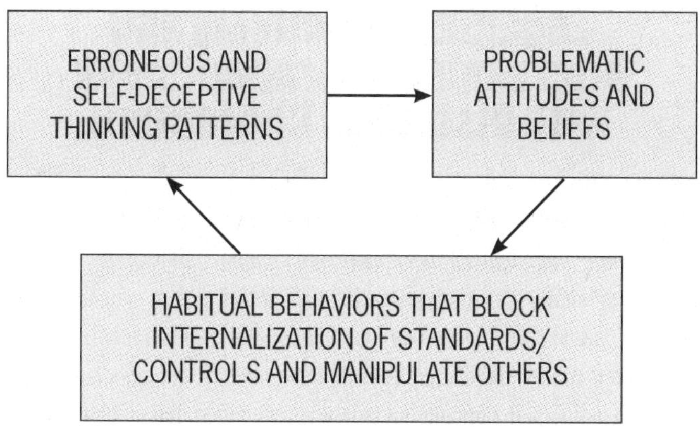

In order for true change to occur in the dysfunctional patterns of disordered characters, this vicious cycle must be broken.

CHAPTER 7

Engaging Effectively and Intervening Therapeutically with Disturbed Characters

As mentioned in an earlier chapter, persons with disturbances and disorders of character require very different therapeutic interventions than do individuals suffering from varying degrees of neurosis. Neurotics need *insight* into the *unconscious* emotional conflicts that underlie their symptoms. Disordered characters, on the other hand, need *corrective* emotional, cognitive, and behavioral experience. Their maladaptive behavior patterns, and the erroneous thinking and attitudes that help foster them, need to be directly but benignly confronted and corrected (preferably, at the very moment they occur). They also need to practice or rehearse more adaptive ways of thinking and behaving. Genuine change always begins in the *here and now* encounter. This can occur in the context of a therapist's confrontation during a session, or any other encounter with an individual willing to address the necessary issues and behaviors. Change also has to be reinforced from time to time in many different venues.

There are many unique principles a therapist needs to employ to effectively promote change in disturbed characters. These same principles must be observed by anyone who wants to deal more effectively with these individuals and avoid victimization by them. For this reason, I've deliberately attempted to make the principles and techniques advanced in this chapter fairly simple and straightforward. In so doing, I hope to help anyone unfortunate enough to know a disturbed character to deal with him or her in a more effective, potentially constructive manner. It should also help you assess whether attempts at promoting change (professional or otherwise) are making any headway.

Many therapists aren't well trained in the art of confronting and correcting maladaptive interpersonal styles. Some actively resist the notion of confrontation. Many others have experienced frustration and failure in their work with disturbed characters, especially if they primarily adhere to and therefore attempted to employ the philosophies and techniques common to traditional psychotherapeutic approaches. As I say time and time again in training workshops, ***trying to treat a disordered character with traditional psychotherapy is like a neurologist trying to perform delicate brain surgery with a dentist's appliances***. Some tools — as good as they might be — simply weren't designed for use in certain circumstances. My years of experience have demonstrated to me that the tools developed to treat neurosis are ineffective at best, and *potentially harmful* at worst, when the therapist's task is to help ameliorate character disturbance. But because many therapists are still primarily versed in and adhere to traditional paradigms, they tend to write off disturbed characters as simply nonamenable to treatment. The reality, however, is that character disturbance can be treated, and often treated fairly effectively, if the right approach is adopted. But when it comes to treating character disturbance — just as when engaging disturbed characters in everyday encounters — almost all the "rules" are different.

Common Attitudes and Misconceptions Impairing Therapeutic Understanding and Intervention. Whether you're a therapist attempting formal intervention or a lay person simply trying to understand and deal with a problem character, some common beliefs and misconceptions can hinder your efforts. Most of these are in large part the result of the lingering legacy of traditional psychology principles, their subsequent acceptance by the general public, and their continued dominance among professionals.

The allegiance many still afford to traditional perspectives has always perplexed me. I've heard many claim that they find traditional paradigms infinitely more "humanistic" and benign than behavioral or cognitive-behavioral approaches. But it was the traditional paradigms that advanced such notions as these: "cold" detached mothers were responsible for producing autistic children; "mixed-message"-giving mothers created schizophrenics; and young girls displaying bizarre behaviors suggestive of incest or other forms of sexual abuse were really children who couldn't come to terms with their own unconscious lust. These days, one would hardly think of such perspectives as humanistic or compassionate. And most of us regard the postulates mentioned above as ridiculously uninformed. Yet, for some reason, other questionable and unsupported principles that flow from the very same frameworks that spawned such unfounded beliefs are still accepted by many as valid and useful metaphors.

Now, I have mentioned before that some principles of traditional paradigms are still potentially very useful when you're dealing with a raving neurotic. But dealing with a disturbed character is much different business. The following are the axioms I've come to believe are the most important to remember:

- They **already "see," they simply "disagree."** So many people, including therapists waste considerable time and energy trying to get disturbed characters to "see" the wrongfulness or harmfulness of their ways. They operate under the misguided notion that, despite the fact that the disturbed character has probably heard the same things from a thousand different people a thousand times before, they still simply don't understand the error of their ways and will finally see the light if the therapist imparts information in a newer, clearer, more cogent way. They fail to realize that most often the disturbed character already understands very well what principles society wants him to accept, but he's simply, for various reasons, still resistant to internalizing those principles. So, successful engagement and intervention requires primarily that the other party simply set firm behavioral limits and expectations for any involvement with the disturbed character, and confront his truth distortions and responsibility-resistance tactics when he displays them. Then, when the disturbed character shows even a slight willingness to modify his thinking or behavior, he can be reinforced for so doing.

- **How they feel is not nearly as important as how they think and act**. Needless attention is often afforded to how disturbed characters must be feeling and how that might bear upon their actions. When working and dealing with disturbed characters, it's important to pay far more attention to the kinds of thinking patterns and attitudes they display, as well as the behaviors they might engage in that block internalizing pro-social values and standards. Their feelings are not the issue. They may claim so, and may also use their feelings to justify their actions. But their feelings are not the main problem. How they think and how they act are what matters most. Once these issues are addressed sufficiently and successfully, attention can be directed to emotional issues, if necessary.

- **Change occurs in the here-and-now**. Here's how you know you're making any headway with disturbed characters: If they're willing to make any changes in their thinking patterns or behavior *at the very moment those problematic patterns appear, and you confront or challenge them about them.* Sometimes, their apparent willingness to modify their behavior is purely superficial and meant to appease (this is the tactic of "giving assent"). However, it's a start, and it can still be reinforced even as you insist on progressively more sincere efforts down the road. When your encounters are still largely dominated by the tactics outlined in the previous chapter, you know the disturbed character remains actively resistant to change. When the tactics become less frequent and less intense, you might indeed be witnessing some authentic change.

- **Remember: position, position, position**. It's very important to keep in mind that most disturbed characters constantly jockey for a position of advantage in all their encounters, and that the "fight" for maladaptive dominance often begins before they even enter the therapy room or engage with you. So, it's extremely important to set the "terms of engagement" very early on (more about this later). It's just as hard for most therapists to adopt an authoritative, confrontational, and directive stance in therapy as it is for most people to take early charge of their encounters with disturbed characters. But anyone in any kind of relationship with a disturbed character, including a therapist attempting to facilitate change, must be willing to assert expectations, enforce limits and boundaries, and employ maximum leverage right from the outset. In traditional therapy, the therapist remains accepting while the client sets the agenda. When dealing with disturbed characters, you must remember that power simply can't be entrusted to those who will almost certainly abuse it. This is a very hard principle for many therapists to accept. They tend to see all efforts to assert authority or control as "counter-therapeutic." But with disordered characters, just the opposite is true. It's imperative that the power rest with the person most inclined to exercise it responsibly. Modeling the responsible, principled use of power is a crucial task for a therapist dealing with a disturbed character.

- **Endorse and enforce values, principles, and standards**. The "old therapy" was deliberately non-judgmental, positively regarding, and open. The purpose was to establish an atmosphere in which even the most guarded and "hung-up" individuals could feel safe enough to bare their souls, and in the process come into conscious contact with the parts of themselves that they had for too long repressed. Disordered characters need to know that *not* anything goes; also they need to understand precisely what values, principles, and standards you expect them to abide by when interacting with you. Nothing is as potentially corrective or therapeutic as making clear what the values and principles of responsible behavior are. You must stand up for them firmly, setting and enforcing appropriate limits and expectations with regard to behavior.

- **Know, honor and use the power of confrontation**. Confrontation has taken a "bad rap" in recent years. Confrontation doesn't mean hostility or belittlement. Confrontation brings a legitimate issue to the fore and deals with it. It's pointing directly at the 800-pound gorilla in the room that many so often choose to ignore. I simply can't stress enough why being willing to confront is so important. For years, clinicians wrote off personality and character disturbances as untreatable. They simply never addressed the core dynamics of a person's dysfunctional style. For example, they might focus on a person's early childhood trauma, "anger" issues, "fear" of commitment, or "insecurity" without ever directly confronting the penchant for habitually seeing himself as superior and entitled, or for exploiting and abusing others. Is it any wonder that the core dynamics of his personality remained unchanged? The fact is that the core dynamics defining dysfunctional personality style were rarely ever confronted, which is a significant part of why they went uncorrected.

  Confronting in a firm and unwavering way, even in the face of a barrage of tactics from the disturbed character, is a true art. This is especially because it's so difficult to do in a truly benign and ultimately loving way. But that's the heart of effective cognitive-behavior therapy with a disturbed character. It's not about the person, his worth, or image. It's about the *behavior*, purely and simply. That's where the focus needs to be. We must call the disturbed character out on it. Do it dispassionately, but do it nonetheless. Expect him to resist and to use every tactic in the book to make you think you're unjustified in taking your stance. But do it. It's the only way change has a chance.

- **Don't accept anything at face value**. Disturbed characters lie, "con," and manipulate a lot. The most disordered of them do so for no apparent reason. For years, clinicians as well as researchers have not adequately reckoned with this reality. Researchers will blindly incorporate self-report measures into their studies without due skepticism, and draw conclusions that are unreliable. Clinicians will often accept without question their clients' reports, not thinking that they might be feeding into a game of impression management or being misled about the real problems that need to be addressed.

  I once consulted to a women's penal institution that, out of necessity, hired a psychiatrist who had never worked with character-disordered individuals before. After he had unadvisedly prescribed a fair number of controlled substances to several of the inmates, I visited with him. I asked what led him to conclude that one woman really needed the prescribed popular drug Valium. He recounted his interview with the woman and the "depression and anxiety bordering on desperation" she reported, as well as the history she gave of being told by many doctors that she "needed" the drug. I asked him if, in his own mind, he had ever questioned the veracity of her report. His reply absolutely stunned me. "Why would she lie?" he asked. You see, in his fashionable outpatient practice, people usually didn't come banging on his door for help unless they had good reason to do so, and unless they were in genuine pain. They didn't typically lie to him. He had worked with neurotics for most of his professional life, and adhered to traditional perspectives. It was beyond his imagination that a person would put on a tearful display and exaggerate their symptoms as part of a con game to "score" some drugs that would be a real hit with the other inmates, and could be "sold" at a premium price. He couldn't fathom that the pathetic-looking person he had tried to help was later bragging to others about how easily "duped" he could be.

When I first started working with disturbed characters, I believed not only most of what they told me, but also the traditional psychological explanations for what made them do the things they do. I believed, for example, that abusers must have been abused themselves; that "bullies" were really cowards "underneath," struggling with self-esteem issues; and that braggarts were really "compensating" for feelings of insecurity. What I didn't know is that disturbed characters are keenly aware of how good neurotics like me tend to think. So, they often told me what they thought I wanted to hear. But over time, the more I checked and cross-checked reliable collateral information about their histories, the less the things they told me made sense. I gradually learned to be more skeptical. Sensing the skepticism, they would often ask what it was I wanted or expected them to say. This was their way of saying that they'd be willing to "give assent" to my expectations while still avoiding the simple truth. Only when they knew for certain that I demanded only the truth, the whole truth, and nothing but the truth did they start to "come clean" with me in any significant way.

- **Take charge and take charge quickly**. Remember, the disturbed character can't be trusted to direct the encounter responsibly, or to wield power or control conscientiously. You must be prepared in advance for your engagements, and have in mind the rules, expectations, boundaries, and limits you want observed. You must also be willing to enforce these from the very outset of your encounter. This is especially true when dealing with the aggressive personalities who lack internal brakes and who go through life like bulls in a china shop. In workshops, I also use the analogy of a locomotive on a mountainside with no brakes. You have to stop such a train when it first starts to roll. Because it gathers momentum quickly, if you wait even a little while to act, you're certain to get run over.

- **Frequently Misused Psychology Terms**. Seeing one's way clear to intervene effectively with disordered characters is not only a matter of abandoning ineffective approaches and adopting a more efficacious paradigm. It's also a matter of correctly labeling and interpreting events. Unfortunately, many mental health professionals erroneously apply certain terms and interpretations to the behaviors frequently displayed by disturbed characters. In my workshops, I humorously introduce a "Top 10 List" of the most frequently misused terms in mental health (I have actually included an 11th one because of its relevance). The list below should be especially helpful to professionals trying to intervene with disturbed characters. But because these terms have been so widely spread among the general populace, the lay person should find the clarifications below useful as well.

1. **Denial** (vs. lying). I introduced this topic earlier. A phenomenon traditionally labeled denial is in essence an unconscious ego defense mechanism. It's the psyche's natural way of protecting a person's conscious mind from the experience of unbearable emotional pain. It's a "this just can't be happening" kind of reaction to an event or circumstance that occurred too suddenly, with such intensity, or was of such an unusually emotionally painful character that the person simply cannot accept its reality without going to pieces. Generally, denial is a temporary psychological state that breaks down with time and acceptance. And true denial

can happen with respect to a person's behavior pattern, also. This is especially true when the behavior is so unusual or so "out of character" that the person simply can't believe he or she did it.

Unfortunately, many times both professionals and lay persons alike misuse the term denial. I frequently hear people say that someone is "in denial," implying that subject is in some sort of altered psychological state with the conscious mind being unconsciously prevented from seeing the reality of a circumstance. In fact, the person purportedly in denial is simply lying.

Lying to avoid punishment is not denial. Neither is lying to control the impression another has of you. Lying to oneself is also not the same as denial. Lying is lying. Denial is something else. Sometimes, habitual liars even begin to believe their lies. Still, this is not the same as denial.

2. **Acting Out** (vs. acting up). This is arguably the most misused term in mental health. In fact, the definition of this term has been modified in various texts and professional articles to such a great extent over the years that it bears little resemblance to its original meaning. Technically, the term refers to unconscious inner emotional conflicts expressed through actions as opposed to other types of bizarre symptoms. Here is an archetypal example:

   After laboring for several days, and staying up all night the night before to complete the task, a man puts a business report on his boss's desk. In typical fashion, the ever-demanding boss retorts: "Well, it's about time. And it had better be good!" Upon leaving the boss's office, the man utters under his breath, "That son-of-a-bitch." Then he enters the men's room and begins washing his hands — and washing his hands — and washing his hands. He washes until his hands are red, raw and blistered. He wants to stop but he can't. He has developed a compulsion or ritual. What's worse, he's completely unaware of the connection between his under the breath comment about his boss, the guilt that this evokes, and the compulsion he feels to make himself "clean" again. This is an example of a person acting out the internal war between his *id* that would like to punch his boss's lights out and his overactive *superego* which demands that he be clean of the stain of such unpardonable urges. So, he washes. His actions are the behavioral manifestation of his inner conflict.

Clinicians and others often use the term acting out to describe when disordered characters are "acting up." Acting up is not necessarily acting out. Most often, it's simply misbehavior. The term started being misused for two reasons: First, instances of acting out are not as clear cut as the one outlined above; and second, for a long time psychodynamic explanations about human behavior were so dominant that almost every behavioral problem was simply assumed to represent the outward manifestation of some inner emotional conflict. There are indeed times when a problematic behavior really represents a form of acting out. For example, a truly depressed youth might be angry over the breakup of his family but conflicted inwardly about his anger. So he might display his frustration through defiant actions that, in a manner completely unconscious to him, keep him from directing even more anger inward (thus becoming more seriously depressed) or toward family members (thus potentially alienating them). His defiant actions might draw his family's attention to him and his problems, thus potentially re-uniting his emotionally-separated parents in a cause to save their child. This kind of situation could still be regarded quite appropriately as a case of acting out. But, of late, the term has become over-expanded in meaning to the point of genuine absurdity. Now, almost every instance of misbehavior is referred to as some kind of "acting out," and the term has found its way into our everyday lexicon. There's even a popular TV commercial for a behavioral therapist's "proven formula" for curing your child's "acting-out" behavior at school. I cringe every time I hear it. There are many forms besides the one I mentioned earlier that true acting out can take. But, for the most part, acting up (misbehaving) is not acting out.

3. **Defensive** (vs. aggressive or combative). Here's one of the most frequent comments I hear from partners in abusive relationships who consult me as a therapist: "Every time I say something to him, he gets so defensive." The term "defensive" as used in common parlance reflects how traditional notions about the inner workings of the human psyche have been so widely but erroneously accepted by the general public. Most of the time, when my clients talked about the "defensiveness" of their partners, they were really describing wanton, intense, and deliberate *combativeness.* Their partners were behaving in a clearly aggressive manner; but, buying into the traditional notion that no one would engage in such behavior unless feeling in some way under attack, they viewed the behavior as defensive in character.

   Here's what generally happens in an abusive relationship (where power is unevenly distributed and the disordered character has the upper hand): Whenever the abused party tries to assert himself, the disturbed character quickly brings out an arsenal of psychological weapons to browbeat the other party into a position of subordination and submission. It's combat, pure and simple. And it's not combat necessarily rooted in a perception that one is under attack and has no choice but to defend oneself. One could say that the disturbed character feels his "position" threatened and acts to remove the threat; but once again this stretches a metaphor beyond the range of its usefulness and accuracy. What's more, buying into this inaccurate perspective only makes the neurotic more likely to feel like the bad guy and cave in. As soon as the neurotic begins to feel like he's the one responsible for inviting the disordered character to feel bad (i.e. the neurotic begins to feel like he's the aggressor), he's very likely to retreat, and allow the real aggressor to regain the upper hand. In fact, the neurotic surrenders the potentially level playing field with the aiding and abetting of traditional psychology.

4. **Shame** (vs. embarrassment at or distaste for being exposed). Therapists often assume that a client won't admit a problem because he feels too much shame and is "in denial" as a result. They then seek to guide the client with gentle encouragement and acceptance through a lengthy period of overcoming that denial (which may or may not actually occur). But what therapists often fail to consider is this: Not wanting to admit problems, and not wanting others to know you for the character you truly are, can be rooted in a host of other reasons other than genuine shame.

I was once a guest at another therapist's group therapy for seriously disturbed characters. I sat passively and listened to group members spew ridiculous excuses for some of the most reprehensible behaviors. After the session, I asked the therapist why some of the lies, obvious errors in thinking, and various irresponsible behaviors I witnessed weren't immediately challenged. He was a therapist overly immersed in and aligned with traditional paradigms. He stated that he had to be very careful to pace his confrontations because all of his clients must certainly be dealing with high levels of shame about their behaviors, and were still very much in various stages of denial as a result.

Let's take a moment and scrutinize this scenario carefully. We have here a group of disturbed characters, most of whom share similar core beliefs, similar patterns of behavior, and a similar degree of comfort with those attitudes and behaviors despite society's disapproval of them. What could possibly be shame-evoking about displaying those attitudes, ways of thinking and behaviors with a bunch of like-minded individuals? Sometimes, there might actually be someone in the group (especially the therapist) who doesn't share the same beliefs and attitudes. In that case, you might observe a person being hesitant to self-reveal. But such a hesitance need not necessarily be rooted in genuine shame. A person can be apprehensive about self-revelation for a variety of reasons besides shame, not the least of which is potentially losing the game of impression-management. Shame is a genuine feeling of not liking the person you are. It can actually keep a person from doing things that most would regard as a negative reflection on one's character. And remember, one of the hallmarks of disturbed characters is their pathological lack of shame.

5. **Splitting** (vs. the tactic of dividing and conquering). Therapists tend to misuse the term splitting the most. Splitting is a very rare and primitive ego defense mechanism: A person unconsciously divides a reality — far too traumatic to reckon with as a single entity — into two or more separate mental images or constructs. For example, a child who is severely emotionally abused, but occasionally showed affection by the same parent, may mentally "split" that parent into internal images of "good parent" and "bad parent." This permits the child to reconcile conflicted emotions by loving the good parent while hating or fearing the bad parent. Victims of horrendous abuse, who feel such self-loathing that they literally cannot stand themselves, might even split their psyches into several parts. This defense, when carried to an extreme, might even result in forming multiple personalities.

   What many therapists erroneously label "splitting," however, is the conscious, deliberate, manipulation tactic of "dividing and conquering," or creating dissention between others as a way of gaining advantage over them. Children learn this tactic early. If mommy says "no," they go to daddy and play the pleading game. Don't even mention that you already asked mommy, and daddy might give you what you want. If you're in an institutional setting, and you have problems with authority anyway, try and divide one camp of the staff against another. Professionals often mislabel this behavior "staff splitting." It's a very unfortunate misuse of the term, and it's not a benign misuse either. An underlying assumption is that the behavior is prompted by the classic and unconscious ego defense mechanism when, in fact, such "splitting" is a conscious and deliberate offensive power tactic.

6. **Passive-aggressive** (vs. covert-aggressive). Passive aggression is another of the most misunderstood and misused terms in mental health. I addressed this earlier in this book, but it bears repeating. Aggression is the forceful energy we all expend to survive and prosper. It usually involves attempting to secure a desired goal, to remove obstacles in the way of achieving those goals, or to remove perceived threats to our well-being. Our language reflects our deep-seated awareness of the true nature of aggression. We say things like, "If you want something, you have to fight for it"; or when we encourage the sick or infirmed to rally their resources and do battle with their cancers, infections, or other diseases. Humans have always done a lot of fighting. It's a big part of life. When we're not making some kind of love, we're generally waging some kind of war.

   How we fight is another matter. It's important to recognize that aggression is not synonymous with violence. Indeed, aggression can be undisciplined and destructive. Aggression can also be carefully tempered with concern for the impact on others, and can be potentially quite constructive in the amelioration of human misery. That's what assertive behavior is all about. Aggression can also be purely reactive: an immediate, instinctual response to a genuine threat. But aggression can also be predatory, or, as some researchers prefer, instrumental. Such aggression is neither prompted by fear or anger, and is not in response to a threat. Rather, it's rooted purely in desire, is strictly "offensive" in character, and the goal is victimization. Aggression can be overt. That is, it can be out in the open, without pretense, apology, or attempt to conceal. Aggression can also be covert. That is, it can be carefully cloaked so that aggressive intent is concealed from open observation. Covert aggression is at the heart of much interpersonal manipulation and emotional abuse. People often get conned and abused by others because they fail to spot their aggressive intentions and behaviors until after they've already been victimized.

One relatively benign form of covert aggression is passive aggression. Passive aggression is, as its name suggests, aggression through passivity. It's not answering your mate when you're mad at him. It's not returning a phone call when you don't really want to connect with the other person. It's "forgetting" once again to pick up the dry cleaning the partner you're mad at asked you to pick up. It can be a fairly powerful and frustrating strategy when carried to extremes. When Gandhi's followers simply stood fast and would not move out of the army's line of fire, although many perished, their "passive resistance" eventually brought an occupying empire to its knees. Most of the time, however, passive aggression is a relatively self-defeating strategy, especially when it comes to getting what you need in a relationship.

Most of the time, when I hear people use the terms "passive-aggressive" or "passive aggression" what they really mean is "covert aggression." The term "passive-aggressive" is used incorrectly to describe the subtle, hard to detect, but yet deliberate, calculating and underhanded tactics that manipulators and other disturbed characters use to intimidate, control, deceive, and abuse others. That's what covert aggression is all about. Although this kind of aggression is often subtle or concealed, there's absolutely nothing "passive" about it. It's very active, albeit veiled aggression.

7. **Passivity** (vs. uncooperativeness). Sometimes, disturbed characters who are deliberately, but not openly, resistant to cooperation are viewed as "passive" and unassertive. Deliberate uncooperativeness needs to be labeled for the combative stance that it is. Resistance-prone characters don't need to be taught assertive skills as much as they need to be confronted about their maladaptive penchant for fighting.

8. **Co-dependence** (vs. dependence or abuse). Perhaps no term is as overused and misused as this term. The term was originally intended to describe the phenomenon by which members of an addict's family of can end up having their lives just as much controlled by the addict's substance of choice as the addict himself. So, whereas the addict becomes substance-dependent, the family members often become co-dependent with the addict on the substance of choice. The lives of co-dependent individuals become so governed by the addict's addiction that they inadvertently give up control of their own lives in service to the addict, thus unintentionally "enabling" the addict's dysfunctional behavior.

   It would take another entire book to address the strengths and weaknesses of the co-dependency metaphor. Suffice it to say that the phenomenon the term was meant to describe does in fact exist. However, the term is often misapplied to behaviors and situations it was never initially meant to define. Most especially, the term is erroneously used to describe "dependency," mutual dependency, or even "abuse." When disordered characters enter into relationships, abusive and exploitative behaviors inevitably follow. When a therapist "frames" a disordered character's refusal to accept financial responsibility, deliberate disinterest and neglect of family needs, and excessive burdening of his partner as a case of "dependence" upon that partner, the entire nature of the relationship becomes distorted. When both the abuser and the victim are seen as "co-dependent" instead of the abusive party being correctly identified as such, and the dependency of the unassertive party (who would likely have set and enforced limits or even left the relationship long ago if it weren't for their excessive emotional dependency) goes unnoticed, the therapist is likely to promote a substantial amount of "enabling" of the abusive situation.

9. **Help** (vs. chasing and enabling). Long ago, one of my colleagues, who just happens to be a clinical social worker, told me a joke that pokes some fun at one of the stereotypes sometimes ascribed to persons who enter the helping professions. It seems there were two social workers walking down a big city street when a mugger on a bicycle rode by and snatched their purses. The social workers took off running in a fruitless attempt to catch up with the robber, all the while shouting to passers-by: "Stop that Man! ... Stop Him!! ... He's obviously in serious need of our help."

   Help is the offer of assistance we extend to those who truly need it and ask for it. Help is not chasing after someone to give them something we think is of value even when they haven't asked for it and show no appreciation for it. Help is not visiting the same issues with someone over and over again when they've already heard the same thing a million times and haven't displayed any motivation to change. Whenever we chase after people to give them something we value but which they disdain, we only reveal our own psychological pathology. And whenever we repeatedly put ourselves in a position to be ignored, exploited, or abused, we only "enable" and encourage disturbed characters to continue their dysfunctional ways.

   I know far too many therapists who sell themselves and their potential tools of empowerment far too cheaply. You have to remember, the disturbed character always wants something for nothing. That's part of what's at the heart of his character defect. Whenever a therapist (or a person with whom he is in a relationship) tries too hard (under the guise of "help"), he enables the disturbed character to continue not working on the necessary tasks of change. In the process, he loses any hope of being afforded any respect. In one of the vignettes presented later in this chapter, you'll get an idea of what rightfully constitutes the "help" people need in their relationships with disordered characters.

10. **Needs** (vs. wants). There are some things that every living creature needs to survive and prosper. Humans have evolved to the point, and learned enough over the centuries, that with only a modicum of mutual cooperation, most human needs can be met with relative ease. In fact, we've reached the point in many advanced societies where we take our basic necessities for granted. Some of us, however, are never satisfied. We want, want, and want still more. Sometimes the things we want are the very last things we truly need (e.g., one more piece of pie, one more relationship on the side, one more luxury condo). Neurotics are notorious for being too apprehensive about getting their basic needs met, and the therapist's job is often to help them assert themselves and learn how to secure their legitimate needs. But when therapists try to help disordered characters find less disruptive ways to get the things they want but don't need, and don't challenge their greediness directly, disaster almost inevitably follows.

    Disturbed characters are more than happy to plead their case and solicit your understanding. They almost always want an "ear" and to have their point validated. They don't want to have their attitudes, beliefs, and ways of doing things challenged. They certainly don't want guidance, direction, and correction. But those things are exactly what they need the most.

11. **Symptoms** (vs. signs). When a person reports his subjective experience of distress to a professional (e.g., "I feel achy all over"), it's called a symptom. When a person displays a physical abnormality, a particular behavior or pattern of behavior, or any observable and objective manifestation of a reality, it's called a sign. The fact that the terms are often misused by professionals is problematic enough. But the problem is exacerbated by the fact that character-disordered individual most often give distorted and sometimes deliberately dishonest reports about their experiences and circumstances. So, the symptoms they report cannot be

trusted. Instead, the clinician often needs to take what clients say with a grain of salt. The therapist must be extra mindful of the *signs* they display, especially the cardinal or most essential signs (e.g., distorted thinking patterns, responsibility-avoidance and manipulation tactics) that signal the presence of character disturbance and other pathologies.

Empowered Engagement with Disturbed Characters

In my first book, *In Sheep's Clothing*, I outlined some of the general rules anyone (layperson or therapist) must observe to empower themselves in relations with disturbed characters, especially manipulators. Those general guidelines include:

- Letting Go of Harmful Misconceptions — especially this tenet of traditional psychology: that everyone is essentially the same and struggling with fears and insecurities.
- Becoming a Better Judge of Character — not necessarily by doing a thorough professional character analysis, but at least by knowing the basic personality features of the persons you're dealing with. Also, decide where they likely lie on the neurotic-character disordered continuum.
- Knowing Yourself — well enough to understand the needs, insecurities, and belief systems that might put you at risk for being taken in by an unscrupulous character.
- Knowing the Twisted Thinking Patterns and Tactics — some people use to avoid responsibility and manipulate others. It's important to know them well, to recognize them the moment they're employed, and to respond to them appropriately.

- o Investing Energy Only Where You Have Power — by choosing battles carefully, avoiding losing battles, and never succumbing to the temptation to take on the burden belonging to someone else. Take charge of your own behavior. Set your own limits and expectations. Leave the burden for change where it belongs — on the person with the behavior problem.

In addition, I outlined some specific rules to observe to remain maximally empowered in any encounter. These rules include:

- o Never accept an excuse. If a behavior is wrong, the reasons for it are irrelevant.
- o Judge actions, not intentions. Never second-guess a motive or accept a promise on the surface. Actions speak much louder than words.
- o Set limits and expectations, and do so very early on in any encounter.
- o Make requests that are clear, simple, and direct.
- o Accept only clear, simple, and direct responses.
- o Stay focused on the here and now.

The Paradigm Necessary for Change

For years an ongoing debate has occurred about whether therapy even works, or if it does work, what makes it work. The question becomes even more salient when we're talking about therapy for disturbed characters — arguably, the most difficult individuals to treat.

In my work over the years, I have found that the art of therapeutic intervention with disturbed characters goes far beyond merely adopting a cognitive-behavioral approach (as opposed to traditional psychotherapeutic approaches). Some of the most important principles are outlined below:

As mentioned earlier, the cardinal principle of intervention with disturbed characters is that *change occurs in the here-and-now.*

That is, every single encounter with a disturbed character not only reflects their interpersonal dysfunction's nature but also presents an opportunity for corrective emotional and behavioral experience. Every interaction, therefore, is an opportunity for change, learning, and growth. If you're ever going to facilitate change, you must literally seize the moment, and refuse to let it go until something different takes place.

My experience includes consulting with therapists of many different training backgrounds, as well as giving numerous workshops and seminars. This has made me aware of how rarely the basic tenets of cognitive-behavioral therapy (CBT) are actually employed, despite the facts that there is fairly widespread knowledge about the paradigm and so many purport to adhere to it. Most clinicians know that CBT is the right answer when you ask them what approach is superior in dealing with character disturbance. Most will even say they employ it. But often, when I scrutinize this claim, I learn that *cognitive* strategies are indeed employed (albeit only at times), whereas behavior modification techniques are usually not employed at all.

Almost every therapist I know has at least a mild aversion to behavior therapy. Most seem to regard it as "cold" and mechanical, and ultimately ineffective because it does not focus on the "whole" person. Some ardently believe it does not attend to the "underlying dynamics" traditional approaches assumed to motivate behavior. Even the common terms associated with behavior therapy, such as generalization, reinforcement schedules, cue saliency, response conditioning, send shivers up the spine of most therapists I know. But behavior therapy has demonstrated its effectiveness and even superiority fairly convincingly, and adding the cognitive component to the paradigm only enhances its effectiveness further. Unfortunately, however, although many therapists will say they do CBT, what they really do is often a mixture of CT (Cognitive Therapy) and traditional PT (psychotherapy). Is it any wonder why many end up pulling their hair out when trying to make headway with a disturbed or disordered character?

Many of the techniques employed in the here-and-now process of emotional, cognitive, and behavioral counter-conditioning are potentially just as useful to the layperson as they are to a therapist. So it might be helpful to see these principles at work in some typical therapeutic encounters. The following altered vignettes are based upon actual cases, each of which exemplifies many of the principles we've covered. The commentaries provided after each vignette are meant to elaborate on the principles employed.

These vignettes depict sessions typically conducted in an outpatient setting. The principles used in these mostly one-on-one encounters can also be applied to group-based interventions and treatments. Sometimes it's even easier to call attention to erroneous thinking patterns, and to confront responsibility-resistance behaviors, when there are others in a group familiar with these things.

The first vignette depicts a real diagnostic interview with an adolescent male and his mother. The young man had been having behavior problems at home and at school. Despite his young age, he was already showing signs of significant character dysfunction. As is generally the case, his mother insisted he come to see a professional. As I typically do, I met initially with both together. The vignette is useful for illustrating the principles outlined earlier in this book, showing how to gain leverage with and deal effectively with character disturbed individuals. As with all of the vignettes in this book, some of the material and identifying information is altered so as to ensure complete anonymity. However, all of the essential psychological dynamics have been painstakingly preserved. I should mention that, although I mean to illustrate methods and principles, I do not mean to suggest that my interventions were perfect. I always see things I would do differently when I review case vignettes. So, this vignette not only illustrates what general principles should be observed, but also what things should be avoided to deal effectively with the disturbed character. After presenting the vignette, I'll discuss some of the general principles and issues that beg further exploration.

VIGNETTE #1

A behaviorally disturbed adolescent brought in by his mother

THERAPIST (addressing adolescent first): What brings you here today?

ADOLESCENT: I have no idea.

THERAPIST: Are you trying to tell me that you're the kind of person who will go places or do things without knowing why?

ADOLESCENT: I don't know what you want from me anyway. If you wanna know anything, ask her (looks glaringly at his mother)!

THERAPIST: I haven't decided just yet whether to consider your input on things, or simply talk to your mother and base my opinions and suggestions solely on what she tells me. But I thought I'd ask you about things first.

ADOLESCENT: She thinks I have an attitude problem.

THERAPIST: I'm not sure what you mean by "attitude problem."

ADOLESCENT: She's always doin' stuff … makes me mad all the time. Sometimes, she makes me real angry.

THERAPIST: Of course, she has no power to *make* you mad. And anger is a normal, healthy human emotion. It's rarely a problem in itself. So, I'm still wondering what the problem really is.

ADOLESCENT: I told you. She knows just what to do to piss me off. And she does it all the time.

THERAPIST: I accept that you need to say that. Maybe you even believe it, I don't know. Maybe you just want me to believe that you believe it. But you should know that I never accept notions like anyone can *make* you feel or do anything. Your feelings belong to you. I also won't accept that anger in itself can be a problem. Maybe you can tell me what you typically *do* when you get angry with your mother.

MOTHER: He curses. He says all kinds of hateful things.

THERAPIST: I think I might understand why you might be willing to speak for your son. But for now, I want to speak to him directly and have him speak directly to me, okay?

MOTHER: I'm so sorry. I didn't mean to… (looks ashamed and hangs head down)

THERAPIST: What do you *do* when you get angry with your mom?

ADOLESCENT: You heard her.

THERAPIST: It's not my intention to fight with you.

ADOLESCENT: I'm not fighting.

THERAPIST: Of course you are, and have been since you got here, perhaps even before that. And I know that you know that. It's quite apparent that you're here against your will. Still, I don't want to fight with you. I will be open, honest, and direct. I will not be disrespectful. There are obviously some problems here, and I'd like to learn more about them. I'm willing to deal with only your mom about them if I have to, but I'd like to get your input.

ADOLESCENT (huffing heavily): This whole thing is because I shoved her once — okay? And it was all because she got right in my face. I've told her a million times not to do that.

THERAPIST: So, you are saying that you have been physically aggressive with your mom.

ADOLESCENT: I just touched her. She wouldn't leave me alone. She knows that sets me off.

THERAPIST: Do you often rationalize — that is, make excuses for — being aggressive?

ADOLESCENT: I'm not making excuses.

THERAPIST: Of course you know what an excuse is and when you're making one, so we certainly won't fight about that. My question is only whether you tend to make these kinds of excuses for your aggressive behavior *often*.

ADOLESCENT: Only when I have good reason.

THERAPIST: I should tell you that unless it's to defend your life against a real attack, I will never accept any excuse for aggressive behavior.

ADOLESCENT: Does that go for everybody?

THERAPIST: For everybody. Has your mother ever aggressed against you?

ADOLESCENT: Well... no.

THERAPIST: So, you are not really the victim here. Your mom says or does things you don't like, and you tell yourself you have the right to aggress against her.

ADOLESCENT: But she knows what she does and how it makes me mad.

THERAPIST: You seem determined to make yourself out to be the victim and to cast blame on your mom. When you aggress against your mom, she's the victim, not you.

ADOLESCENT (more forcefully): She never has anything nice to say. She's constantly on my back. It's always this and always that.

MOTHER: Maybe he has a point. It could be partly my fault.

THERAPIST: What do you think is your fault?

MOTHER: I don't know. Maybe because I just don't know what to do anymore. I've tried taking away privileges, talking to him calmly. He just seems to get so mad. It's hard to talk to him. Maybe I end up saying too many negative things.

THERAPIST: The issue I want to focus on right now is the aggression. How often has he been aggressive with you?

MOTHER: Not that often.

THERAPIST: How often would that be?

MOTHER: Four or five times, I think. But nothing as bad as the other night. That's why I called you. I was really afraid he might hurt me that time.

THERAPIST: What do you do when he aggresses?

MOTHER: Try to calm him down. Try to talk to him. Try to understand what's making him act that way.

THERAPIST: You don't have the power to calm him down. What do you do to protect yourself?

MOTHER: Do you think I need to?

THERAPIST: If you don't do what you have power to do, and keep trying to change things you can't control, you'll get angry, frustrated, and depressed. Then, you won't think straight or have the energy to handle the situation properly. You have power over your behavior. That's why I asked you what you do when he aggresses.

MOTHER: What can I do?

THERAPIST: Have you considered calling the police?

ADOLESCENT (bursting out and glaring at mother): That's it! Now, I suppose you'll go hollering to the cops and get me in trouble with the law any time I say a cross word!

MOTHER: Don't you think that would be a little much. A little cruel?

THERAPIST: I think what your son just did is cruel. And covertly aggressive (manipulative). He's casting himself as the injured party while at the same time trying to beat you up with guilt and shame — insinuating that you're the kind of person who will over-react and get him into unwarranted trouble over a trivial matter. What do you usually do when he tries to intimidate you like this?

MOTHER: (starts to cry, says nothing)

ADOLESCENT: That's what she does.

THERAPIST (to adolescent): Do you ever let yourself think of just how wrong and harmful it is for you to fight like you have in here today. Rationalizing behavior you know is wrong, but making excuses for it anyway; minimizing the seriousness of some of your actions; using tactics such as making yourself out a victim; intimidating your mother; spending all that energy to have the upper hand and not doing one minute's work to learn how to control yourself. Do you ever think about how wrong all of that behavior is?

ADOLESCENT: (gets a bit somber, remains mute)

THERAPIST: I'm going to give you my opinions now about what I see as problems; what I think each of you needs to do about it; and what I'll be willing to do to help.

MOTHER: Okay.

ADOLESCENT: (looks up and sits attentively)

THERAPIST: I think things are upside-down in this family. This young man acts like the boss and sometimes bullies, (addressing mother) and you don't know what to do to gain the upper hand. Have you ever been in a situation like this before?

MOTHER: (with head down low and in a soft voice): Uh … my first husband.

THERAPIST: So, you need to get much better at recognizing and dealing with aggressive behavior. This young man will naturally fight for the things he wants and test all the limits. He doesn't know yet how to handle power, and you haven't learned yet how to effectively wield it.

MOTHER: I don't want to make him hate me.

THERAPIST: You don't have the power to make him hate you.

MOTHER: Maybe he will anyway.

THERAPIST: Are you saying if you stop tolerating abuse, set limits, and provide direction, you're worried your son will hate you for it?

MOTHER: Maybe.

THERAPIST: And you might tolerate abuse just to avoid feeling hated?

MOTHER: I just want him to know I love him and to appreciate me.

THERAPIST: You don't have power over his attitudes or feelings.

MOTHER (tearfully): What if he just leaves?

THERAPIST: You don't have power over what he does, just how *you* respond to it. You have the power and responsibility to set a good example, to set limits, expectations and consequences, beyond that you have no power. But the power you do have is significant.

MOTHER: What should I do?

THERAPIST: I'm willing to provide you supportive counseling, and help you learn better ways to empower yourself and to be better able to handle yourself in the difficult job of parenting this young man.

ADOLESCENT: You mean I don't have to come (looks glad at this point)?

THERAPIST: I mean, at this time, I'm choosing not to work with you.

ADOLESCENT: What if I want to come anyway?

THERAPIST: Should the time come when I think it could possibly be of benefit, I might agree to see you.

MOTHER: So, should I come next time?

THERAPIST: Yes. I'll give you some things to look over that can serve as a springboard for the work we will be doing.

ADOLESCENT: I think I'll come next time, too.

THERAPIST: You may come, of course, but I will not see you. You can sit in the waiting room and read a magazine.

ADOLESCENT: All you'll do is talk about me and say things behind my back that aren't true, and I won't be here to defend myself.

THERAPIST (turned toward mother but speaking loud enough for son to hear): We will focus only on the issues I spoke about earlier. We will leave him out of it.

(Turned toward son): I think it would be nice for us to visit under the right circumstances. I have a lot of things you may find useful in making important changes in your life.

ADOLESCENT: I know what you're trying to do. You're trying to get me to change by making me feel bad. Well, it won't work!

THERAPIST: I don't have the power to change you. I only have the power to assist people who want to change. As I see it, there are things both of you need to change. And I respect that you don't see the need for doing things differently just now. So, for the time being, your mom and I will work on the things she wants to change.

ADOLESCENT: I still may want to come sometime.

THERAPIST: I think that would be really nice under the right circumstances. When I think the time is right, and if I'm convinced it could be of benefit, I'll be glad to give it a shot.

Let's take a step-by-step look at the interpersonal processes going on in this vignette. Both of the individuals in my office that session had their own reasons for being there. I almost always ask individuals making an appointment to see me what their purpose is in seeking me out. The adolescent's response to my opening question is telltale. His brief response is packed with tactical maneuvers and reveals much about his as yet unspoken agendas. He responds by saying he has "no idea" why he's there. Keep in mind, I rarely listen that closely ***to*** what a person says. I usually listen ***for*** the kinds of things he or she might say (i.e. the tactics of manipulation and impression management they might employ), and what the underlying agendas most probably are. Now, it's remotely possible that the exact purpose of this specific visit wasn't spelled out by his mother, but I feel it quite safe to assume that this young man has a pretty good idea why he's in a counselor's office. So, I make the following suppositions, merely on the basis of his opening remark:

1. He's using the tactic of feigning ignorance (i.e. "playing dumb").
2. His use of the tactic means he's fighting. He doesn't really want to be there, and he certainly doesn't want to submit himself to my authoritative counsel (i.e. he's already fighting with me and wants to control the encounter).
3. He's of insufficient character to be entrusted with the leadership role in his interactions with me. I need to set all the terms of engagement, and assume an authoritative stance quickly.

Now, my response to this young man's opening remark is not typical of how I operate these days. The question I asked had a more provocative tone than I usually find necessary. Sometimes provocative questions are necessary and helpful, but I don't use them as often anymore. By implying that he is trying to cast himself as someone who simply goes where he's told to go and does what he's told to do without any awareness of the purpose, I'm casting him as a passive or deferential type of person, when in fact I suspect quite the contrary. This provocative technique can be used with individuals who are, in fact, quite aggressive in interpersonal style; but they attempt to cast themselves as passive, and to cast those who are suffering in relationships with them as villains. By using this technique, I'm signaling to this youngster that I believe him to be actively engaged in impression management and manipulation, as opposed to being willing to engage in discourse. By stymieing that effort, I increase the chances he'll take a different course.

Next, this young man attempts to direct attention to his mother, and to take more solid control of the interview process. He also puts her on notice with a glaring glance (i.e. uses the tactic of covert intimidation). My response is to assert who will control the interview process, and what kind of behaviors I will or won't tolerate. Such things always need to be done firmly but matter-of-factly, with no displays of hostility or malice. Asserting control over the process must also be done without hesitation. I also use the "leverage" technique of suggesting two possible outcomes, one clearly less desirable than the other, and present the youngster with a choice. By insinuating that he might not be given a voice in matters that concern him, he is prodded to make a better choice. I don't engage in this level of leverage anymore because it is too akin to manipulation, i.e., making a covert or veiled threat. So, although I move quickly to establish that I make the decisions about the process, I don't red-flag outcomes as leverage. I merely assert that I'll be making a decision regarding with whom I will work.

In the case at hand, the young man takes the bait, and for the first time offers up some information. The way he frames it, however, is to insinuate that his mother harbors an erroneous belief that he has a problem with his "attitude" (engaging in covert belittling). His tactics are to again divert attention to his mother, to cast her as a villain, and to cast himself as an innocent victim.

I take the opportunity to invite the young man to elaborate on just what the "attitude" issues are, but he quickly blames his mother for "doing stuff" and "saying things" that upset him. He uses the tactic of overgeneralization to exaggerate any legitimate issues (i.e. "she is *always* doing stuff"), and tries to put the blame for *his* responses squarely on her. I then firmly take a stand behind this principle: No one bears responsibility for behavior other than the person engaging in the behavior. I also take a stand on the principle that human emotions, including anger, are not the cause of human suffering. I put the focus squarely on thinking patterns and most especially behavior, not emotions.

As I increasingly pin the youngster down on the relevant issues, and have nearly successfully zeroed in on the specific problem things he does, look who comes to the rescue! Good ol' mom speaks up and says what he easily could have admitted himself some time ago. I begin to learn a lot about her and her penchant for rescuing. When I benignly confront her about that, her behavior of wanting to crawl into a hole and hide tells me almost everything else I need to know about her and her own character.

I then get back to the matter of confronting the problem behavior for which the mom dragged this young man into my office in the first place. Along the way, I confront the resistance of this young man directly. I indicate that I have no intention of becoming ensnarled in a fruitless power struggle. He eventually acknowledges that the proverbial straw that broke the camel's back, prompting the visit to my office, is that he has become physically aggressive with his mother. He then launches a literal barrage of responsibility-avoidance and manipulation tactics: He trivializes (i.e. uses the tactic of minimization by saying "only once" and "not hard") the importance of his physical misconduct, and attempts to re-assign blame to his mother (e.g., "only because she was in my face"); he casts himself as a victim, and rationalizes (makes excuses). Disturbed characters use these tactics because they're generally quite effective (exemplified by some of the mother's later statements). I can't count the number of times workshop attendees have told me that they might strive to find out if, in fact, the mother ever really did get in this lad's face. But that successfully leads them off the topic at hand; it shapes their impressions of the situation in the manner the young man is seeking to shape impressions. I make it clear, however, that I never entertain an excuse for physical assault. It's wrong, period. I make it crystal clear the principle I stand on, and that I'll accept no excuse for violating the principle.

An important thing to note: When I next confront the young man's excuse-making, I don't accept his "denial" (i.e. lying) about the fact that he's been physically aggressive. I don't buy into the potentially fatal notion that he's most likely ashamed of himself and can't believe he's really done such a thing; or that his conscious state is so altered that he truly thinks he hasn't done it. Rather, I assume he knows full well not only what he's done, but that society generally frowns on such actions, and would negatively appraise his character. So, I don't assume his "denial" is motivated by the pain of guilt or shame. I instead assume that he's actively engaged in defiance of a principle, resisting submission to the notion that such behavior is simply not okay. He's simultaneously attempting to manipulate me into a more favorable assessment of his character, not wanting me to think of him as the type of person who's comfortable aggressing against people simply because they called attention to his character flaws.

I then witness what happens when the young man more intensely takes aim at his mom, using a barrage of tactics and casting her as the villain. Eventually, she caves. She accepts not only the notion that she's at fault, but that she's at least partly responsible for his aggressive conduct. She's willing to take on too much responsibility; he's taking none — an archetypal dysfunctional relationship and a perfect example of what happens when the overly conscientious neurotic is in a relationship with a person of deficient character.

Eventually I decide that the person to work with first is mom. I do so for three main reasons:

a. She's in more immediate pain and discomfort and will be motivated to seek relief;

b. She's fairly neurotic (she has character issues, but on balance her over-conscientiousness exceeds the level of her character deficiency) so she's more amenable to traditional counseling;

c. The balance of power in the family is pathologically skewed and needs re-alignment. Mom is not supposed to be perfect, just the authority figure. Instead, she's in the one-down position. I don't want to "enable" the balance to remain unhealthily skewed. And I'd like to facilitate the process of mom gaining mental and emotional strength for both her own benefit and that of her son. Despite the fact that he's nearing adulthood, he desperately still needs authoritative guidance.

In fashioning the initial plan of treatment, I also had to take into serious consideration the mom's unhealthy emotional dependency, and how she might tend to overly rely on my support as opposed to doing what's necessary to empower herself.

Traditionally-oriented therapists might easily be uncomfortable with the fact that I did not initially conduct therapy sessions with the "identified" client (i.e. the adolescent brought in by his mother). The traditional approach would be this: Set an atmosphere of positive regard and willingness to "help"; then the young man would eventually "overcome his resistance" and forge a therapeutic alliance with me. However, I might offer some fairly provocative points of explanation: (1) It was particularly respectful of me to accept this young man at exactly the place that he was with respect to receptivity to change. (2) His mother bears primary responsibility for guiding his character formation *and* she really needs help right now. (3) Denying a visit to the adolescent, setting strict terms of engagement, standing up for principle, making clear that my support was freely available under the right terms — all this was, in fact, one of the most *corrective* and, therefore, *therapeutic* things I could have done. (4) My commitment to principle, willingness to call both parties out on their various pathologies, and work over a several-month period with the mother demonstrated my professional credibility as well as my trustworthiness. This greatly enhanced the likelihood that the young man would seek me out when the time came to want help for himself, if necessary.

Now, I did eventually see this young man professionally. In fact, I saw him several times. The first time was when he begged for a session, primarily because he'd lost a lot of leverage with his mother, and was seeking to re-tilt the balance of power. I saw him once but refused him regular counseling at that time. The second time, he was having some problems at college and was in danger of being tossed out. I agreed to see him, but again I limited contact to the initial visit. Why? His motivation was primarily to alleviate his immediate distress. He had insufficient desire to work on the character traits that created the problem in the first place, and he was well aware that I don't engage in "crisis management," but rather "character development." He was aware, however, that my door was always open to him for the right kind of work.

He came to see me when his first marriage was on the rocks, making some degree of investment in therapy; but when he came to grips with how much work (i.e. changing) he had to do, he departed prematurely. After the breakup of his second marriage, a bitter divorce, self-sabotage in his first career, and a few other major failures, he came back again, this time to really work. And work he did. I should say that, in addition to his brief earlier visits with me, he had made the rounds of counselors, including psychiatrists, and was offered all kinds of opinions about the nature of his problems and how to overcome them. He was given just about every kind of diagnosis along the way, from adult ADD to Bipolar Disorder, and was prescribed various medications. His relationship difficulties were framed as anything from "fear of intimacy" to "low self-esteem." But he himself had the answer when he brandished the worksheets I had long ago given his mother on thinking errors and responsibility-avoidance tactics. Waving them in front of me, he stated emphatically, "This is me. These sheets say it all. These are the kinds of things I've always done. I've always had this kind of thinking and I've always used these kinds of tactics to kid myself and manipulate others. My whole life has been a train wreck just waiting to happen, and I always knew it but wasn't ready to give in (note how he frames the issue as a matter of capitulation — NOT insight). I just want to make my life different now. I hope it's not too late."

So, he knew in his heart what the problem was all along. *Awareness* was *never* the issue. *Acceptance* or the lack thereof was the major obstacle, finally overcome. And, as has been proven to me countless times, I believe this is why he came back to me instead of to someone at the other places he'd been: He knew he could trust me to confront the key issues directly, without undue whitewashing or politically-correct mis-framing. He knew where I stood and what my principles were. I'd confronted him on what I believed to be his most important issues before, and he knew early on whether or not my assessment was on the mark. This meant he had good reason to trust me, and there's no possibility of a truly therapeutic relationship without trust. If I'd tried to candy-coat his behavior by attributing it to low self-esteem, depression, a chemical imbalance, or past trauma, I would have had absolutely no credibility. In all of his encounters with me, I must have sounded like a broken record, always espousing the same principles and never succumbing to his vigorous attempts at impression management. When the time was right, he knew he could count on me for the honest confrontation and authoritative guidance he needed. I gladly obliged him. Because his motivation was internal, the effort on my part from that day forward was minimal.

If this were only one shining example of success in a sea of treatment failures, it would certainly not serve as a support for the philosophy I advocate. But I've been around long enough now to see scenarios similar to this one repeated many times.

The following is another vignette that illustrates well the thinking patterns and attitudes common to the disturbed character. It also shows the tactics they habitually and automatically use to resist accepting responsibility, and to manipulate and manage others' impressions. It is a sort of "composite" vignette containing a few snippets from several different, but very similar, interviews woven into the principal character's dialogue.

The vignette is of an interview between a prison social worker and an inmate. The inmate is a female who has been in trouble with the law on numerous occasions, but has come to prison for the first time. The prison social worker is attempting to learn something about the woman's background to assist placing her in programs that will help her earn the earliest possible parole.

VIGNETTE #2

A newly incarcerated female with a history of antisocial conduct and drug abuse

INTERVIEWER: Tell me how you happened to come to prison.

INMATE: To tell you the truth, I think my probation officer had it in for me. She just doesn't like me.

INTERVIEWER: How is that?

INMATE: Well, I was keeping my appointments and doing everything I was supposed to do; but then I caught a silly drug charge, and she revoked me and sent me here.

INTERVIEWER: A drug charge?

INMATE: Yeah. I got pulled over and the cop found a little weed in my car. They didn't even ask me whose it was or how it got there.

INTERVIEWER: So you were charged with possession?

INMATE: Actually, they got me for distribution.

INTERVIEWER: Why distribution?

INMATE: Well, because some of the weed was in little bags.

INTERVIEWER: Why in little bags?

INMATE: (Shrugs her shoulders)

INTERVIEWER: How many bags?

INMATE: About 50.

INTERVIEWER: Fifty is quite a few bags. Would you say that you were probably going to distribute those bags?

INMATE: Not that day.

Let's take a good look at this very illuminating scenario. Here we have a social worker trying to do something potentially quite helpful for this woman. In order to get her into the right program in a timely manner, the social worker needs to know what this woman is all about. She needs to know her criminal history, the kinds of problems and issues to address, and how serious the problems are. Gaining access to the right programs and completing them with a favorable rating can result in considerably less time of incarceration for the inmate. So, the social worker is trying to "help." Meanwhile, from the very outset this inmate is engaged in a game of impression management, manipulation, and responsibility-avoidance. It's exemplified by the thinking patterns she displays and the tactics she uses.

When the social worker asks why the woman has come to prison, the first thing the inmate does is blame her probation officer. (Actually, the very first thing she says is "to tell you the truth," which in the case of a disturbed or disordered character, represents your first clue that a lie is about to follow.) She paints a picture of herself as a compliant, dutiful probationer who had the "bad luck" to be assigned a probation officer who didn't like her, and so recommended revoking her probation for no good reason. She then casts herself as the victim of even worse luck by being stopped by a police officer (she skirts the issue about why she was stopped) who stumbled upon "a little weed" in her car. She also implies (misleads through insinuation) that, had the officer asked about how it might have gotten there, she might have been able to offer an exculpating explanation. So right off the bat, she externalizes the blame, minimizes the nature of her wrongdoing, and casts herself as a person of generally good character who has been treated unfairly by the system.

Now, you should know that the social worker has this woman's complete criminal record and history in a fairly thick informational "jacket," and has been perusing through it while asking the woman questions. Also, upon minimal further probing, more of the truth comes out (although there is still a substantial amount of lying by omission and distortion going on). Given these facts, it would have been much easier, simpler, and less time consuming for the inmate to have simply acknowledged to the social worker that she has a habit of drug trafficking, and got "busted" once again — and that's why she's in prison. All this will be learned in short order anyway, so one has to wonder why this woman simply doesn't fess up.

Therapists aligned with traditional psychology models would automatically assume that this woman feels too guilty and ashamed "underneath it all" to simply self-reveal so bluntly, and is probably still "in denial" to some degree about the nature of her life and circumstances. But what the woman has to say later in the interview challenges those kinds of assumptions:

INTERVIEWER: So I'll bet you're going to think twice about having anything to do with drugs again when you get out, huh? I'm going to recommend that you get into the substance-abuse treatment program. That'll look good on your record, too.

INMATE: I don't need any treatment. I ain't got no real problem. I'm not an addict or nothin'. Look, everybody does a little weed sometimes, and there's nothing wrong with that. Everybody I know does weed. And I ain't no big time dealer, either. I know lots of people who sell all kinds of heavy stuff for lots of money, and they didn't catch the charges I got or get the time I got. The cops take bribes from the real pushers and leave them alone. Anyway, I didn't catch a lot of time, so I'll be out soon enough. I'd rather do my time and get out than have to be in one of those [more colorful language deleted here] programs where they make you talk about God and higher powers and [stuff] like that, and make you say you're an addict and you don't know how to run your own life anymore."

Diehard traditionally-minded therapists would still insist that this woman's apparent "denial" of the extent of her "problems" is proof of her underlying emotional pain. But the reality is more likely this:

1. This woman does not feel badly about her behavior. She only regrets that her life has now been interrupted.
2. She has no genuine remorse, not only with respect to the wrongfulness of her behavior, but also for the potential negative impact it had on others and society at large. The social worker asked her about who was caring for her two young children. Her response was that it was no big deal because her mother had always pretty much cared for them. That fact reflects on her lack of concern for the impact of her conduct. Again, traditionally-minded therapists might frame the fact that her mother has to care for the kids as an instance of "dependency." But "using" others as vehicles to enable your irresponsible lifestyle is not the same as true dependency.
3. She's going to do what she has always done when she gets out, because she hasn't submitted herself to the principle that her behavior is wrong or harmful. She's still at war with principles she knows society wants her to accept.
4. She attributes the causes of her misfortune to external sources, not to her wrongful thinking and behavior.
5. She detests the notion of subordinating her will to any kind of "higher power" whether within some kind of program or not.
6. She's nowhere near uncomfortable or troubled enough emotionally or mentally to be motivated to change her modus operandi.
7. This woman has been around. She's familiar with drug treatment programs and the tenets of several of them. She also understands that other people take issue with her attitudes and beliefs toward drug use. There's nothing

> at this point that anyone can say that she hasn't heard a thousand times before, and that might make her "see" what she's doing and its consequences. She already *sees*, but she still disagrees with some fundamental principles about how to function in a civilized world.

A major question in most people's minds might be this: Why doesn't this woman just say from the beginning what she obviously knows, and then more clearly admits toward the end of the interview? Of course, the traditional assumption is that she's "in denial" which blocks her insight. But it should be evident, when taking a careful look at the whole of this encounter, that she's simply accustomed to using certain tactics to justify her behavior, to resist change, and to manipulate the impressions of others about her character. In fact, such tactics often work, at least in the short-run. So, she uses the tactics to keep doing as she damned well pleases, without concern for the impact of her behavior on others. It should be noted that this woman is one of many inmates who, when given a choice between submitting to some kind of correctional program to gain earlier release, will forego that opportunity. When they are released, they don't want anyone looking over their shoulder (i.e. a parole officer) to whom they'll have to answer. Remember what I said about aggressive personalities: They find it anathema to be in a situation in which they have to recognize or submit to a higher authority.

VIGNETTE #3
An adult male referred for evaluation by another therapist

CLIENT: Hey, how's it goin' George? Well, today's the day, huh? The big shrink's gonna tell me what he thinks (smirks).

THERAPIST: As I promised you last time, I am going to share with you my opinion about what I see as a problem. And I'll give you some suggestions about what you would need to work on in therapy. Then, I will give your therapist a copy of my report.

CLIENT: Well, what's the verdict, doc? You're a doctor of what... philosophy.... psychology? Is that like a real doctor, or what?

THERAPIST: As we talked about the first time, I'm a psychologist. I'm not a medical doctor. All of my training is in psychology. My area of specialty is personality and character. As we have discussed this at length before, perhaps we'd better get on with my assessment.

CLIENT: Go ahead. Shoot.

THERAPIST: I think that, for you to have fewer of the kinds of problems you've been having, and in order to be a better person in general, you need to make some changes in the kind of person you are — some basic changes in your personality. At your age, that won't be easy, but I think that's what you'll need to do.

CLIENT: What about my personality?

THERAPIST: Mostly, you lack good "brakes." Also, you tend to think too much of yourself, and you tend to pay too little heed to others in your life and their needs.

CLIENT: I'm not sure what you mean, bad brakes.

THERAPIST: I think you understand that when you want something, or want to do something, you don't hesitate or stop and think about it first. In fact, you don't stop at all. You don't back-up, back-off, or give-in when you should. You're in full-throttle mode in the very times you really need to be thinking about applying the brakes.

CLIENT: And you can tell all this after just a couple of visits?

THERAPIST: As we discussed earlier, I consider much more than just our visits, which is why I've consulted with your therapist, interviewed some of your family, looked at your history, and given you some tests. I've also made some important observations about the kinds of attitudes you display and behaviors you exhibit. I consider my opinion accurate.

CLIENT: Even if no one else has ever told me that before? Dr. Brady thinks I probably have depression. But you think I'm just a bad person. So, he's wrong and you're right, huh?

THERAPIST: I can't speak for anyone else. I'm giving you my opinion. And, of course, you didn't hear me say you were a bad person. I said you're a person with poor brakes. I meant exactly what I said.

CLIENT: Dr. Brady says my anger is a symptom of depression. Maybe that's what it is. Maybe all I need is a pill.

THERAPIST: Anger can indeed be a sign of depression, especially when it is out of character for the person. But I've carefully reviewed your history. There were many times when you were on a mission of sorts — taking no prisoners — fighting hard to get what you wanted — and you weren't angry at all. Many times, when you showed anger, it seemed more to intimidate those who opposed you — a tactic as opposed to a genuine feeling. You seemed to do whatever you had to do to get what you wanted without care for whom you hurt, and you ended up losing in some way. If you had put on the brakes, you might have really won. Then you got upset because you'd made a mess of things. How long have you had a problem putting on the brakes?

CLIENT: I just don't see how you could be so sure after just meeting me. You don't really know anything about me. I mean, you're saying some pretty heavy things here. Besides, I like me. Lots of people like me. They love me at work, and I do great at my job. Make good money. But you tell me I'm all messed up.

THERAPIST: You ask how I can be so sure. I think you would know better than anyone else whether any of what I have said to you makes sense. And, of course, you know that I'm not suggesting you need to change *everything* about yourself. What I am saying is that, as an aggressive personality, you have to learn when and when not to pull out the stops, and when and when not to put on the brakes. You also need to get a more balanced sense of self-worth. It seems to have really riled you that anyone might have accurately assessed your character.

You actually helped confirm most of my hunches when you started out this session using the tactic of leveling; that is, trying to intimidate me by subtly denigrating my credentials, trying to throw me on the defensive. I think you need to stop all the very destructive behavior that I outlined for you on the worksheets I gave you, and which I'm sending to your therapist as well. If you don't work on correcting those things, you'll keep hurting people and making a mess of your relationships. It won't be easy, but you can do it. And you can start by doing some things differently right here and right now.

Now, my question to you, if you remember, is how long you've had this problem.... I mean, with your brakes.

CLIENT: My whole life.

The scenario depicted above illustrates several of the points I've already made about the nature of encounters with disturbed characters, especially the egotistic and aggressive personalities.

First, posturing and jockeying for position was evident from the very beginning of the encounter. As I've mentioned before, in the client's mind, the "fight" had already started, even before the formal encounter began.

Second, you can expect folks who like who they are, and who are relatively entrenched in their way of doing things, to resist the notion that they need to change. They're very happy to frame whatever is going wrong in their lives as almost anything else (e.g. a depression) than to face the daunting task of real change. Unfortunately, sometimes professionals can enable that resistance.

Third, at some level, the disturbed character really knows what the real issues are. He will eventually demonstrate respect and some degree of amenability if the person confronting him stands on principle and holds ground. Just because clients resist, saying all kinds of things and using all kinds of tactics, doesn't mean they don't deep down know the truth. If you don't nail them on the truth, they have absolutely no reason to respect or trust you.

Fourth, basic personality tendencies can change if you'll actually give them some attention. And change always occurs in the here and now. When the client in the vignette above finally capitulates (it might have been an instance of "assent" only), he is in fact doing something different from what he usually does. This small step is actually a big deal, which needs to be recognized and reinforced. That would send a message to him that the world will not come to an end if he considers modifying his *style* of relating. The more the dysfunctional aspects of his style are confronted and corrected, and the more reinforcement he gets for modifying his usual modus operandi, the more he will grow and change. If a lot of time were wasted in therapy talking about the things that depress him, as well as his fears or insecurities, not much about his personality would change.

This case underscores a couple of very important points made earlier about some disturbed characters, especially the egotistic and aggressive personalities. Remember, it's always about three things: position, position, and position. Right from the outset, this individual tries to put me in a place he wants to prescribe for me. He doesn't want to see me as an authority. He especially doesn't like the notion that I might have some advantage over him by "having his number." He uses the tactic of "leveling" not only to even the field of contest between us, but also to put us on an equal level of stature (e.g., he calls me by first name and engages in subtle mockery of my professional status). He also can hardly allow himself to believe that someone else could have the upper hand in an encounter with him and could be so astute as to see through his game of impression management, and get to the core of his character issues. But in the end, it is the truth and the willingness to stand up for it that saves us both from further, destructive combat.

VIGNETTE # 4
A mother seeking a second opinion about how to help her daughter

This very brief vignette helps illustrate how some of the principles of traditional psychology have not only gone too long unquestioned by professionals, but also have been generally accepted by laypersons, much to their detriment in trying to understand and deal effectively with disturbed characters.

CLIENT: She must have really low self-esteem. She'll tell me I think she's stupid whenever I try to offer constructive criticism. She says her teacher has it in for her, too. She says the teacher's a jerk and lets the other kids pick on her, and she's the one who gets in trouble when she defends herself. She can't possibly feel good about herself. She gets so defensive whenever I try to correct her.

THERAPIST: What do you mean "defensive?"

CLIENT: If I say the slightest thing about her behavior, she flies off the handle. She'll say I hate her, or that I never have anything good to say about her. She'll kick and scream. Sometimes she'll hit me. I don't want her to feel so badly that she has a meltdown. So, I keep my distance. But I know she needs help. The other therapist says it all stems from her low self-esteem. But I don't know what to do.

Like many, this mother (as well as her child's therapist) believes that no one would react so intensely to criticism unless "underneath it all" they didn't have a poor opinion of themselves. Also, she appears to believe that the child perceives the efforts others have made to help her as an "attack" on her worth, meriting a "defensive" (albeit spirited) response. But in my work with this family, it became quite clear that this child was anything but self-unsure in character or "defensive" in posture. She was the consummate fighter, and had reason to be confident that she could take on the best of opponents. To be sure, she lacked the wisdom of life experience necessary to see the ultimate shortcoming of her ways. But for now, she perceives herself as winning, and she feels pretty good about it. So good, in fact, that she's outpaced her mother in strength, power, and influence. That's a recipe for disaster in any family. Kids can't forge a decent character on their own. They don't have the moral maturity or the wisdom to do it. They need authoritative guidance. With this child, mom ends up backing off, because she knows neither how to interpret nor deal with her daughter's tactics. So, she ends up facilitating the creation of a monster.

VIGNETTE #5
A long-term client actively working on his character development

CLIENT: I'm not sure what I need to work on today. It's been a crazy week. And I'm sure you can tell I'm just a bit hyper today. So, if I start rambling, you'll just have to stop me. No... I already know what you're going to say, I need to stop myself. Okay. I'll try.

THERAPIST: That's great.

CLIENT: I didn't go to my computer class today because the professor is such a jerk and has given us a bunch of busy work, and we've not been learning the really important stuff, anyway.

THERAPIST: (Gives only a familiar glance)

CLIENT: Okay. I know. I'm rationalizing.

THERAPIST: So why didn't you go to class today?

CLIENT: I wanted to spend some time with Marcie. She's a lot more interesting! I probably shouldn't have trashed Professor Bartlett like that, just to make an excuse for choosing time with Marcie over computer class. He's actually an okay guy. And besides, I probably need to be better about my attendance anyway because I need the grade. I'm actually doing okay, just not as good as I could be.

THERAPIST: I like how you took ownership of your decisions, both good and bad. What do you think you'll do to keep yourself on track better?

CLIENT: Well, Marcie's schedule is different from mine. There's a lot of time when she doesn't have class when I do. So, I'm probably going to get tempted to skip again. When that issue comes up and I make the right choice, I'll treat me and her to a beer at Charlie's (a popular hangout). When I don't, I'll make myself put in an extra hour of study.

THERAPIST: That sounds good.

CLIENT: You don't seem all that impressed.

THERAPIST: You know why I resist being too demonstrative in my support for you.

CLIENT: Yeah. You want me to recognize myself and not have to depend so much on others to encourage me.

THERAPIST: Right.

CLIENT: But you can't blame me for wanting you to be impressed.

THERAPIST: Blame you, no.

CLIENT: But you still want me to recognize myself.

THERAPIST: Right. This is all about you and how you value your own efforts to be a better person.

Now, this is a young man with whom I had worked for many years since his early childhood. During that time (as is typical for any child going through the process of character development) he developed a fair degree of dependency upon the support, guidance, and direction he was afforded. There were times that I confronted him directly and frequently about his various behaviors, tactics, and thinking patterns interfering with his efforts to build character. But in the end, the material I gave him on his worksheets became his to learn and internalize. It also became incumbent upon him to be more self-observant, and to catch and correct maladaptive patterns as they emerged. Sometimes, when he'd forget to "catch" himself exhibiting a maladaptive behavior, a glance from me would be all it took to remind him. My job then turned primarily to reinforcing him for his efforts (like I did with the brief verbal praise in my first two responses).

Eventually, however, even the task of reinforcement had to become his. He is a living example of how the behavioral principles of covert self-monitoring and self-reinforcement for correcting behavior can be powerful instruments of change.

VIGNETTE #6
A snapshot of a husband and wife in a joint counseling session

WIFE: I want you to do better about not calling me names, cursing, and belittling me when we have things to discuss.

HUSBAND: And I suppose you're going to tell me you've never cussed before or anything. There's no winning with you. I can't do anything right. I always end up looking like the bad guy.

WIFE: I'm sticking to my issue here. I'm not accepting that this is about me, or which one of us is the better person, or that you're a victim in any way. Despite the fact that you've improved on the name-calling, I want you to do better. I just want you to work harder at not calling me names or belittling me when we have a discussion.

HUSBAND: Okay, okay, *okay*!

WIFE: And I don't just want you agreeing to get me off your back [using the tactic of "assent"]. I'm going to be watching for this to get a lot better over time and to last.

The woman in the scenario above "gets it." She anticipates tactics and is not swayed by them. She has a legitimate concern and makes a legitimate request. And she takes ownership of setting her own reasonable expectations and limits. She has no need for hostility or for defensiveness. She knows what to expect and what to do. As she mentioned to me many times, life has completely changed for her.

EPILOGUE

Neurosis and Character Disturbance

The Most Pressing Issue of our Time

There is an old saying that "all roads lead to Rome." That is, many issues can be traced to a single source. When you seriously examine our most pressing social problems, whether political, interpersonal, occupational, or even economic, the problems can eventually be traced to impaired individual responsibility. Like it or not, character matters. It affects everything we do, and character-deficiency lies at the root of many woes we face. Even the biggest financial crisis since the Great Depression was mostly caused by the greed, dishonesty, and irresponsibility of a handful of character-deficient bankers and executives.

Where Is the Outrage?

For months, the public was subjected to endless warnings about the dangers of a possible swine flu epidemic. Industries and public agencies rallied. But the problems posed by this virus pale in comparison to the pain, misery, and social costs incurred every day by the character crisis facing the industrialized world. Yet, we hear no public outcry. In fact, we've become all too accepting of the fact that the responsible among us are dwindling in number. We seem to regard it as an inevitable feature of the human condition. We might get outraged when a horrendous character like Bernie Madoff rips off millions of hard-working Americans, but we don't seem too interested in how such a person becomes a problem character in the first place. It's important to realize that character disturbance is not only a very serious issue, but also a phenomenon we can actually do something about. But first, we must become oriented toward addressing the issue.

The Wrong Way to Attack the Problem

For quite some time, western societies have sought legislative solutions to the character-disturbance problem, almost always with unintended, and sometimes disastrous results. We have more rules on the books than a reasonable person could possibly count, and we attempt to enforce new rules every day. We behave as if the solution to our ills is more and tougher rules. But the fact is this: The irresponsible people among us don't pay attention to the rules, nor are they particularly influenced by the potential consequences of breaking them. Those of us who live in a righteous spirit do not act responsibly because of the rules or for fear of breaking them. To make matters worse, however, we are overly and unfairly burdened by the rules we devise in our fruitless effort to control the irresponsible among us.

To prove the point that trying to "legislate" morality almost always has unintended and sometimes disastrous consequences, I offer the following example: A seven-year-old boy was observed giving a girl at school a kiss on the cheek. This violated the school's "no-tolerance" guidelines on "sexual harassment," and resulted in the boy's suspension. The rule was well-intended. True sexual harassment is an insidious behavior that needs to be dealt with firmly. But the way the rule was crafted defies common logic. And remember what I said about all roads....Well, here's the reason we can't leave it to principals, superintendents, or school boards, to exercise discretion: We don't trust that people put in those positions will always have the integrity of character, the soundness of judgment, and the appreciation of shared principles necessary to exercise good discretion. So, we make blanket rules that affect everyone "equally," with "no-tolerance," and set up firm, inflexible guidelines that all authority figures must follow. (Most states even mandate that judges sentence criminals within certain guidelines.) In the end, we erroneously place our trust in "the rules" instead of people — competent adults we would like to fairly interpret, administer, and enforce the principles the rules were meant to advance.

Our misplaced trust in rules impairs us from exercising necessary discretion. Also, since we cannot specifically target every possible act of social irresponsibility, many people escape so-called justice because no specific statute covers their alleged act of wrongdoing. So, even though almost anyone with a brain knows that it's wrong to steal, "con," or cheat, irresponsible people spend their time finding ways to do all such things that are not covered by a specific statute. An example of this is the near-collapse of the American capitalization system and the economic recession (nearly depression) it spawned. There were rules in place to keep "regular" banks from engaging in risky behavior with other people's money, but those rules didn't cover financial institutions who largely act like banks but aren't technically banks. Unscrupulous money managers stayed within the law but engaged in horribly reckless behavior for personal profit. Their behavior might not have been illegal but it was reprehensible. All roads lead to...

The incessant overburdening of the responsible folks among us will eventually prompt a more wholesale abandonment of responsibility, i.e. leadership burnout. Those who have always taken their social responsibilities seriously are becoming sick and tired of carrying the burden for everyone else. They'd like a break every now and then. Some seem to be so endowed with intellectual capacity, endurance, and the penchant for multi-tasking, they can handle the increasing burden without succumbing to depression and defeat. But many are not fairing very well under the ever increasing weight placed upon them. They labor with a large sense of unfairness and resentment about those they carry on their backs. Nature has a way of intervening to stop imbalance. This trend will have to end. And when circumstances finally force the issue, it will not be pretty.

What's Happened to Punishment?

There is a popular perception that punishing people for wrongdoing is simply ineffective. There is a grain of truth to that notion. Punishment is by no means the ideal way of shaping human behavior or building character. Reinforcement is a more powerful behavior modifier. And nourishing empathy and teaching mutual regard are better shapers of character. But punishment's recent "bad rap" has much more to do with how western societies typically penalize than with the nature and potential value of punishment itself.

Even when punishment is administered effectively, it appears to only deter, suppress, or inhibit behavior. It doesn't have the power to eliminate it or curb it indefinitely. So, I'm not advocating punishment as the ideal behavior shaping tool. But the fact that punishment can indeed help humans *inhibit* their behavior (especially by strengthening inhibitory neural networks during the formative years) is of significant value. For punishment to be effective, however, (whether it involves introducing an aversive consequence or removing a positive one), it must meet some specific requirements. It needs to be *immediate* (the optimal interval between an act or impulse and an aversive consequence is actually somewhat less than one second), *certain* (i.e. occurring across a wide variety of situations and circumstances any time the misbehavior is exhibited), and of *sufficiently aversive* quality to deter the person from exhibiting the behavior again.

In my quarter century of working with clients ranging from parents and children to prison inmates, I've seen that punishment is almost never immediate. The neurotics among us have seen to it that the wheels of justice turn exceedingly slowly. And for a variety of reasons we have come to particularly disdain corporal punishment, even though when it's appropriately done during the most appropriate developmental years, it can at least provide an immediate consequence to a child's wrongful actions. Someone who commits a crime will wait months or even years (depending on their resources for appeal) to face the consequence of their conviction.

And, as every criminal knows, getting caught and actually having to face deserved consequences is anything but certain. The "system" is overloaded, jails and prisons are overfilled, and all kinds of deals are cut to get out of the rightful consequences of misbehavior. Children learn early how unreliable it is these days that parents, teachers, and other authority figures will agree, not only on whether a behavior merits sanction, but what that sanction should be. Long gone are the days when children were told that persons in authority were always "right" as far as they were concerned; and that any trouble a child got in with another parent, guardian, teacher, or coach would only be met with stiffer consequences from his or her own parent. Lastly, some of the ways we "punish" are so devoid of aversive quality that it's laughable. Despite the salacious and distorted reports of what life is like in prison, with a few notable exceptions, many inmates enjoy a life behind bars (with free health and dental care, better and more reliable housing, clothing, and nutrition) than they were ever used to in the "free world." So, many criminals not only don't mind coming back to prison, but some even deliberately sabotage their paroles and probation to regain entry. And we call this punishment?

The Disappearance of Basic Rules of Human Decency

Gone are the days that some very basic rules for decent conduct were known and respected by a majority. In former days, a child could expect most parents to respond in a similar way to concerns about their behavior. And they could also expect their parents to back up the observations or the discipline of other authority figures such as aunts, uncles, neighboring parents, or teachers. Beginning with the rebellious '60s, all the rules became much less clear. Now, authority figures in children's lives undermine each other with regularity.

The Right Way to Address the Problem

It all starts with individual responsibility. The only time-tested effective training grounds for that is a stable, intact home. Children can only learn to be responsible when they "bond" emotionally to caretakers that model for them firm commitment, adherence to principle, and the willingness to accept obligation freely and with love and joy. In their early years, children are very dependent upon their caretakers. This dependency must eventually be overcome, but it also serves a vital purpose early on. A child who depends upon external support will experience unsettlement, anxiety, and distress when that support is withdrawn. Looking at years of research about the most important factors necessary for kids to emerge as responsible adults, one could rightfully conclude that two factors appear of the greatest importance: (1) the children were afforded love and affection *liberally* and *unconditionally*, and (2) support and approval for their behavior was very *conditional.*

A child who knows in his soul that he is truly loved will not only bond emotionally, but also will become unnerved when sensing parents' disapproval. This is the greatest shaper of character known to exist. A properly bonded child might kick and scream during various phases of the socialization process; but she will eventually "cave-in" to the demands when seeing that the caretaker's discipline is rooted in loving concern. Even those who "rebel" as adolescents will eventually come back to the principles they were taught as younger children, especially once they begin learning that their parents weren't as stupid as they once thought.

We don't need more rules, more institutions, more programs, or more psychological experts paid to try and repair (and inadvertently "enable") the damage done by character dysfunction. Rather, we need to pay attention to our children, and what really helps their character develop in the first place. We must stop divorcing each other so frivolously, take our parental responsibilities much more seriously, agree with and support one another on the most basic principles of civil behavior, and instill an appreciation for those principles in our children early on. We must bring back a sense of right and wrong, as well as a sense of shame. And when some person, company, or entity engages in behavior that promotes or "enables" the erosion of these principles, we should call them out and let our outrage be known. We should also support all those making genuine efforts to do the responsible thing, backing them not only verbally, but also emotionally and even financially.

The Need for an Honest Discourse

Humankind has always faced challenges to its survival and prosperity, but today's challenges are particularly daunting. If we're to have a prayer of truly recognizing and overcoming our difficulties, we simply must do two things: People of integrity and character must come together, and they must engage in an *honest* discussion of the issues. These two requirements are inextricably interdependent. There has to be sufficient integrity of character among those talking (i.e. the participants must necessarily have faced and overcome their fears, biases, insecurities, and misperceptions) for the truth of important matters to emerge, and to be appropriately accepted and revered when it does.

All too often these days, concern over political correctness (i.e. how socially "enlightened" or acceptable we think others might regard the position we take) and the tendency to put personal beliefs and interests ahead of the general welfare impair our ability to conduct an honest discourse and debate. It's natural for people to strive to advance their causes. But when they distort important aspects of a situation in order to "frame" the debate in a manner that gives them an edge, everyone loses. Too often, people let their biases, underlying motivations, and unholy determination put a self-serving "spin" on the issues they seek to confront or address. And although politicians have raised this tendency to an art form, they're not the only ones too cowardly and self-serving to acknowledge, speak, and respect the simple truth.

As individuals, we must become more aware and honest about the fears, biases, and distortions that we let close our minds and impair our judgment. Getting honest with ourselves about who we really are: This is essential for psychological health and personal growth. And becoming much more honest with one another about our mutual problems and concerns is essential to avoiding further social fragmentation and polarization. Confronting issues and one another in a frank yet benign way has never been easy. But the bottom line is this: If we don't get honest *with ourselves about ourselves* and *with one another about one another* and soon, we're pretty much done.

The Road to Riches

There are some things in life whose value is almost impossible to measure. In my life, I've been in many places psychologically, spiritually, and financially. My present-day life is abundantly rich in many dimensions. But there were times when this was not the case. Looking back on those times, it's sobering to realize how pivotal a role my character defects played in creating and maintaining the difficulties in my life. I am by no means a person of enviable virtue. I have plenty of shortcomings and vices. But I owe everything of value I have in my life to reckoning with my most serious character defects, and making sincere efforts to change. I also owe a supreme debt to those who labored on my behalf to instill any sense of character in me. Some people express gratitude by saying: "I don't know where I'd be" without the love and support of their family, friends, and other supporters. But I know exactly where I'd be if I hadn't come to appreciate the character-shaping lessons I've been given. I've been in the abyss before. It wasn't pretty. And I don't want to go back. I know I still have a long way to go. I am still a very flawed creature. But I am determined to continually do better, and most especially, to *be* better. I'm determined because I know in the deepest recesses of my soul how much character matters. And I hope that, in some small yet significant way, this book has helped impress the importance of character upon you as well.

ENDNOTES

1. Peterson, C., & Seligman, M., *Character Strengths and Values: A Handbook and Classification*, (American Psychological Association and Oxford University Press, 2004), p. 5.
2. Adams, J., Address to the Military, October 1798.
3. Millon, T., *Disorders of Personality*, (Wiley Interscience, 1981), p. 4.
4. Millon, T., *Disorders of Personality*, (Wiley Interscience, 1981), p. 198.
5. Hare, R., *Without Conscience: The Disturbing World of the Psychopaths Among Us*, (Guilford Press, 1991).
6. Simon, G., *In Sheep's Clothing: Understanding and Dealing with Manipulative People*, (A.J. Christopher & Co., 1996).
7. Shapiro, D., *Neurotic Styles*, (Basic Books, 1999).
8. Shapiro, D., *Neurotic Styles*, (Basic Books, 1999), p. 1.
9. Millon,T., *Personality Disorders in Modern Life*, (Wiley, 2000), p. 2.
10. Millon, T., *Personality Disorders in Modern Life*, (Wiley, 2000), pp. 60-61.
11. Millon, T., *Personality Disorders in Modern Life*, (Wiley, 2000), pp. 210-213.
12. Millon, T., *Personality Disorders in Modern Life*, (Wiley, 2000), pp. 315-317.
13. *Diagnostic and Statistical Manual of Mental Disorders*-Fourth Edition-Text Revision, (American Psychiatric Association, 2000), pp. 789-791.
14. Millon, T., *Disorders of Personality*, (Wiley Interscience, 1981), p. 246.

15. Erikson, Erik H., *Childhood and Society,* (Norton, 1950).
16. Erikson, Erik H., *Childhood and Society,* (Norton, 1950).
17. Adler, A., *Understanding Human Nature,* (Fawcett World Library, 1954).
18. Millon, T., *Personality Disorders in Modern Life,* (Wiley, 2000, p. 278).
19. Samenow, S., *Inside The Criminal Mind,* (Random House, 1984).
20. Yochelson, S., Samenow, S., *The Criminal Personality, Vol. I: A Profile for Change,* Aronson, 1976).
21. Simon, G., *In Sheep's Clothing: Understanding and Dealing with Manipulative People,* (A.J. Christopher & Co., 1996, pp. 24-30).
22. Millon, T., *Personality Disorders in Modern Life,* (Wiley, 2000, pp. 110-113).
23. Millon, T., *Personality Disorders in Modern Life,* (Wiley, 2000, pp. 107-108).
24. Simon, G., *In Sheep's Clothing: Understanding and Dealing with Manipulative People,* (A.J. Christopher & Co., 1996).
25. Cleckley, H., *The Mask of Sanity* (4th Edition, Mosby, 1964).
26. Stout, M., *The Sociopath Next Door,* (Random House, 2006).
27. Hare, R., *Without Conscience: The Disturbing World of the Psychopaths Among Us,* (Guilford Press, 1991).
28. De Becker, G., *The Gift of Fear: Survival Signs that Protect Us from Violence,* (Little Brown & Co., 1997).
29. Simon, G., *In Sheep's Clothing: Understanding and Dealing with Manipulative People,* (A.J. Christopher & Co., 1996, pp. 145-146).
30. Samenow, S., *Inside The Criminal Mind,* (Random House, 1984).
31. Samenow, S., *Inside The Criminal Mind,* (Random House, 1984).
32. Samenow, S., *Inside The Criminal Mind,* (Random House, 1984).
33. Samenow, S., *Inside The Criminal Mind,* (Random House, 1984).

ABOUT THE AUTHOR

Dr. George Simon received his Ph.D. in clinical psychology from Texas Tech University. He has spent much of the last 25 years studying and working with persons with disturbed characters and their victims. He enjoys encouraging others and spends much of his time writing articles, giving instructional seminars, consulting to therapists, businesses, and organizations, and composing inspirational music.

Dr. Simon is an accomplished speaker and has made appearances on national television networks such as *CNN* and *Fox News Network* as well as numerous regional TV and radio talk shows.

Dr. Simon is the principal composer of *Anthem for the Millennium (America, My Home!)*, which gained popularity after the attacks of September 11, 2001, and has been heard in various performance venues by over one million people.

Dr. Simon, his wife, and family make their home near Little Rock, Arkansas.